LONDON RECORD SOCIETY
PUBLICATIONS

VOLUME XVI
FOR THE YEAR 1980

LONDON AND MIDDLESEX CHANTRY CERTIFICATE 1548

EDITED BY
C. J. KITCHING

LONDON RECORD SOCIETY
1980

Acknowledgements

The Editor wishes to thank the custodians of the records used in the compilation of the calendar, particularly at the Public Record Office, the British Library Department of Manuscripts, Guildhall Library, the Library of St Paul's Cathedral and the Worshipful Company of Drapers. Crown copyright material in the Public Record Office is reproduced by permission of the Controller of Her Majesty's Stationery Office. The publication of this volume has been assisted by a generous grant from the Twenty-Seven Foundation.

Printed in Great Britain by
W & J MACKAY LIMITED, CHATHAM, KENT

CONTENTS

ABBREVIATIONS

APC	*Acts of the Privy Council of England*, ed. J. R. Dasent and others (46 vols, 1890–1964)
BC	PRO, E 301/88, Brief Certificate of Colleges and Chantries in London and Middlesex
CPR	*Calendar of Patent Rolls*
Dugdale	W. Dugdale, *History of St Paul's Cathedral*, ed. and continued by H. Ellis (1818)
E 101	PRO, Exchequer Various Accounts. (Those cited are the pension rolls for London, E 101/75/21 and Middlesex, E 101/75/22 respectively)
E 117	PRO, Exchequer King's Remembrancer, Church Goods
E 135	PRO, Exchequer King's Remembrancer, Ecclesiastical Documents
E 301	PRO, Exchequer Augmentation Office, Certificates of Colleges and Chantries
Guildhall	Guildhall Library
Harley 601	British Library, MS. Harley 601
Hennessy	G. Hennessy, *Novum Repertorium Ecclesiasticum Parochiale Londinense* (1898)
Husting	*Calendar of Wills Proved and Enrolled in the Court of Husting*, ed. R. R. Sharpe (2 vols, 1889–90)
LP	*Letters and Papers, Foreign and Domestic, Henry VIII*, ed. J. S. Brewer and others (21 vols, 1864–1920)
LR 2	PRO, Exchequer Office of Auditors of Land Revenue, Miscellaneous Books
PRO	Public Record Office
PROB 11	PRO, Prerogative Court of Canterbury, Registered Copy Wills
Sparrow Simpson	*Documents illustrating the History of St Paul's Cathedral*, ed. W. Sparrow Simpson (Camden Society, new series, xxvi, 1880)
SC 6	PRO, Special Collections, Ministers' Accounts. (Those cited are the accounts for Michaelmas 2 Edward VI for London, SC 6/Edw. VI/293 and Middlesex, SC 6/Edw. VI/298 respectively)
t.	In the tenure of
Valor	*Valor Ecclesiasticus*, ed. J. Caley and J. Hunter (6 vols, 1810–34)

WD 26   St Paul's Cathedral Library: the original return of the
               dean and chapter to the commissioners in 1548
Walters   H. B. Walters, *London Churches at the Reformation*
               (1939)

*   faded
**   badly faded; almost illegible

INTRODUCTION

The reports of the royal commissioners appointed in 1546 and 1548 (pursuant to acts of Parliament in 1545 and 1547 respectively) to survey colleges, chantries and kindred endowments form one class of the records of the Exchequer Augmentation Office at the Public Record Office, collectively known as Certificates of Colleges and Chantries.[1] Their importance as historical source material has long been recognised, and a number of local record societies have included among their publications texts or calendars of the certificates for their counties,[2] which constitute a useful corpus of comparative material for the present calendar. The Certificate which forms the subject of this volume, that of 1548 for the cities of London and Westminster, the county of Middlesex and chantries supported by London companies (E301/34), is already well known. Many extracts have been published, with varying degrees of faithfulness to the original text, and writers on the history of individual parishes and institutions have regularly had recourse to the original.[3] Never before, however, has it been fully calendared or analysed. This is due in part to its considerable bulk, and in part to its physical condition: whilst some of the membranes present no difficulty to the reader, parts of others remain largely undecipherable even under ultra-violet light, and in those cases the fragments of script which do emerge have to be substantiated and supplemented by reference to other contemporary sources, some of which are based on, or closely related to, the Certificate. Fortunately also, some portions of the text were transcribed by earlier writers when it was less faded.

The Chantry Acts
The two acts of Parliament[4] which gave rise to the chantry surveys of 1546 and 1548 were quite different in emphasis. The Henrician act fulminated against the misappropriation of godly endowments for colleges, chantries, hospitals, free chapels, gilds and stipendiary priests, and enabled the crown to appropriate all their revenues that were being poorly governed. It did not proscribe similar foundations where misappropriation was not suspected, but merely authorised the issue of commissions of investigation. The commissioners were thus not empowered to dissolve, but only to report on, the foundations, and it is their reports which constitute the Henrician 'chantry certificates'. Henry's act lapsed with his death, and by the end of 1547 when the subject was again raised in Parliament the mood

---

1. PRO, E301.
2. For an incomplete list see Conyers Read, *Bibliography of British History: Tudor Period* (2nd edn, Oxford, 1959), no. 2100.
3. e.g., see J. M. Sims, *London and Middlesex Published Records: a Handlist* (1970), 8–9: and Hennessy, *passim.*
4. 37 Henry VIII c.4; 1 Edw. VI c.14.

had decisively shifted. Endowments concerned with prayers for the dead were now denounced as intrinsically superstitious and were to be dissolved, provided that any by-products beneficial to society at large—such as education, poor relief and chapels of ease—were protected, and the rights of cathedrals and corporations safeguarded. Endowments for obits and lamps were added to the list of proscribed foundations, but hospitals were taken off the list. Those priests who were considered supernumerary to the needs of a parish were to be pensioned off—a provision unnecessary in the Henrician act. As before, commissioners were to report on the foundations.

The Chantry Commissions

Commissioners under the 1545 act were appointed on 14 February 1546 in twenty-four circuits covering the whole country.[5] Those under the 1547 act were appointed exactly two years later: on 14 February 1548.[6] In the former case each commission was nominally headed by a bishop, but in 1548 bishops were not enlisted, and there was instead an increase in the number of officials of the court of Augmentations. Procedure was much the same throughout the country in both years. A written questionnaire, identical for each parish, was sent to parish officials, and a written return had to be brought in to the commissioners at an appointed place and date. The commissioners' scribes made fair copies or abstracts of the parishes' original returns, and it is these abstracts which, strictly speaking, constitute the 'chantry certificates'. The original returns for 1546 survive for nine companies and thirty-eight city parishes in three books now among the records of the auditors of land revenue,[7] and there are other isolated examples extant. For the later survey very few original returns survive; no doubt most were destroyed when the Certificate had been written up.

The Henrician commission was directed to the Lord Mayor (Sir Martin Bowes), the bishops of London and Westminster, and the following: Sir Roger Cholmeley, Sir Richard Gresham; Wymond Carew, Robert Brooke, William Stamford, Nicholas Bacon and Thomas Mildmay, esquires: a team of able administrators and lawyers well suited to the task in hand. Two of the Henrician commissioners, Sir Roger Cholmeley, Chief Baron of the Exchequer, and (the now knighted) Sir Wymond Carew, Treasurer of First Fruits and Tenths, were called to serve again under Edward. Their new colleagues were Sir Nicholas Hare, a Master of Requests who already had wide experience of the stewardship of crown lands; Sir John Godsalve, Clerk of the Signet (who had also served in 1547 as one of the commissioners in the royal visitation of the diocese of London but had been recalled to urgent business in the Signet Office);[8] Richard Goodrick, the Attorney of Augmentations and Hugh Losse, the royal surveyor for the area; John Carrell and Richard Morrison, esquires. There could hardly have been a team that better knew the importance of keeping a precise record of their proceedings.

Thanks to the survival of an agenda book of one of the 1546 commis-

5. *LP*, xxi pt i, no. 302 (30).
6. *CPR 1548–9*, 135 *et seq.*
7. LR 2/241–3.
8. *APC 1547–50*, 517.

sioners or their scribes,[9] we have a clear idea of procedure under the earlier commission. No equivalent document is known for 1548, but glimpses of the work are afforded by surviving churchwardens' accounts and company records. For city parishes in 1546 the commissioners first met at Guildhall to sign warrants to the aldermen of each ward ordering them to deliver to every parson, vicar or curate and churchwardens a copy of the official questionnaire or 'Bill of Articles'.[10] A great deal of paperwork was called for in the preparation of one warrant for each ward and one Bill of Articles for each parish and company, but whereas all the commissioners signed the warrants, they appear to have split up into sub-commissions of five men to sign the Bills.[11] All were actively involved, as is attested by their signatures at the end of each main section of the Certificate. By the time the investigation began in earnest, the chantry act had been public knowledge for two months, so the parish and company officials had had some intimation of what to expect. Nevertheless, the fact that they received only a week or ten days' notice to present their written replies to the commissioners under a pre-arranged timetable must have imposed considerable strain on those who had to account for many endowments. There were few negative returns.[12]

In 1546 the recipients of the Bills of Articles, together with all masters, wardens and governors of colleges, hospitals, gilds, fraternities and the like, and all chantry and stipendiary priests, had to appear to present, or to hear presented, the answers to the articles, and to be further questioned if necessary. Some were sent away to bring back more detailed reports on particular foundations. Entries in wardens' accounts show that in 1548 procedure was modified. It was a royal pursuivant and not the aldermen who warned officials to make their returns—for whose services, incidentally, the recipients of the Bills were usually charged at least a shilling, as though being cited to appear in a court of law. The venue of the commissioners' sessions was also different in 1548. In 1546 they had been at Guildhall, but we now find them in several other places, including the halls of the Saddlers and Haberdashers, and even the house of Hugh Losse.[13] They could more easily be peripatetic in 1548, since they were content to see only representatives of the parishes and companies, rather than the many officers who had been compelled to attend in 1546. Since the clergy had recently undergone the royal visitation it was no doubt a relief to them not to be rounded up yet again.

In 1546 work began at the very end of February, ward by ward, starting with Limestreet and Billingsgate. The whole city was covered, even taking account of adjournments and requests for clarification, by mid April, when the commissioners' attention was turned to Middlesex, hundred by hundred.

9. LR 2/243 fos 1–7.
10. e.g., LR 2/243 fo. 15.
11. e.g., see E 301/126; LR 2/242 fo. 74.
12. Those which have come to my attention at the PRO are St Mary Mounthawe (E 135/8/47); St Bartholomew the Great (LR 2/242 fo. 74); and the Companies of Curriers (E 301/90), Pewterers (E 117/13/4) and Poulters (E 117/13/5).
13. Saddlers' Hall, see the accounts of St Margaret Pattens (Guildhall MS. 4570/1); Haberdashers' Hall, see the accounts of the Merchant Taylors (Guildhall Microfilm 298).

The London companies came under scrutiny only in the first and second weeks of May, and thus had rather longer to prepare themselves. Finally, the dean and chapter of St Paul's were visited from 19 May onwards.[14] The timetable for 1548 cannot be reconstructed with any precision, but evidence from other circuits throughout the country suggests that most of the work was again completed within the three months of March, April and May.[15]

The costs incurred by parishes and companies in making their returns varied in proportion to the extent of their endowments and the state of their records. On receipt of the Bill of Articles they began a frenzied search for deeds, wills, rentals, royal licences and any other muniments which might establish the age and reputability of a foundation. In 1548 St Botolph Aldgate held a general parish meeting to discuss the reply.[16] More commonly, wardens enlisted a few worthy helpers to draft their returns after poring over the documentation, often in the presence of a lawyer and/or scrivener. Those involved might seek consolation and sustenance, at parish expense, in some nearby hostelry. The wardens' accounts for St Dunstan in the West in 1546[17] record payments of £2 16s 6d for one dinner at the Queen's Head to discuss the return, 8s 8d for another dinner at the Rose tavern to amend it, and 2s 8d for breakfast at Guildhall when it had been safely delivered to the commissioners. Expenses were more modest there in 1548, no doubt because most of the answers were to hand from the previous enquiry; but the Queen's Head was again patronised, at a cost of £1 9s 8d, and more remarkably twelve rabbits and two capons were provided by the parish for a dinner for the commissioners at Mr Losse's house. Among the parishes, expenses of this order were exceptional, though small sums for identical ends are frequently entered in wardens' accounts.

The drafting and writing of the returns could also be costly. In 1548 it cost St Mary at Hill £1 for the advice of a counsellor and £1 6s 8d for a scribe.[18] For All Hallows Staining, with less to declare, the return cost only 4s 4d,[19] and for St Andrew Hubbard 2s 8d.[20] On the other hand, St Michael Cornhill employed 'the scrivener in Fleet Street', paying him £4 2s 4d.[21] Considering the many other expenses incurred at about the same time through legislation affecting church fabric and fittings, it was a heavy burden.

Turning to the companies, we find much the same reactions, though naturally on a somewhat larger scale. Muniments had to be sought: the Merchant Taylors, for example, paid Thomas Argall, the registrar of the Prerogative Court of Canterbury, to search out a will relating to one of their endowments.[22] The Recorder of London was called in to help some

14. Southwark was surveyed by the Surrey commissioners.
15. The return for St Peter Paul's Wharf is dated 16 March (Guildhall MS. 12140/3) and that for the Armourers' Company 20 April (MS. 12140/2).
16. Guildhall MS. 9235/1.
17. Guildhall MS. 2968/1.
18. Guildhall MS. 1239/1 pt 3.
19. Guildhall MS. 4956/1.
20. Guildhall MS. 1279/2.
21. Guildhall MS. 4071/1.
22. Guildhall Microfilm 298.

companies,[23] and hospitality was arranged. Occasionally, a company dinner afforded the opportunity to discuss the return, or indeed the very implications of making a return at all, since most of the companies feared for their non-religious endowments despite saving-clauses in the acts. In 1548 the Vintners held two dinners:[24] one in the Mermaid for £1 1s 8d, and the other in the Three Cranes for only 9s 8d. On a more extreme level, the Merchant Taylors in 1548, when summoned to appear at Haberdashers' Hall, claimed that they could not complete their return in time. So they 'rewarded' the pursuivant with 3s 4d and paid one of the commissioners' clerks a further 1s 8d to make a new date when they could have a dinner in their *own* hall for the commissioners: in the presence of the Lord Mayor, and at a cost of £7 18s, as it turned out.[25]

The 1548 Certificate: condition of the document
With this sketch of the procedural background we are in a better position to understand the 1548 Certificate. It consists of the commissioners' digest of the returns submitted by the parishes and companies. Forty large parchment membranes, approximately 19 inches wide and 30 inches long, were needed to contain the full Certificate. These were assembled one behind another and stitched together along the top, the whole document then being rolled. The membranes are, for the most part, covered with writing on both sides. The first and last are badly faded owing to their exposed position, and the tops and bottoms of many others are now also difficult to read. A few margins have been worn away, and here and there the modern reader's task is impeded by the application of gall, long since, in an endeavour to resurrect fading words and phrases. It has been necessary to study much of the document under ultra-violet light, and to compare it with related material to verify doubtful readings and fill some of the lacunae. By contrast, much of the interior of the document is still clearly legible, and it has been well repaired, so potential readers should not be deterred by the preceding remarks.

Other principal sources consulted
Foremost among the supporting material used in the preparation of this calendar is the 'Brief Certificate', a further report compiled by the chantry commissioners themselves from the original returns for the guidance of those who were to assign pensions for the dispossessed priests and issue warrants authorising the continuation of schools, poor relief, and clergy to assist the cure in populous parishes. The Brief Certificate for London and Middlesex at the Public Record Office[26] names, parish by parish, all those who received any regular income from the proscribed endowments, and adds a few recommendations for continuation, which are discussed below. A record of the pensions actually paid in London and Middlesex immediately after the dissolution is enrolled in two of the Exchequer Various Accounts in the Public Record Office.[27]

23. e.g., the Grocers (Guildhall MS. 11571/5) and Merchant Taylors (Microfilm 298).
24. Guildhall MS. 15333/1.
25. Guildhall Microfilm 298.
26. E 301/88.
27. E 101/75/21 and 22.

As already hinted, a good many original returns survive, in the Public Record Office, in Guildhall Library, at St Paul's cathedral and among company records. Those which have come to my attention are mentioned in the footnotes to the appropriate section of the calendar, and have been carefully compared with the Certificate. It has not, however, been practicable to annotate every variation between the sources, and readers wishing to follow up entries for particular parishes are recommended to consult all the alternative sources.

The accounts of churchwardens and company officials, many of which are preserved at Guildhall, shed further light on the ceremonies being observed on the eve of the dissolution, whilst the wills of many benefactors are abstracted in R. R. Sharpe's calendar of wills enrolled in the Husting Court. The Certificate itself is often a signpost to the existence of a will, mortmain licence, or other supporting document which may prove useful to those wishing to trace the earlier history of a foundation. In a few instances comparison with the Valor Ecclesiasticus of 1535[28] has been instructive, but this must be used with caution: a lot of water had flowed under the bridge in the intervening years. More useful in several respects are the Ministers' Accounts of Augmentations for the first year following the dissolutions.[29] They supply details on some of the individual properties that had yielded rent to the dissolved foundations, together with a good deal of topographical detail wanting in the Certificate. A somewhat later, and only partial, abridgement of the main Certificate, entitled 'The foundation of all the chantries in London and Middlesex', whose *raison d'être* I have been unable to discover, is now among the Harleian Manuscripts at the British Library.[30]

The function and limitations of the Certificate
The Certificate should be judged on its own terms: as a summary of the endowments proscribed by the 1547 chantry act and therefore liable to confiscation. It was intended only as a general guide to the crown and the court of Augmentations on the likely yield, and hence as a basic reference work when the property was to be disposed of. It is better understood as the first major document in the story of the expropriation of the chantries than as the last one in that of their working days, though of course it does contain many indications of that earlier history if treated with caution. It is a monument to the industry not only of the commissioners and scribes but also of the parishioners and company officials who made the returns. Yet it has to be said that the Certificate was a hastily prepared abstract: the magnitude of the task in hand for London and Middlesex militated against those telling asides found in some other Certificates as to the worthiness of certain foundations to continue. We tend to be presented with the bare bones, and the meat may sometimes be found in the complementary sources mentioned above. To take just one example, the Certificate rarely mentions the names of the saints in whose honour altars, chapels and masses were dedicated, even when dealing with St Paul's cathedral; this is

28. Ed. J. Caley and J. Hunter (6 vols 1810–34).
29. SC 6/Edw. VI/293 and 298 respectively.
30. Harley 601.

not a suggestion that devotion to the saints had lapsed, but merely a result of the summarising process. The commissioners were responsible for this basic limitation on the information they transmitted, though it is only fair to note that there were often deficiencies also in the source material from which the returns were compiled: when wills and foundation deeds could not be found,[31] or when re-foundations or augmentations of earlier endowments were mistaken by parishioners for the original foundation. Neither should we expect a high degree of consistency in terminology and presentation: the returns came in from hundreds of different people who interpreted the questions in a variety of different ways.

Sections of the Certificate
The Certificate falls into three distinct sections which digest, respectively, the returns submitted by the city of London churches including St Paul's cathedral (**1–116**), by Middlesex parishes (**117–190**), and by the city companies (**191–224**). The entries within each section appear to be in random order. Each section is followed by a summary of the total value of the endowments it has just listed, with the signatures of the commissioners.

Institutions omitted from the Certificate
Negative returns—if there were any in 1548 as there certainly were in 1546 —do not appear in the Certificate. This probably explains the lack of any entry for St Mary Mounthawe and St Katherine Colman, and many of the lesser companies. With the single exception of St Helen Bishopsgate (**101**), where two chantries were supported by the crown itself, none of the surviving ex-monastic, now parochial, churches is mentioned. Even Westminster, now a cathedral, is omitted. Most of the assets of these monasteries had, of course, been confiscated already, and in this respect a further survey may have been deemed superfluous, though it is hard to believe they had nothing to declare by way of lights, obits and lesser endowments, even if they no longer had any active chantries. Hospitals, too, are omitted, including St Katharine by the Tower and the Savoy, the latter in any case being within the Duchy of Lancaster. The absence of a return for St Bartholomew the Less may also reflect the connection with a hospital. Whilst hospitals were exempt from the survey in 1548, there is no reason to suppose that any chantries within them were to be allowed to continue, and we know from the 1546 return that in St Katharine's at any rate, there were two chantries.[32] The reader will search in vain for any trace of institutions which had already surrendered to the crown, notably the college of St Martin le Grand. It is impossible to calculate how many further endowments were deliberately concealed from the commissioners.

Format of entries in the Certificate
The information in the Certificate is generally presented in columns. At the left-hand margin is a note of the parish or company concerned. There

31. For one endowment at St Michael Bassishaw the wardens 'could not tell where to find the same to make thereof plain declaration without further respect of time for better search' (E 301/89 fo.2v).
32. C. Jamison, *The History of the Royal Hospital of St Katharine* (1952), 57.

follows a brief description of each endowment there, and in the next column its total gross value. A further column provides a break-down of expenditure, with its own separate total on the right-hand side, below which is set out the 'Clear remainder', or net total once the expenses have been met. Where more, or less, had to be said about a given foundation, the columns were ignored and the entry made in a continuous statement reading across the membrane. Each parochial entry concludes with a section of 'Memoranda' answering further questions from the Bill of Articles.

The donor
Although it is possible to verify many of the names of original donors as stated in the Certificate from Husting wills, this is by no means always the case, for donations might be made during a man's lifetime, or as a result of some devise: it was common for endowments to be made, at least technically, by persons other than those for whose souls a chantry was nominally established. Frequently an initial bequest proved insufficient to support its desired objective, and then further benefactors might spring to the rescue with supplementary endowments. It can be unsafe to take the Certificate alone as evidence of the name or date of the original foundation, or indeed of the original intention, even when the ostensibly unambiguous formula 'given by A.B. for his soul for ever' is employed. The entry for the Grocers' Company (**212**) records lands given by John Billesdon for his soul for ever, but Billesdon's will makes clear that the bequest was principally for Sir Thomas Lovell's soul, which is not mentioned in the Certificate. The entry for St Peter Wood Street (**99**) has lands and tenements given by 'one Farrendon', but the original return for 1546 shows that they were actually given by John Foster and Thomas Polle to find a chaplain to sing 'for the prosperous and good estate' of King Henry IV during his life, for his soul after death, for John and Thomas themselves, and only in the last place for Nicholas Farrendon, whose name alone has passed into the Certificate. In the calendar the phrase 'bequeathed by' has been used where the original has 'given by A.B. in his will'. But even where there is no mention here of a will or bequest, the donation may actually have been made in this way.

The foundation
The Certificate then sets out the intention of the foundation, and care has been taken in the calendar to use the exact word found in the original to describe the nature of the endowment, even though it is certain that the terminology is quite imprecise.

Many endowments said to be for a *priest* or *chaplain* were in fact chantries,[33] but if the word is not used in the Certificate it has not been used in the calendar because there was at least a theoretical distinction between, for example, a *chantry priest* and a *stipendiary*. Whatever else he did in the parish, a chantry priest had a specific obligation to celebrate masses for particular souls, and his chantry might own property or draw rents, whereas a stipendiary, as the title suggests, was one who received a stipend

33. For example, we know from other evidence that Cresswick's 'chaplain and obit' at St Katherine Cree (**61**) was known as Cresswick's 'chantry' (PRO, Chancery, Town Depositions, C 24/23).

in cash, not necessarily derived from any specific properties set aside for the purpose, and was often appointed with the intention that he should assist the parish clergy in divine service and possibly with the cure of souls. In its original return[34] St Michael Bassishaw was insistent that it had no *chantries*, but rather three *stipendiaries*, two of them financed by the Yarford bequest, and added that 'the parish of St Michael's could not have been well served nor maintained in the service of God if this godly and blessed intent and mind of this foundation of Sir James Yarford had not been founded'. The Certificate, however, merely calls them *priests* (**74**). All Hallows Bread Street reported in 1546 that it had four priests 'but whether they be chantry or stipendiary priests they know not'.[35] In 1548 the Certificate records in this parish (**90**) only one *priest* and one *chaplain* (besides four *priests* maintained there by city companies, which may help to explain the bewilderment). It was to become an extremely important point of law whether a priest merely received a cash stipend from an individual or corporation, or whether he received profits from specific lands or rents given to maintain his foundation. The city companies were to insist, in their long battle with the crown over the confiscation of their 'chantry' endowments, that when they maintained chantries they were only paying fixed cash stipends from their overall revenues. Even if someone had given them specific properties with a view to their maintaining a chantry from the proceeds, they held that the lands thus acquired became a full part of the company's overall estates, and were not appropriated to that specific objective. The crown was to take the opposite view at the dissolution, and the companies were compelled to buy back the lands and rents in question. It is noteworthy that in the companies' section of the Certificate the entries uniformly speak of payments to 'A.B., priest, for his stipend' even where *lands and tenements* are said to be the source of income.

There is occasional mention also of *conducts*, priests hired on a more casual basis for particular services, or to swell the numbers in the choir and teach children. Most of them were sufficiently part of the parochial establishment to receive a regular, if small, income, and thus to qualify for a pension after the dissolution. The Brief Certificate clearly distinguishes them from the other types of clergy,[36] though it appears to use interchangeably the terms *chantry priests*, *chaplains* and *stipendiaries*, and frequently adds to the confusion by speaking of the 'chantry of A.B.' in one breath, and describing its priest as a *stipendiary* in the next. The title *Sir*, applied haphazardly to priests in the Certificate, was not confined to those of any particular standing, and its omission in many instances is insignificant. We find it used of graduates and non-graduates alike.

Obits or *anniversaries* (the terms appear to be used interchangeably) were annual commemorations of the deceased on the anniversary of his death or on some other convenient day. They might be conducted by the parish clergy, chantry priests or others hired for the occasion. The associated ceremonies and benefactions varied considerably with local custom and

34. E 301/89.
35. LR 2/243 fo.23.
36. In the pension lists (E 101) they are described as 'ministers', as are lesser officials such as singing men and sextons.

the generosity of the funds left by the donor, but a common practice was to begin with the singing of vespers on the eve of the celebration, including the antiphon *Placebo*,[37] and to continue with matins and lauds on the day itself with the antiphon *Dirige*,[38] with or without a requiem mass. Payments might be made not only to the officiating priest, but to others present, ranging from the lord mayor and sheriffs for the obit of a distinguished citizen, to the choir, clerk and sexton. Alms were distributed to any poor persons present, or in some cases to a specified number of poor persons or children, sought out and paid either by the executors or the parish priest. In the case of obits supported by the city companies the solemnities were often made the occasion of a company feast. The Certificate is usually content to give merely the total sum spent on the obit, without a breakdown of the expenditure, and this is another instance where any surviving original returns or company accounts can throw more light on what actually happened.

Brotherhoods and *fraternities* are further terms used interchangeably in the Certificate, and may apply to men, or women, or both.[39] We shall return to these below. Endowments will also be noted for *lamps*, and for particular liturgical observances such as the singing of *anthems* and *Salves*.

It should perhaps be mentioned here that in some instances, whilst clear provision is made for endowments, and an annual income recorded, there is no actual statement that the money was being spent in the way originally intended. The entry for St Sepulchre Newgate (**13**) looks impressive on paper for all its priests, yet only paragraphs 1 and 6 of the entry actually state that the priest in question was being paid, and only two priests are named in the Brief Certificate. Some endowments had lapsed, and this was a case where others had been merged or augmented to ensure enough income for a more limited number of priests than originally envisaged.

The source of income

The commissioners chose not to record precise details of sources of income, but distinguished only between real estate and ready cash. Endowments in the form of real estate are mainly entered as consisting of *lands and tenements*, a generic term which ought not to be too strictly interpreted. The Ministers' Accounts show that an endowment comprising only land, or only houses, might well be described as *lands and tenements* in the Certificate. Occasionally more specific information is given: houses, shops, cottages, and so on, in which case more significance may be attached to the descriptions. Care has been taken in the calendar to preserve the distinction between endowments in real estate and those in cash (including rents), by commencing the entries with the description of the property followed by the stated value in the former case; and by placing the value first in the latter case. The commissioners did not use the Certificate to pinpoint the

37. Psalm 115 verse 9.
38. Psalm 5 verse 9. See *Lincoln Diocese Documents*, ed. A. Clark (Early English Texts Society, vol. 149, 1914), 8. *Dirige* might be said on the eve with mass on the day itself, see *The Medieval Records of a London City Church*, ed. H. Littlehales (EETS, vol. 128, 1905), p. li.
39. e.g., see the usage in **21** and **22**.

exact location of properties eligible for confiscation: they were content with a general description, sometimes to the extent of recording the parish in which property was situated. Hence the Certificate is not a good hunting-ground for topographical detail, save in those few instances where it steps beyond its normal limits. For example, we read once of a 'tenement in the parish of St Mary Magdalene Old Fish Street, at the corner of Dolittle Lane' (**8**). In all, forty tenement names or signs are recorded, though not always with the name of the street or parish. They are included in the subject index.

Disbursements

In every case the figures recorded in the Certificate have been faithfully reproduced even if the sums do not correctly add up. Errors in the original have been indicated where noted. The profitability of endowments varied considerably. Rents might fluctuate from year to year; expenditure on maintenance or repairs was sporadic: several years might elapse with nothing to be spent, and then massive bills might be incurred in a subsequent year. There were often commitments outside the immediate foundation, for example in the form of quitrents to other landowners, and tenths (payable on perpetual chantries) to the king. The founder's aim would have been to provide an income sufficient to maintain his objective and leave enough over to meet likely costs. This profit, described as the *clear remainder* might be quite handsome in some years, whilst in others there might be a deficit. Among the Harleian manuscripts[40] there survives 'A remembrance of the charges and receipts of the chantries of Chalton and Illyngworth' in St Alban Wood Street, which observes that 'the receipts are more than the payments every year by £13 4s 8d, which if the lands be well guided were sufficient every year to bear the vacations and reparations'. For Wodcocke's chantry in the same church the profit recorded is only 13s 10d, 'which is not able every year, one with another, to bear the vacations and reparations, as will appear every year by the reckonings'. Since the Certificate provides us with the figures for only one year, they are not necessarily indicative of the health of a given endowment, but of course where the clear remainder is recorded as *Nil* (which in the Certificate often hides the fact, revealed by the sub-totals, that there was actually a deficit), financial collapse may have been imminent. In good years, or in the case of wealthy endowments which were unlikely ever to sink into deficit, it was sometimes possible to provide for extra clergy out of the surplus, as at St James Garlickhithe (**16**).[41] Foreseeing the possibility, some founders sought to place controls on any surplus revenue. John Bottesham and Alice Potyn gave two tenements to St Dunstan in the East to house a chantry priest and a parish clerk (**21**). A box was to be kept for the residue of the profits from which loans could be made to the poor, and the cost of repairing the tenements met. The rules were still stricter at St Andrew by the Wardrobe, where any surplus from John Parraunt's chantry was to be put away in a chest with three locks, one

---

40. MS. Harley 604/17 fos 51v–52; cf. **57**.
41. Cf. LR 2/242 fo. 55v: a detailed account of how the wardens at St Andrew by the Wardrobe spent the surplus funds from John Lee's chantry.

key kept by the chantry priest, one by the parish priest and one by the churchwardens.[42]

The Memoranda: Housling people

Parishes were asked to include in their returns the total numbers of *housling people*, and in most cases their answers appear, among the *Memoranda* at the foot of each entry, calendared here as 'communicants'. It may be assumed that the figure sought was the total number of those eligible to receive communion: in other words, the maximum number of persons to whom the clergy had to administer the Sacrament on Easter Day, when all those eligible to receive were expected to do so. This was some measure of the number of clergy required to minister in the parish. The Somerset return uses the phrase 'partakers of the Lord's Supper',[43] and that for Hertfordshire 'people that receive the Holy Communion'.[44] Whilst some of the figures given look like exact computations, which may indicate that they represent the actual number who received Communion, the majority appear to be nicely rounded approximations, and as such cannot be used with any precision as a basis for calculating the total population of the city, even if we could be sure what was the ratio of communicants to the total population. In fact, no consensus exists on this ratio. William Page, editing the Yorkshire Certificates, thought that the housling total should be doubled to arrive at the total population.[45] J. E. Brown, working on Hertfordshire,[46] favoured adding only a quarter to the housling total given, to account for those under fourteen years of age, and therefore below the normal age for receiving communion. In a recent study, Kevin McDonnell uses a multiplier of 0.75 on the housling totals to calculate the numbers of those aged under fourteen.[47]

The Certificate gives a housling total of 3,400 for St Sepulchre Newgate **(13)**, whilst the Brief Certificate speaks of 4,000 'people' in the parish. This is not a sufficient basis for any calculations since either figure, or both, may have been an approximation. There is no other internal evidence available from the Certificate, and the different methods outlined above yield very different population totals, as may be seen by taking a sample parish with a notional total of 200 housling people. By Page's method there would be 400 people; Brown would suggest 250 and McDonnell 350. The totals given for housling people at the end of the London Certificate are 41,664, and at the end of the Middlesex Certificate 22,079. By the various methods just described this would give a range for the total population of from just under 50,000 to well over 80,000 in London; and from 26,000 to 44,000 in

42. LR 2/242 fo. 52.
43. *Survey and Rental of the Chantries . . . in the County of Somerset*, ed. E. Green (Somerset Record Society, 1888), e.g. p. 25.
44. *Chantry Certificates for Hertfordshire*, ed. J. E. Brown [c. 1910], p. viii.
45. *Yorkshire Chantry Surveys*, ii, ed. W. E. Page (Surtees Society, 1895), p. xvi.
46. See above, n. 44.
47. *Medieval London Suburbs* (1978), 120. Peter Laslett suggests, in *Household and Family in Times Past* (Cambridge, 1972), ch. 4, that an average household comprised 4.75 persons; and the *Oxford English Dictionary* ('housling') cites an example from Ulcombe in Kent which suggests that there was roughly one householder to every 4 communicants there. If the latter sort of ratio were also true in London this would provide another basis for calculations.

Middlesex. Since the figures are almost certain to exclude those temporarily resident, including foreign merchants and other visitors, something approaching the higher figure may well be more realistic.

The Memoranda: Parish Clergy

The memoranda for each parish include, where supplied, the name of the 'parson'. Since the Certificate often speaks of the king or some impropriator as 'parson' the word has been calendared throughout as *rector*. Additional comments about serving the cure have to be treated with caution, and in some cases are tantalisingly ambiguous. In a few cases the meaning is clear, as where the rector 'serves the cure himself without any help',[48] or at the opposite extreme 'is never resident'.[49] But the words 'AB, rector, who findeth no one to serve the cure', may simply mean that the rector is resident and does not pay a curate, whilst 'AB, rector, finds a curate in his absence' may mean either that AB is normally absent so finds a curate, or that when AB happens to be absent he finds a curate. The Certificate cannot be used on its own, therefore, as an indicator of clerical non-residence in 1548.

The Memoranda: Schools

Parishes were also asked to note whether they had any grammar schools, and to this article they practically all made a negative return. The commissioners began the Certificate by including these pieces of negative information, but quickly realised that it was a waste of ink and stopped doing so. Therefore the absence of a specific statement on schools in the Certificate does not mean that the question went unanswered. It should be noted that the question was not whether any of the priests taught.

A comparison with other sources

Enough has now been said to indicate the degree of caution that is appropriate for the reader approaching the Certificate for the first time. The following case study demonstrates how fresh light can be shed by the complementary sources, in some instances showing that the Certificate, if used on its own, may be positively misleading. For the parish of St Peter Paul's Wharf we have not only the Certificate (**60**) but also, in Guildhall, the original return.[50] It is particularly fortunate that this parish also received contributions from the Armourers' Company, whose original return also survives in the same series at Guildhall.[51] We can therefore easily check the thoroughness of the Certificate.

When making their original return, the rector and churchwardens of St Peter's observed at the outset that they used to have three chantries, but that the costs of maintenance, including the payment of tenths to the crown, had compelled them to merge the revenues and maintain only two priests. They supplied full details of the bequests that had established the chantries, and produced the original wills for the commissioners to see. They itemised the tenements and rents involved and gave the names of

48. e.g. **81**.
49. e.g. **91**.
50. MS. 12140/3.
51. MS. 12140/2.

current occupiers. They named the two priests as James Payne and Thomas Potter, giving their respective ages as sixty-eight and forty-six, and commenting 'their qualities be sufficient to serve their charges; their understanding in the Latin tongue is indifferent'. The three chantries had been set up by (i) William Barnard in 1310 with an annual quitrent of £4 6s 8d; (ii) Walter Kent in 1361 with property now yielding annually £7 4s; and (iii) William at Stoke *alias* Essex in 1430 with an annual quitrent of £10 divided between a chaplain to sing for John Trygges and others including William himself (£6 13s 4d), an augmentation for Barnard's chaplain (£2 6s 8d) and an obit of £1; the £10 was now being paid by the Armourers, Trygges' chantry being the one that had lapsed, its endowments being used instead to maintain and repair the other properties.

If we now turn to the Armourers' return and look for their account of the £10 just mentioned we find more detail. William at Stoke had financed his bequests merely by a rent-charge issuing from his property: he had not given the property itself to his chantry. But forty-eight years later, in 1478, the then owner of the property, Everard Frere, had bequeathed it to the Armourers' Company, asking them to set up another chantry for the soul of Katherine Alyard after her death, and to distribute bread to five poor men every Sunday. On reflection, however, the company had decided that the revenue was insufficient both to maintain William at Stoke's bequest and to establish a new chantry, so with Katherine's agreement they provided the poor men with their bread but did not endow a priest for her.

Now what does the Certificate tell us of all this? The entry for St Peter Paul's Wharf (**60**) records in the merest outline the chantries of William Barnard and Walter Kent, and the totals agree with those in the original parish return. Only one of the two priests is named, and no account of their ages or standing is given. No details of the founders' wills are noted. There is no mention of the payment made by the Armourers, because it appears later in the Certificate in the entry for the company. In that entry (**215**), we read that the endowment of a priest in St Peter's and the augmentation of Barnard's chaplain were financed from 'lands and tenements' bequeathed by William at Stoke, that James Payn, priest, receives £6 13s 4d, and that a further £2 6s 8d is given to augment Barnard's chaplain. The Certificate's shorthand has become distinctly misleading. For, as we have seen from the originals William at Stoke did not give land, but only a rent-charge; it was Everard Frere who had given the land, and he had not given it to the chantry but to the Armourers' Company. James Payne and Barnard's chaplain were one and the same. Nor is any mention made of the prayers for John Trygges and others that were an integral part of William at Stoke's chantry foundation. The information submitted has not only been précised: it has been conflated to some extent. But there is no confusion over the total sum involved, and this emphasises the basic function of the Certificate.

This short case study is given not to undermine the reader's confidence in everything that the Certificate will try to tell him, but merely to stress the caution that is necessary in interpreting the information, and the need to consult as many other sources as possible. By contrast, there are cases where the Certificate tells us more than some of the supporting sources. For example, the will of William Newport as enrolled in the Husting court[52] includes donations to be 'devoted to the good of his soul' by his executors. The Certificate (**4**) shows that a *Salve* was sung before the image of the Virgin in St Nicholas Olave, and a lamp kept burning there.

Despite its shortcomings, the Certificate has the over-riding advantage that it fills in more of the picture of the chantries for the whole of our area than do any of the other sources taken individually. And although every element of its information must of course be subject to careful scrutiny, this is equally true for the other sources (and indeed for any other major administrative record of the period). A glance at each section of the Certificate in turn will help to redress the balance in its favour by showing some of the wider issues on which it throws some light.

The London returns
The heyday of chantry foundations in London as elsewhere had been the late fourteenth and early fifteenth centuries, after which the rate of new foundations steadily declined down to the Reformation. In the fourteenth century in particular the city authorities had fought to defend the right of those who held property within the city to devise it to the church without applying for royal mortmain licences, and although the crown, by repeated inquisitions and legal proceedings, made all potential donors think twice about their rights, the position was substantially maintained, subject to scrutiny by the mayor and recorder of all wills containing such devises before their enrolment at the Husting court.[53] The wills themselves provide a valuable source for the history of many such foundations.

Perpetual endowments (whether by gift, or devise, and whether by royal licence or not) are only a part of the story, though naturally the best documented part. It was possible to pay a lump sum for a single mass, or for that matter for as many masses as desired. Few aspired to the 1,000 masses sought by William Staundon, grocer, in 1412.[54] But a mass might be had for a few pence,[55] and thus came within the pocket of lesser men who could not afford perpetual endowments. For the same reason of economy, lamps and torches were very popular; even those parishes which had no chantry endowment to report often had to make some return about a lamp or some other lesser observance.

Smaller and short-term endowments of obits, masses and prayers virtually supplanted the long-term and perpetual endowment by the early sixteenth century. Fashions and fortunes had changed: families had grown larger, leaving less disposable income to spend on religious endowments.[56] And when church lands, and the very doctrine of purgatory, came under

52. *Husting*, ii, 336.
53. H. M. Chew, 'Mortmain in Medieval London', *English Historical Review*, lx (1945), 1–17. For two recent studies of London chantries see Rosalind Hill, 'A chaunterie for souls' in *Reign of Richard II*, ed. F. R. H. Du Boulay and C. M. Barron (1972), 242; and L. S. Snell, 'London chantries and chantry chapels' in *Collectanea Londiniensia*, ed. J. Bird *et al.* (1978), 216.
54. *Husting*, ii, p. iv.
55. e.g. **98**.
56. J. A. F. Thompson, 'Piety and charity in late medieval London', *Journal of Ecclesiastical History*, xvi (1965), 191.

threat as Protestantism spread, it was hardly to be expected that long-term endowments would continue to find favour. W. K. Jordan has noted that prayers for the dead were still 'at once numerous and generous' in London in the period 1511–40, though a 'remarkably slender portion' of all that was bequeathed went into chantry and other religious observances.[57]

From the 1520s there was a steady infiltration of Protestant ideas into the capital. Writers and preachers challenged parishioners to cease believing in purgatory and prayers to the saints. There was sporadic image-breaking, and the crown itself began to place curbs on certain types of endowment.[58] The dissolution of the monasteries sealed the fate of those chantries which had been maintained by the monks themselves within the walls, unless founders' families or trustees intervened to remove the endowment to a parish church.[59] But many a founder had alternatively given lands or money to a monastery on condition that it maintained a chantry in his memory in a parish church from the profits, the remaining income being devoted to the monastery itself. (The practice exactly parallelled that of giving land to one of the city companies with similar provisos.) In such cases, when the crown confiscated the monastic revenue it honoured the commitment outside the walls by paying the (continuing) chantry priest an annual stipend from the court of Augmentations, demonstrating that as yet there was no intention of declaring chantries illegal.

Yet despite this apparent leniency the crown gradually introduced further restrictions on the endowment of religious observances. By 1538 it was illegal to keep lamps burning before images.[60] So it would be surprising if by the 1540s there had not been some falling off in the old observances, the endowments being withdrawn or witheld for other uses. The Certificate contains a few pointers to this, though they cannot all be taken at face value as symptomatic of rising Protestant feeling, or even of a fear for the safety of investments. Some decay of the old foundations resulted from sheer financial necessity, the funds being needed elsewhere. Such might have been the case with the endowment for one of the brotherhood priests at St Dunstan in the West, which had been diverted for the past twenty years to the repair of the church (**20**). And we are sometimes witnessing nothing more than the normal life-cycle of such endowments, which had come and gone in their scores throughout the middle ages. This, no doubt, explains many of those instances in the Certificate where, although there is provision for a priest, nobody is actually named as holding the post. But there are other examples which do suggest a growing fear for the investments. It was just two and a half years since the money set aside for a lamp in St James Garlickhithe had been channelled instead into poor relief (**16**). Robert Brocket had left money for a chantry priest at St Martin Pomery but made alternative provision for donations to prisoners and poor relief if it proved impossible to maintain a respectable priest 'for lack of honest behaving himself'; in 1548 it was the prisoners who were drawing the money

57. *Charities of London, 1480–1660* (1960), 276, 22.
58. e.g., see Statute 23 Hen. VIII c.10.
59. e.g., Thomas Roger's obit maintained by the Vintners (**193**).
60. *Visitation Articles and Injunctions of the Reformation Period*, ed. W. H. Frere and W. M. Kennedy, ii (1910), 38.

(223). One donor at St Martin Outwich had requested that land be bought to secure the future of his obit, but his wishes had not been honoured.[61]

Yet even amid all the Protestant preaching and exposition of the scriptures,[62] there was little relenting in the daily round of chantry masses and obits. In 1542 Brinklow's *Lamentation of a Christian against the City of London* still found it necessary to protest against the continued support given to chantries,[63] and the Certificate amply testifies to the continuing devotions in almost every parish. There was scarcely a church in the city that did not have something to declare to the commissioners, even if it were only an occasional obit or a lamp burning before the sacrament. There were many parishes where the old traditions were quite unabated. St Magnus had a dozen or so priests and conducts if we include those ministering to its fraternity (24–5). St Dunstan in the East had ten priests (21), as did St James Garlickhithe (16), and several others could boast half a dozen or more.

It is noteworthy that in London many of the parish churches outshone the 'collegiate' foundations, which were on a small scale compared with St Stephen's in Westminster or the great secular colleges found in other counties. Whittington college in St Michael Paternoster Royal had a master and six fellows, four choristers and a handful of casually hired conducts (96). The collegiate foundation in St Lawrence Pountney comprised, in addition to the rector, only three fellows and four lesser officials (71). The 'colleges' associated with St Paul's cathedral were no more than communal lodgings for the clergy associated with particular chantries (113). The college in the Guildhall, which unlike Whittington and St Lawrence Pountney colleges had no parochial responsibilities, had only a master and three fellows (92).

The Certificate is therefore more concerned with chantry and similar foundations. The clergy who depended on them for a living are shadowy figures about whom little beyond a name is known. Only in a handful of cases did information about their age and standing—even though it was specifically sought in the Bills of Articles—filter through to the Certificate. Such a sample is statistically insignificant, though it records men of all ages from their twenties to their seventies, none of whom had more than a modest level of education: 'a base singer and simply learned . . . of poor quality and learning . . . of good conversation and learning touching ordinary service', and so on. They were legion, and a glance through the index of names suggests that there was no noticeable degree of pluralism among the chantry and stipendiary priests named in the Certificate. This suggests in turn that there was a plentiful supply of candidates for such posts.

The Brief Certificate, which contains rather more names than the Certificate, gives 266 chantry priests, stipendiaries or chaplains in London excluding St Paul's, and a further 69 conducts. In St Paul's, in addition to the cathedral's regular team of canons and petty canons, there were 48 chantry priests. This gives a grand total of 383 lesser clergy in the capital whose jobs

61. **91**, and compare Mr Cote at St Vedast (**5**).
62. See Claire Cross, *Church and People 1450–1660* (1976), 72–3.
63. *VCH London*, i (1909), 281.

were simultaneously under attack, and only a handful of whom remained in post after the dissolution. In Middlesex there were only a score or so of chantry priests and 4 conducts, excluding the staff of St Stephen's college, Westminster (who were all pensioned off: dean, 11 canons, 11 vicars and 4 chantry priests). If we recall the omission from the Certificate of the cathedral at Westminster and of certain other foundations noted above, the total number of clergy affected by the dissolution in our area alone may have been as high as 450, most of whom were pensioned off. The dissolution therefore created considerable upheaval, even though there were many clerical opportunities in the capital on a permanent basis, in private and hospital chaplaincies, or more temporarily during vacancies and at particularly busy seasons such as Easter. Few chantry priests drew less than £6 13s 4d yearly, and this wage seems to have been the norm in the city. Although it was not a fortune by contemporary standards it was enough to live on, and was no doubt supplemented in many cases by re-muneration for other casual employment, sometimes by the inclusion of a room or house rent-free,[64] and in the case of some ex-monks by royal pensions drawn in addition to the chantry stipend.[65]

In London as elsewhere it is debatable to what extent chantry priests and stipendiaries became involved in the regular services and ministry of the parish. It was implicit in many foundations that they should. For example, Agnes Palmer left money to the Fishmongers' Company to maintain a chantry and obit for her husband in St Peter West Cheap, requiring the priest to be perpetually resident and present at all divine service 'at the hours and times convenient'.[66] Many foundations were made deliberately to increase the number of masses available to the parish at large: this is particularly true of donations for the morrow mass. At Holy Trinity the Less **(85)** the rector gave an extra 16s yearly and a chamber to one of the privately endowed stipendiaries so that he would in addition help him to serve the cure,[67] whilst at St Leonard Foster Lane the parishioners them-selves raised the money to find a stipendiary to help the parish priest minister to his 450 communicants **(65)**. Several other returns, explicitly or implicitly, indicate that such priests were assisting the parochial ministry.[68] Naturally, the busiest time came at Easter when all of age to receive com-munion were expected to do so and every available priest was needed to help. At St Mary Woolchurch, with 360 communicants and three chantry priests in addition to the rector and curate, the parishioners still observed that at Easter 'all the priests we have do not suffice' **(36)**.

But it was one thing to assist at the canonical hours and to sing the services hitherto laid down, helping out with other duties at busy times, and quite another to engage fully in the pastoral ministry. In compiling the Brief Certificate and making their recommendations for the continuation of some clergy in populous parishes, the commissioners recognised either

64. This was by no means always the case. The stipendiaries at St Michael Bassishaw, for instance, had no rooms 'but such as they hire and pay rent for' (E 301/89 m.3r).
65. See Subject index: Augmentations, pensions.
66. E 301/120.
67. See also St Matthew Friday Street **(69)** and St John the Evangelist **(70)**.
68. Particularly **2, 34, 82, 88, 95, 107.**

little need for regular assistance or little potential in the particular clergy available to provide it as a result of the dissolution. Exactly what criteria they employed in making their decisions is not clear, but only two London parishes, both outside the walls—St Botolph Aldersgate with 1,100 communicants and St Sepulchre with no fewer than 4,000—secured one assistant each. Why was no similar provision felt necessary for St Giles Cripplegate (2,440), St Bride (1,400), St Botolph Aldgate (1,130), St Dunstan in the East (900) or St Dunstan in the West (900)?

There were financial and disciplinary reasons why the commissioners might have felt constrained to keep their recommendations down to a minimum, regardless of the merits of individual clergy or the needs of particular parishes. A commitment to pay an assistant to the cure instead of pensioning the same man off gave the crown a long-term financial obligation to the parish. And whatever the ultimate goal of the dissolution, it was certainly not to find a means of retaining the maximum number of clergy associated with the old foundations. The greater the number of those left in post, the more difficult it would be to ensure that the proscribed ceremonies were actually stamped out. It was probably also in the commissioners' minds that the ill-educated clergy they for the most part found in these positions were not the men needed for a vigorous pastoral ministry in future.

If the chantry priests and stipendiaries had been regularly assisting with education in the parishes, the Certificate is remarkably silent on the subject. But most of the clergy were probably like those we have already met at St Peter the Less, whose understanding of the Latin tongue was indifferent. The well established St Anthony's school is mentioned in the return for St Benet Fink (**55**) without further comment, but otherwise teaching is referred to in only four London parishes. In every case it was almost certainly confined to children who sang in the choir. Rice Williams was 'schoolmaster of the children' at St Mary at Hill, where there was a dispute in the court of Augmentations before it was determined to cease paying him.[69] The rest seem to have faded out gracefully: James Rimyger, organist and 'master of the singing children' at St Dunstan in the East (**21**), Hugh Jones who taught singing children at St Mary Woolnoth (**40**), and Peter Jackson, an ex-monk, at St Gregory (**10**). Outside London, the Mercers maintained a school at Farthingho, Northants, and the Goldsmiths one at Stockport, Cheshire, both of which are recorded (**194, 222**). The Chantry Certificate is, of course, the wrong place in which to look for evidence of schooling unconnected with chantry foundations. The Brief Certificate does not single out any schools as worthy of continuation.

In addition to noting potential assistants to the cure, and schools worthy of maintaining, the Brief Certificates made a point of recording donations to poor relief, which were exempt from confiscation under the chantry act, and which the government intended rather to encourage and augment. Poor relief flowing from chantries and fraternities, as has often been remarked, was very haphazard and did little to penetrate the roots of poverty. As an extreme example we may take the parish of St Sepulchre which was said to have no fewer than 900 poor people, and yet declared

69. BC.

only 4s set aside for their relief (**13**). The scale of contributions and the status of those eligible to receive them depended on the individual benefactor, who also dictated whether the relief should be in the form of a direct cash 'dole', or goods such as food, clothing or fuel, or relief from the payment of Easter dues and the like.[70] Many bequests were once-for-all gifts to those who attended the testator's funeral, and therefore do not appear in the Certificate, which speaks only of the regular contributions being made annually, usually in association with obits.

The Brief Certificate summarises contributions to the poor as follows: a yearly total of £134 from the London parishes and only £12 from Middlesex, to which must be added a further £116 in benefactions to named individuals sponsored by five London fraternities and one in Middlesex, together with the almshouses attached to St Stephen's college, Westminster. The latter distorts the general picture, for almshouses as such were exempt from the act: the one at St Stephen's is only mentioned because the college itself was dissolved. One of the bedesmen there received £5 12s 8d yearly, six others £5 6s each and the eighth £5 3s 4d: sums which compare favourably with the earnings of the chantry priests: 'poverty' here was a relative term. Out in the parishes it was a different story. The fraternity of Corpus Christi in St Giles Cripplegate, for example, supported eight poor persons with grants of from 6d to 10d each per week, a further two at half a mark per quarter, and one more at 5s per quarter. A shilling or so a week seems here to have been considered generous as the contribution to a bedesman on a fraternity's roll. But it would again be wrong to assume that the Certificate tells the whole story: it speaks only of the lasting endowment or regular contribution which the crown scrutinised. We may safely assume that many contributions among fraternities to the support of their own members in true need did not arise from any endowment, but from *ad hoc* collections which did not attract the commissioners' attention.

It would be as unsafe to use only the Certificate to calculate the total number of fraternities in city churches as it would be to use only this source for the number of city companies in existence. For that would be to forget that the Certificate deals only with the tangibles: goods, money and lands to be forfeit to the crown. Associations with no regular endowments completely escaped attention, or made negative returns which are not here recorded. Only thirty or so fraternities are mentioned, finding priests for special masses, or supporting lamps, obits and liturgical observances.[71]

St Paul's cathedral
The section of the roll covering the chantries and obits of St Paul's includes some of the least legible passages of the whole Certificate. Fortunately, however, John Caley, keeper of the records in the Augmentations Office, transcribed this section early in the nineteenth century for Henry Ellis's continuation of Dugdale's history of St Paul's. A comparison of Caley's readings with the more legible parts of the roll reveals a few minor errors of transcription, and although Caley's version has been used in the prepara-

70. See Subject index: poor relief.
71. On the wider rôle of fraternities, see S. L. Thrupp, *The Merchant Class of Medieval London, 1300–1500* (Ann Arbor, 1962), 34 *et seq.*

tion of this calendar, it has been checked against what becomes legible of the original under ultra-violet light.

Several other sources furnish information which may be used to check and supplement that given in the Certificate. The cathedral library still retains a copy of the dean and chapter's original return made to the chantry commissioners.[72] Thomas Fuller examined it when compiling his *Church History* and abstracted a certain amount of information: 'enough to acquaint us with the nature of all the rest'![73] He added, 'It seems the chapter would not go to the cost of true arithmetic; some of the sums being not rightly deducted: whose mistakes I chose rather to follow than to vary any whit from the original'. In fact, there are few such errors, and the return contains far more detailed information than the Certificate itself. For the commissioners' purposes, no more than the usual abstract of the terms of foundation, and summary totals of income and expenditure were officially needed, whereas the chapter had made a comprehensive return to each of the questions asked, including full details of the dates and terms of each chantry endowment, stating not only for whose souls prayers were to be offered, but also the names of the actual founders: we have seen that these were often quite different, though the commissioners lightly disregarded the distinction. The majority of the foundations within the cathedral were in memory of its own ecclesiastical dignitaries: bishops of London, deans and canons; and whilst a few had been planned in the lifetime of the donor many were created after the death of the person they commemorated, usually by his executors. The chapter also recorded the names of the altars or chapels at which the chantries and obits were celebrated, but this information did not find its way into the Certificate. They further gave precise details of property, including the names of tenants and full rentals. The names of chantry priests, which are in places omitted from the Certificate, are also to be found in the original, which contains in addition an inventory of the cathedral's plate.

The Brief Certificate and pension list happily present the names in the same order as the Certificate, which facilitates cross-checking of doubtful readings. The Ministers' Accounts for Michaelmas 1548 too are in the same order.

The obit list as given in the Certificate (112) is particularly badly faded at the top, but may be checked against Caley's readings, against earlier mentions of obits in Dugdale, and against printed lists of the obits celebrated.[74] The scribe of the Certificate was inconsistent in his rendering of early surnames,[75] but the readings given in the calendar retain the form he used.

The dean and chapter exercised general oversight of the cathedral's fifty or so chantries, and as many obits. Some of the foundations had been in existence since the twelfth or thirteenth centuries, and only two were sixteenth-century creations.[76] If the income of a particular foundation

72. WD 26.
73. T. Fuller, *The Church History of Britain*, ed. J. S. Brewer, iii (1845), 469.
74. Sparrow Simpson, 74.
75. For example, he has 'Richard Elye' but 'Henry *de* Cornhill' (112).
76. Those of FitzJames (108) and Dowman (109).

became too small to support the donor's intention, the dean and chapter could reduce the number of clergy provided for, or alternatively add resources of their own, annex one or more further endowments, or take some of the income from a comparatively rich endowment to help out a poorer one. When the income from Sir John Poulteney's chantry became inadequate to maintain its three priests and the overheads, three more ailing chantries were annexed to it (**108**). When Roger Waltham's chantry was in financial straits they added to its revenue a portion of the endowment intended for the chantries of Fulk and Philip Basset (**110**). A couple of the chantry foundations incurred a small yearly deficit, and a few others barely broke even, but if the 1548 figures are typical, the dean and chapter made a net annual profit of over £200 from the overall chantry account, from which, however, they had to meet any repairs and other fluctuating costs of maintenance.

Although it is not made apparent in the Certificate, the chantry priests played a full part in the general services of the cathedral. In addition, several of the chantry foundations made provision for regular payments to support the choir or ministers of the cathedral, and finance exhibitions for the further education of poor choristers. An obit list from the Brief Certificate, printed in Dugdale, further shows that officials who attended obits held in the cathedral also received considerable bonuses: the 30 canons £64, 12 petty canons £28 11s 6d; 6 lay vicars £19 11s 0½d; 10 poor choristers £27 2s 10d; 4 virgers £2 12s 7d; 2 bellringers £1 7s 4d and 4 poor servants of the church 13s 4d.

In two cases, founders had established buildings in the cathedral precinct to house the priests of their foundation. These became known as Lancaster college and Holmes college after their creators (**113**). The other chantry priests had no 'mansions' or lodgings as of right, but some were able to procure rented rooms within the Priests' House, also known as Peter college, owned by the dean and chapter for use by the cathedral clergy. The rents (or at least the contributions provided for them in chantry foundations) seem to have varied: Wyther's chantry paid £1 1s 4d for two chambers, More's £1 3s 4d for four.[77]

Neither in the Certificate nor in the dean and chapter's original return is any mention made of the age or standing of the priests. They are all uniformly referred to simply as 'Sir'. If the Brief Certificate's silence on the point is trustworthy, none of these men was an ex-monk receiving a pension. Only three had stipends lower than £6 13s 4d, and the highest recorded was only £9 3s 4d. However rich the foundations, then, it does not seem that the chantry priests received unusually high remuneration because they happened to be attached to the cathedral.

Middlesex and St Stephen's college, Westminster
Of the twenty-six pensionable priests recorded in the Middlesex section of the Certificate (see Table), all but five were found in Westminster or the London suburbs and those densely populated areas stretching east along the Thames and north along Ermine Street. Three suburban parishes, however, were exceptional in having no chantries to declare in 1548:

77. **WD 26.**

St Martin in the Fields (with 700 communicants), St Giles in the Fields (305) and St Mary Matfelon (670). Further afield, Harrow-on-the-Hill, the only other substantial township, supported a Lady mass priest; Uxbridge with an unspecified number of communicants had two priests and Hillingdon (with 320) one. The priest at Littleton was paid by the court of Augmentations, whilst the one at West Brentford was apparently not a cantarist at all: Joan Redman had left some lands to endow a priest there to administer the sacraments and, according to the Brief Certificate, the parishioners subscribed 1s 4d a week to maintain him, evidently the only priest serving in their chapel. The commissioners felt it 'mete that there be a priest'.

TABLE

Distribution of chantry priests in Middlesex, 1548

PARISH	COMMUNICANTS	PRIESTS
St Margaret Westminster	2,500	6
St Clement Danes	1,400	2
Stepney	1,360	1
Enfield	1,000	2
Harrow	1,000	1
St Leonard Shoreditch	800	3
Hackney	600	3
Edmonton	600	2
Hillingdon	320	1
Uxbridge	not stated	2
St Mary Strand	280	1
West Brentford	120	1
Littleton	100	1

About forty of the county's seventy parishes had under 200 communicants, and whilst parishes with comparable populations in the city might support several chantries, this does not seem to have been the case in rural Middlesex. Possibly the capital itself acted as a magnet drawing benefactions to its churches even from the wealthier residents of the surrounding county, many of whom must surely have had regular contact with the city and its institutions. The small rural parishes were manageable units for one priest unassisted, and there was little need for chapels of ease or assistants to serve the cure. It seems unlikely that there had ever been many more chantries than those recorded in 1548, though winds of reform had certainly left some traces. At Hornsey (**129**) land given for an obit had for the past five years been devoted to the poor or spent on the repair of highways instead. Finchley reported an endowment for a priest 'if the king's majesty's laws will suffer it' (**157**). Tockington free chapel in Harrow parish had already been surrendered to Henry VIII (**162**). But there are few other signs suggesting the recent removal of endowments.

Although they did not support chantries, many of the small parishes nevertheless reported lesser endowments, for obits, lamps and the like, and there are several references to animals (instead of land or money) being donated to support religious observances or poor relief. Generally, they were hired out at an annual rent, the revenue being put to the desired end: a common rural phenomenon widely noted in other counties. At Tottenham there were as many as thirty-three cows, and at South Mimms twenty-four. The revenue from such sources varied: at Kingsbury the yearly rent was 1s per cow, at South Mimms 1s 4d and at Chiswick 2s. At West Brentford a cow had been sold for £1 to provide cash for an endowment, whilst Hampton reckoned its cow worth a total of 12s.

The return omits the precinct of St Katharine's by the Tower, and the parishes of Little Greenford (Perivale) and Clerkenwell. The grand total given for communicants is 22,079, though the commissioners' addition cannot be checked because the returns for Hounslow, Hanworth and Uxbridge omit the number of communicants. No mention is made in the Certificate of the chapels at Kilburn, Twyford or Kingsland; and Haliwell chapel in the parish of St Leonard Shoreditch is mentioned only in the return of the Grocers (212), save for a comment that it had lead still standing on its roof (190b): a sure indication that the crown had eyes on it. The return may have been more hurriedly compiled than that for London. No details are given of the ages and learning of the chantry priests in the county. There is no mention of any school, and only one of a sermon (125).

Poor relief is largely haphazard. At St Margaret Westminster (139) four poor people were maintained for life. At Hounslow (153) there was an almshouse for the poor and sick. The brotherhood at Uxbridge (119) let out a tenement rent-free to a poor blind man, whilst at Kensington (154) the church house was occupied by the poor. Elsewhere there was no large-scale offering for poor relief, apart from the casual doles regularly associated with obits. We do, however, get a good idea of the parish church as the focal point of the local community, often with further buildings or rooms where the parishioners might meet together and 'common of matters as well for the king's business as for the church and parish'.[78] And donations for the repair and maintenance of the church fabric are reminders of the heavy costs borne by parishioners in the upkeep of the church building itself, let alone any chantries within.

The commissioners had little to say about what ought to be permitted to continue after the dissolution. Apart from the priest at West Brentford mentioned above, they made special mention in the Brief Certificate of one other priest, serving the chapel at Stratford Bow, two miles or so from its mother church of Stepney and in a 'great thoroughfare and much people there inhabiting'. Surprisingly, no comment was made about the effect on St Margaret Westminster (2,500), St Clement Danes (1,400), Harrow (1,000) or Enfield (1,000) of removing the services of chantry priests without making any provision for assistance to the parish clergy. As in London, we are left wondering what were the commissioners' motives.

The royal college of St Stephen Westminster was the richest single foundation described in the Certificate (190). With revenues, spiritual and temporal, drawn not only from London and Middlesex but from eleven other counties, and totalling over £1,000 yearly, it was one of the wealthiest

---

78. As at Hackney (151), St Clement (152), Finchley (157), Hanworth (167) and Kingsbury (178).

collegiate churches in the country, richer than most of the dissolved monasteries. Its officials were a dean, 11 canons, 11 vicars, 4 chantry priests, 4 lay clerks, 7 choristers, a virger, a sub-sexton and a clock-keeper, whilst 8 poor folk (7 men and one woman in 1548) were, as we have seen above, maintained in the almshouse, with weekly cash allowances and contributions towards their clothing and fuel.

A foundation of this magnitude really merited a chantry Certificate of its own, in which greater detail could have been recorded, but it was actually entered, in a much abbreviated form, at the end of the Middlesex section of our Certificate. Whatever the original method of founding chantries within the college, the accounts were rendered without accrediting particular lands to particular chantries: the total revenue, received partly from the college's own bailiffs and partly through the sheriffs of York, Essex and Hertfordshire, was evidently paid into a central fund from which the officials received their fixed yearly stipends, ranging from the dean's £105 to the clock-keeper's £4 9s 8d. No separate mention is made of the chantries save to record the payment to their priests, and only passing mention is made of obits and lights. This rather truncated account of the college was probably the best that could be quickly put together for the chantry commissioners' deadline.

The London companies
The final part of the Certificate is devoted to returns made by the companies of the city of London, which had been a major channel for the endowment of chantries and other religious observances in city churches. With the notable exception of the Parish Clerks (**218**), who were deemed a fraternity wholly liable to dissolution under the terms of the chantry act because of their essentially religious function, the companies' status as associations of traders and craftsmen was not challenged, and those of their corporate lands which were not, in the crown's view, firmly tied to proscribed religious objectives were exempt under the terms of the act.

As with the parishes, so with the companies, the Certificate includes no Nil returns. Thus, what we have is a digest of the positive returns that came in, from all twelve Great Companies, and twenty-two lesser ones. The companies sponsored priests and obits in over sixty parish churches in the city, a few in the suburbs and a handful elsewhere. The assets they devoted to these objectives amounted to just over £1,000 a year: that is, between a fifth and a sixth of the overall value of chantry endowments in London. Stipends paid to the priests varied according to the generosity of the original donor, usually a former member of the company who had given money or lands to support these objectives, but about half of all priests supported by companies received the £6 13s 4d per year common throughout the city, and only three received less. At the top of the scale, the Merchant Taylors (**211**) sponsored nine priests, twenty obits and two lights; at the bottom (of those who declared any contribution), the Coopers (**200**) maintained only one single obit.

It is not always possible to determine from the wording of the Certificate the churches in which the observances were held, and the parochial entries avoid all mention of the chantries supported by the companies there. But the Brief Certificate, tackling the clergy parish by parish includes the company priests under the church in which they served.

Note on editorial method

A transcript of a short section of the Certificate (**54**) is supplied below to demonstrate the method of calendaring. The general order of presentation has been discussed above. In the original document the London and Middlesex parishes have been numbered in a later hand, and since these numbers have been extensively used for reference in the past they are retained as the numbers (in bold type) heading each section of the calendar. The numerical series has been extended in the calendar to cover also the entries for the city companies, which are not numbered in the original. The membrane numbers are indicated in the text in square brackets. The nature of each endowment is first set out in italic. In the ensuing description single inverted commas enclose words or phrases quoted verbatim from the original. Double inverted commas are used only where the original spelling has also been retained. The spelling of forenames has been modernised but surnames are transcribed exactly in the calendar (even though comparative sources show wide variation in forms). Placenames are given in their modern form (followed by a transcription in round brackets in the event of a significant variant appearing in the original). Unidentified places and field names are given in double inverted commas. Square brackets indicate editorial interpolation. Badly faded entries are preceded by an asterisk, or in extreme cases by two asterisks. Where only parts of words or phrases are legible, three dots indicate omissions unless an attempt has been made (in round brackets) to supply the illegible portion.

54. The paroche of St Mertens Vintry
Scilicet: William Clovyle John Cornewalles & Gilbert Admershe gave unto the parson and churchewardens of the seid churche for the meynten[a]unce of a priest and an obite for ever twoo tenementes by yere viij li. Wherof: To Sir Jeffrey Davy singing for the said persones of thage of liij yeres havyng no other promocion but this his stipent vj li xiijs iiijd. In thexpences of the said obite viijs iiijd. To the Kynges Ma[jes]tes [sic] for quitrent xxs. And to the parische of Saynt Johns in Walbroke iijs iiijd. Total viij li vs. And then remayneth clere [Blank].

The howse called Whyttington Colleage have geven yerely amonge the pore of the said parische the day before the feast of Seynt Michell Tharchaungell in money vjs viijd.

Memoranda: There is of howselyng people within the seid parische the nomber of iiij^c lx. Sir Edwarde Saunders is parson of the same parische churche and the yerely value of his parsonage is xviij li xiijs iiijd and that no priest is founde ther by hym but servythe the cure hym self

LONDON AND MIDDLESEX CHANTRY CERTIFICATE, 1548

(PRO, E 301/34)

'The City of London and the County of Middlesex: A brief declaration made by us Sir Roger Cholmeley, knight, Chief Baron of the king's majesty's Exchequer; Nicholas Hare, Wymonde Carewe and John Godsalve, knights; Richard Goodricke, John Carrell, Richard Morrison and Hugh Losse esquires, commissioners of our sovereign lord the king within the city of London and the county of Middlesex for the (?execution) of an Act made in the first year of his highness's reign concerning colleges, free chapels, chantries, fraternities, gilds, brotherhoods and other lands whatsoever given for or towards the finding of any priests, obits, lights, lamps and such other like uses as in the king's commission unto us directed in that behalf more plainly appeareth; declaring as well the true value of all such colleges, free chapels, chantries, fraternities, brotherhoods, gilds and such other, with (? the yearly reprises) and annual deductions going out of them, as also of all such sums of money coming and growing to the king's said majesty by reason of the forenamed Act of Parliament, as hereafter more plainly may appear.'

1. ST AUGUSTINE BY PAUL'S GATE[1]

*Chantry and obit:** 2 tenements in the parish of St Mary Magdalene Milk Street, t. Richard [Barnes],[2] given under royal licence by Henry Rede, £11 6s 8d p.a. Of which, 2s quitrent to the king; 13s 4d tenths to the king; £6 13s 4d to Sir William Browne, chantry priest aged 47, of small learning and having no other living; 10s obit; ... ; total deductions £8 17s 4d. Clear remainder £2 9s 4d p.a. ... .

Priest, obit and lamp: a tenement in the parish, t. Thomas [Rydley],[3] given by John [Ryvers],[4] £5 10s p.a. Of which, 10s obit; 6s to the poor; £1 light; £1 6s 8d to a chaplain praying for the soul of Richard [Cocke];[5] total deductions £3 2s 8d. Clear remainder £2 7s 4d p.a. ...

Taper weighing 1 lb to burn before the image of Our Lady: a tenement in the parish, t. Robert [Goslyng],[6] given by John Burten, £5 6s 8d p.a. Of which, 7s taper; 4s quitrent to the late house of Burton Lazars; total deductions 11s. Clear remainder £4 15s 8d p.a.

Paschal light: £2 p.a. rent from his manor of [Fulbrook],[7] Oxon., given by John Malte. Of which, £2 paschal light. Clear remainder Nil.

*Priest for 3 years for the soul of the said John Malte:** [£20] cash given by the same. Nothing has been paid to Sir William [Seyman],[8] priest, aged 63 ...[9] Clear remainder £20.

*Memoranda:** no brotherhoods or schools; ... communicants. John Royston, rector, is not resident and finds a curate to serve the cure. Value

1

of the living not known. No other priest besides the curate and chantry priest ... .[10]

1. Cf. (for 1546) LR 2/242 fos 58–64.
2–4. SC 6.
5. LR 2/242 fo. 61.
6. *CPR 1549–51*, 129.
7. Will of John Malt, 1547 (PROB 11/31 s. 39).
8. BC.
9. Some 3 lines illegible.
10. Two further memoranda, one concerning jewels, ornaments and plate, are largely illegible. The living was valued at £19 16s p.a. in 1535 (*Valor*, i, 375). John Aungell, conduct, is also listed here in BC.

2. [m.1d] ST ANDREW BY THE WARDROBE[1]
Priest and obit: (?lands) given by John Parrante,[2] £12 3s 4d p.a. Of which, 10s quitrent to the king; £6 13s 4d to Thomas Morres, chantry priest; 8s obit; total deductions £7 11s 4d. Clear remainder £4 12s p.a.
Priest and obit: lands which Humphrey Talbot, kt., willed to be amortised to find a priest for his and other souls, the grant being assured by Thomas [Ashurst][3] for ever, £7 6s 8d p.a. Of which, £2 to augment the salary of Thomas Morres above; 6s 8d obit; total deductions £2 6s 8d. Clear remainder £5 p.a.
Obit and alms: lands, tenements and a free rent of 14s 3d from a tenement now t. one Decro, given by John Lee, £9 5s 8d p.a. Of which, 5s obit; 8s to the poor; £1 quitrent to the king; total deductions £1 13s. Clear remainder £7 12s [8d][4] p.a.
Rood lamp: 6s 8d p.a. rent from a tenement in the parish owned by the Lady Anne of Cleves and t. John Puddell.
Lamp before the Blessed Sacrament on the choir altar: 6s 8d p.a. rent from a tenement of the dean and chapter of St Paul's in the parish, t. Nicholas Spackman.
Memoranda: no brotherhoods or grammar school; 450 communicants. Robert Hope, rector, receives £17 17s 6d p.a. In his absence a curate serves the cure with the help of the chantry priest. An inventory of chalice, vestments etc. kept by the churchwardens has been made and nothing surrendered.

1. Cf. (for 1546) LR 2/242 fos 50–7.
2. Name verified in SC6 and *Husting*, ii, 423.
3. SC6.
4. Margin wanting.

3. ST BENET PAUL'S WHARF[1]
Chantry: foundation unknown[2] for lack of sight of the evidence; lands reckoned among other church lands which amount in all to £14 13s 4d p.a. Of which, £1 5s 3d quitrent to the king; £6 13s 4d to Sir [blank][3] Goche, chantry priest aged 40, a base singer and simply learned, who also receives £6 13s 4d p.a. pension from the late house of St Neot's, Hunts; total deductions £7 18s 7d. Clear remainder £6 14s 9d p.a.
Memoranda: no brotherhoods or grammar school; 336 communicants.

Walter Major, rector, receives £12 18s 2¼d p.a. No other priest except at Easter; nothing surrendered.

1. Cf. (for 1546) LR 2/243 fo. 42.
2. Morley's chantry in LR 2.
3. William (BC).

4. St Nicholas Olave
Lamp and 'Salve' before the image of Our Lady: 10s p.a. rent given by William Newport for ever from a tenement in the parish of St Michael Queenhithe.
Memoranda: no brotherhoods nor grammar school; 163 communicants. Edward Cowper, rector, receives £11 10s 11d p.a. and finds another priest to serve the cure: Sir Alexander Bull aged 40, whose qualities and learning are indifferent. Nothing surrendered.

5. [m.2] St Vedast Foster Lane
*Chaplain:** lands given by William Trystor for his soul for ever, which, together with rents given by [Simon Atwell]¹ to overcome the insufficiency of the former, amount to £18 5s 2d p.a. Of which, £1 13s 4d quitrent to the king; 13s 4d tenths to the king; £6 13s 4d to Sir [Albert]² Copeman, chantry priest aged 39, of poor quality and learning and having no other income; 13s 4d obit; £1 to the poor; total deductions £10 13s 4d. Clear remainder £7 11s 10d p.a.
Priest: lands given by Geoffrey Gate for his and his wife's souls for ever, £8 6s 8d p.a., augmented by further lands given by Christopher T[yrry],³ £6 3s 4d p.a.; total £14 10s p.a. Of which, 13s 4d quitrent to the king; 5s quitrent to the dean and chapter of Westminster; £6 13s 4d to Sir John [Merkhame]⁴, chantry priest aged 59, of mean quality and learning and having no other income; total deductions £7 11s 8d. Clear remainder £6 18s 4d p.a.
Obit and lamp: a tenement given by John Russell for the soul of Andrew (?Secheford), £3 p.a. Of which, 3s 4d obit; 6s 8d lamp; total deductions 10s. Clear remainder £2 p.a.
Jesus Mass and Lady Mass: £100 was given by Dame Elizabeth Thurston, widow, to buy lands to maintain the 2 masses and certain 'Salves' for herself and others: £5 6s 8d⁵ p.a.
Priest: £160 given 16 years ago by Mr Cote to buy lands to support a priest singing for Cote and others: no lands yet bought. Mr Hartop pays a priest with the interest from the money.
Memoranda: 460 communicants. Sir Richard Ridge, rector, receives £33 5s 10d p.a. and serves the cure himself with the help of a curate and the chantry priests.⁶

1. Harley 601.
2. BC.
3. *Husting*, ii, 629.
4. BC.
5. Marginal note: £5.
6. For other priests serving here, see **222**. BC also names William Peryman, conduct.

6. ST BOTOLPH BILLINGSGATE¹
Priest before the Lady Altar, and 7 tapers: tenement given by John Pickman, £10 p.a. Of which, £6 13s 4d to Sir Thomas Serle, priest² aged 50, of good conversation and learning touching ordinary service and having no other income; 9s 4d tapers; total deductions £7 2s 8d. Clear remainder £2 17s 8d p.a.
Priest and obit: land and tenements given by Thomas Aubury for his soul, £8 6s 8d p.a. Of which, £7 6s 8d to Sir Thomas Barnston, priest³ aged 60, a man of good conversation and learning and having no other income. Clear remainder £1 p.a.
Augmentation of a priest's wages: tenement given by Richard Cockes, £6 p.a.
Augmentation and poor relief: tenements given by Roger Smalwood for his soul, £2 6s 8d p.a. Of which, 2s alms. Clear remainder £2 4s 8d p.a.
Obit: £1 10s p.a. rent given by Nicholas West for his soul for ever.
Obit: 13s 4d p.a. rent received from the chamberlain of London, given by John Renewell for his soul. Of which, 13s 4d to the poor. Clear remainder Nil.
Priest: Thomas [Wall]⁴ gave to John [Collet]⁵ and Katherine his wife a tenement in Thames Street called the Sun, and to William Saunderson and Jane his wife and the survivor of them, and to their heirs and the survivor of them, to maintain a priest in Grundisburgh (Grounesborough), Suff., or in default of this in St Botolph. Not paid for the past 2¼ years.
Memoranda: 300 communicants. Nicholas Archebolte, rector, receives £23 6s 8d p.a. For the fraternity here see next entry.

  1. A recently discovered return for 1546 is among the Chantry Certificates at the PRO, E 301/132. It covers both the parish and the fraternity (see **7**), and gives more detailed accounts of the properties of both.
  2. Thomas Lane is named as priest in BC and E 101.
  3. William Bell is named as priest in E 101. The endowment is omitted from BC, which, however, has an additional conduct, Thomas Bird.
  4–5. Names verified from E 301/132 and the will of Thomas Wall (PROB 11/24 s. 6).

7. ST BOTOLPH BILLINGSGATE: FRATERNITY OF OUR LADY AND ST JOHN BAPTIST¹
Fraternity lands: £14 p.a. Of which, 17s 6d quitrent to the king; £8 6s 8d to Sir William [Lucar],² priest, of small learning and having no other income; 6s 8d to the poor; total deductions £9 10s 10d. Clear remainder £4 4s 2d p.a.
*Memorandum:** plate, jewels and ornaments belonging to the fraternity are in the hands of Nicholas Reve and Edward ... , as in an inventory³ in the hands of Hugh Losse Esq.

  1. See **6** n.1.
  2. E 301/132.
  3. The inventory submitted in 1546 is attached to E 301/132.

8. [m.2d] ST BENET SHEREHOG¹
Priest: £3 6s 8d p.a. rent given by Ralph Faber from a capital messuage in the parish, for his soul for ever. Of which, £3 6s 8d to Anthony Coplyn, priest, now deceased. Clear remainder Nil.

Chaplain to sing divine service: £4 8s p.a. rent given by John Freshe from a tenement in the parish of St Mary Magdalene Old Fish Street, at the corner of Dolittle Lane.

Memoranda: 300 communicants. Anthony Richardson, rector, receives £7 p.a.

   1. Cf. (for 1546) LR2/243 fos. 43–4.

9. St Mary at Hill[1]

Priest and Lamp: £8 2s 6d p.a. rent given by Rose Writell from her tenements in Thames Street to Robert Haymond and Margery his wife and the heirs of Margery's body, to pay a priest 6 marks p.a. and maintain a taper of 4 lb before the image of Our Lady. Of which, £4 to Christopher Burley, priest aged 43, a good singer and well learned, having no other living except the further £4 recorded below; 2s 6d tapers; total deductions £4 2s 6d. Clear remainder £4 p.a.

Priest, obit, torches and other charges: lands and tenements given by John Weston, £8 13s 4d p.a. Of which, £4 to Christopher Burley; 11s 8d obit and torches; 3s 4d church works; 13s 4d quitrent to the master of the Bridgehouse; total deductions £5 8s 4d. Clear remainder for the relief of the poor £3 5s p.a.

Priest, obit and lamps: lands and tenements given by John Cawston for his soul for ever, £20 17s 8d p.a. Of which, £6 13s 4d to Edmund Alston, priest aged 36, a good singer and handsomely learned, having no other living; 13s 4d to the king in right of Bermondsey (Barmesey); 4s 10d obit; 5s quitrent to the king; 6s quitrent to the wardens of St Magnus; £1 tapers; total deductions £9 2s 6d. Clear remainder for repairing the houses £11 15s 2d p.a.

Priest: lands and tenements in the parish given by John Nasinge for his soul for ever, £12 3s 4d p.a. Of which, £6 13s 4d to Thomas Lewes, priest aged 42, a good singer, a player on the organs and prettily learned, having no other living; £1 2s quitrent to the king; total deductions £7 15s 4d. Clear remainder £4 8s p.a. for the repair of the houses.

Priest and obit: lands and tenements given by William Cambridge to find a priest well learned in divinity for his soul for ever and to maintain other charges specified in his will, £10 6s 8d p.a. Of which, £6 13s 4d to Matthew Berye, priest aged 40, a good singer and indifferently well learned, having no other living; £1 1s 8d obit; 6s 8d to the poor; 6s quitrent to the king; total deductions £8 7s 8d. Clear remainder £1 19s p.a. for the repair of the houses, any surplus to be given to the church.

Priest, obit and light of 5 tapers: tenements given by Richard Gesseling for his soul for ever, £9 p.a. Of which, £6 13s 4d to John Sherpyn, priest aged 44, a teacher of children, having no other living in certainty; £2 12s to the poor; 2s 10d wax; 4s 5d obit; total deductions £9 12s 7d. Clear remainder Nil.

Priest, obit and lamp: lands and tenements given by John Bedman for his soul for ever, as specified in his will, £13 6s 8d p.a. Of which, £6 13s 4d to a conduct;[2] 6s 8d obit; £2 12s to the poor; total deductions £9 12s. Clear remainder £3 14s 8d p.a.

5

Church lands:[3] £24 3s p.a. claimed by the churchwardens as church lands, but there is no evidence to prove title. From this 3 conducts receive £8 p.a. each: William Rice, Robert Tanner and William Hamounde. Clear remainder 3s p.a.

Memoranda: 400 communicants. One chalice held by the churchwardens to the king's use. Sir Alan Percye, rector, receives £40 p.a. There are no other priests besides the rector, curate and certain conducts to sing and help the choir, who are paid £16 p.a.

> 1. Cf. Guildhall MS. 1239/1 pt. 3 fos 705 ff. In that account the stipends of the priests differ from those given here; fo. 713 contains an obit calendar.
> 2. Bedman (Bidham)'s chantry in BC has no priest recorded against it. It is probable that one of the 3 conducts in the next paragraph served this chantry.
> 3. In BC the scribe at first wrote 'the king's title cannot appear for lack of evidence: respect' quousque examin' in Cur' '. But a subsequent note reads that Rice Williams, schoolmaster of the children, had received £8 10s p.a. and was awarded a pension of £5; Robert Tanner had also received £8 10s and Hamounde £8. In addition the parishioners paid Thomas Martin, parish clerk, £6 13s 4d and Thomas Mundy, sexton, £4.

10. [m.3] St Gregory

Chantry priest: lands and tenements given by Robert Rasamond for his soul for ever, £13 18s p.a. Of which, £6 13s 4d to Peter Jackesonn, chantry priest aged 39, a teacher of children, who also has £5 6s 8d p.a. pension 'for that he was a religious person'; 2s quitrent to the king; total deductions £6 15s 4d. Clear remainder £3 12s 8d p.a. towards the repair of the houses.

Memorandum: 600 communicants. Sir John Wakelinge, rector, receives (?£19) 18s p.a.

11. St Michael Cornhill

Priest, obit and other charges: lands and tenements given by William Rus for his soul for ever, £27 13s 4d p.a. Of which, £8 to Sir William Penne, priest aged 38, of indifferent learning and having no other living; £2 12s to a bedesman; £2 in coal to the poor; £3 for 3 lamps; 15s quitrent to the king; total deductions £15 7s [sic]. Clear remainder £12 6s 4d p.a.

Priest and obit: lands and tenements given by Andrew Smythe for his soul for ever, £12 p.a. Of which, £7 6s 8d to John Paddye, priest and conduct aged 26, indifferently learned and having no other living; 2s quitrent to the king; total deductions £7 8s 8d. Clear remainder £4 11s 4d p.a.

Chaplain and obit: tenements given by Simon Mordonne for his soul for ever, £9 p.a. Of which, £6 13s 4d to John Campyon, priest and conduct aged 66, a good singer and indifferently learned, and having no other living; 3s quitrent to the king; total deductions £6 16s 4d. Clear remainder £2 3s 8d p.a.

Conduct and obit: tenements given by John Langhorne for his soul for ever, £10 8s p.a. Of which, £6 13s 4d to Robert Morecock, conduct aged 36, whose quality and conversation is as the other,[1] and having no other living; 3s quitrent to the king; total deductions £6 16s 4d. Clear remainder £3 11s 8d p.a.

Augmentation of Walter Bullingham's chaplain and obit: tenements given by Thomas Baker for his soul, £2 18s 8d p.a. Of which, £2 to Ralph More, chaplain aged 50, who has been bed-ridden for 18 years and also receives £4 13s 4d p.a. pension from the king; 4s 4d to the poor; total deductions £2 4s 4d. Clear remainder 14s 4d p.a.

Obit: tenements given by Dame Ursula Lile for her soul for ever, £8 13s 4d p.a. Of which, 6s 8d quitrent to Westminster [sic]; £1 quitrent to the king; £6 0s 8d to the poor; total deductions £7 7s 4d. Clear remainder £1 6s p.a.

Lamp and obit: tenements given by Roger Stockeden for his soul for ever, £7 4s 8d p.a. Of which, 7s obit; 10s lamp; total deductions 17s. Clear remainder £6 7s 8d p.a.

Obit: a tenement in the churchyard and a tenement in the parish, given by Thomas Irelonde for his soul for ever, £3 10s p.a. Of which, 3s 4d quitrent to the king.[2] Clear remainder £3 6s 8d p.a.

Obit and paschal lamp: tenements given by Robert Drope, £6 13s 4d p.a. Of which, 13s 4d paschal lamp; 3s 4d to the poor; total deductions 16s 8d. Clear remainder £5 16s 8d p.a.

*Obit:** £6 13s 4d p.a. rent paid by the Drapers' Company for [William] Combton.[3] Of which, £6 13s 4d to Thomas Baker, priest aged ... Clear remainder Nil.

*Memoranda***[4]

1. Presumably Campyon above.
2. No payment recorded for the obit.
3. Harley 601 has this name altered to Comerton.
4. For a detailed rental see Guildhall MS. 4071/1. The rector was John Willoughby (Hennessy, 332).

12. [m.3d] St Michael Cornhill: Fraternity of St Anne and Our Lady[1]

Chaplain: [A tenement in Gracechurch (Gracious) Street, t. William Gurley, £7 6s 8d p.a.; another tenement there, t. William Austley, £6 6s 8d p.a.; a tenement in the parish of St Botolph Bishopsgate, t. James Sweper, £1 6s 8d p.a.; 4 tenements in St Michael's churchyard, t. Sir William Leekes, £1 9s 4d p.a.]; total £16 9s 4d p.a. Of which, £8 to Sir John Thomas, priest aged ... , indifferently learned and having no other living; £1 quitrent to the king; £1 10s to St Bartholomew's hospital; 2s to the king; total deductions £10 12s. Clear remainder £5 17s 4d p.a.

Chaplain: a tenement in Lombard Street, t. Robert [Clerke], £8 p.a.; a tenement in the parish of St Mary at Hill, [in Love Lane, t. Henry Smyth][2] £6 13s 4d p.a.; a tenement without Bishopsgate called the Half Moon, t. Robert Woode, £3 p.a.; total £17 13s 4d p.a. Of which, £8 to Sir William Brickes, chaplain aged 33, ...ly well learned and having no other living; 18s quitrent to the king; 16s alms to the poor; total deductions £9 14s. Clear remainder £7 19s 4d p.a.

Memoranda: plate and ornaments in the hands of Thomas Judge and George Hinde, churchwardens, to the king's use, as shown in an inventory made by Hugh Losse.[3]

1. Much of this entry is now illegible, and the gaps have been supplied as indicated from Harley 601, which ascribes the first endowment to the fraternity of St Michael here, as does BC.
2. Also named as one of the priests here in E 101.
3. For a later copy of the inventory, see Walters, 641–2.

13. S⊤ SEPULCHRE WITHOUT NEWGATE

Priest, obit and church repair: tenements given by Geoffrey Churche for his soul for ever, £5 6s 8d p.a. Of which, £3 13s 4d to the priest;[1] 4s 8d obit; total deductions £3 18s. Clear remainder £1 8s 8d p.a. for repairs.

Lady altar: augmentation of a priest's salary: tenement given by Thomas Whitton for a priest celebrating mass and other divine service, £5 p.a. Of which, £1 3s 4d quitrent to Eton college. Clear remainder £3 16s 8d p.a.

Lady altar: augmentation of a priest's salary: 2 tenements given by Roger Marks for his soul for ever, £2 p.a.

Lady altar priest: tenements given by William Harsham towards a priest's salary, for his soul for ever, £1 p.a., and further tenements given by Thomas Eydon, £4 6s 8d p.a.

Obit: 10s p.a. rent given by John Pecket from a tenement in Smithfield, for his soul for ever. Of which, 4s alms to the poor. Clear remainder 6s p.a.

Priest and obit: tenements given by William Newcastell for his soul for ever, £19 14s 8d p.a. Of which, £3 6s 8d to the priest; 6s 8d obit; total deductions £3 13s 4d. Clear remainder £16 1s 4d p.a. for the repair of the church.

Priest, and church repair: a tenement in Smithfield Bars, t. Thomas Parker, given by Abred Apulbie, £2 p.a.

Maintenance of the ornaments: 13s 4d p.a. rent given by William Cressewicke from a tenement in St John's Street called the Castle.

Obit: £2 p.a. rent given by John Staunton for his soul for ever.

Memoranda: 900 poor are relieved in the parish; 3,400 communicants. The king is rector by impropriation and receives £42 14s 10½d p.a. William Cloplonde, vicar, receives £20 ... p.a. A brotherhood is described below.[2]

1. Peter Deakon (BC). He appears to be the only priest maintained from the endowments described in this section; but see also **14** and **15**.
2. BC also has John Merten, conduct, here.

14. S⊤ SEPULCHRE WITHOUT NEWGATE: BROTHERHOOD OF OUR LADY AND S⊤ STEPHEN

Brotherhood lands:[1] 6 cottages at the Barbican in the parish of St Botolph without Aldersgate, t. John Twyforde and others, given by John Austen and others, £5 11s (?4d)[2] p.a.

[m.4] *Obit:* a tenement given by William Kenns for his soul for ever, £2 13s 4d p.a. Of which, 3s alms to the poor. Clear remainder £2 10s 4d p.a.

Priest and obit at the Lady altar: tenements given by John Jenour for his soul for ever, £1 10s p.a.

Obit: a tenement given by Robert Sibson for his soul for ever, £3 p.a.

*Obit:** a tenement given by William [Rawlyn][3] for his soul for ever, £1 6s 8d p.a. Of which, £1 to the poor. Clear remainder 6s 8d p.a.

*Memorandum:** the plate, goods and ornaments are in the hands of Richard ... and ... , as shown in an inventory in the hands of Hugh Losse Esq., the king's surveyor.

1. BC names Michael Wingate as priest of the brotherhood.
2. Edge torn off.
3. Harley 601.

15. ST SEPULCHRE WITHOUT NEWGATE: STIPENDIARY LANDS*
[*Priest to sing in the Lady chapel:* tenements][1] given by Walter [Bruce],[2] £8 12s 4d p.a. Of which, 3s quitrent to the king. Clear remainder £8 9s 4d p.a.
Priest: tenements given by William Andrewe, £13 6s 8d p.a. Of which, £7 6s 8d to John Lowe, priest aged 35, of honest qualities and having no other living; £1 6s 8d ... ; 9s ... ; 1s ... ; total deductions £9 3s 4d. Clear remainder £4 3s 4d p.a.
Priest at the altar of the apostle ... and obit: lands and tenements given by John Knyf for his soul for ever, £8 16s 8d p.a. Of which, £6 13s 4d to a priest;[3] 13s 4d ... ; total deductions £7 6s 8d. Clear remainder £1 10s p.a.

    1. Harley 601.
    2. BC.
    3. John Hope (BC).

16. ST JAMES GARLICKHITHE[1]
*Morrow mass priest:** lands and tenements given by Thomas Lincoln and Richard Lyon, £22 2s 8d p.a. Of which, £8 to Sir John ...,[2] priest; (?£3 16s quitrents to the king); £1 quitrent to ... ; 6s 8d obit; 6s 8d to the poor; total deductions £13 9s 4d. Clear remainder £8 13s 4d p.a.
[*Priest and obit*]:* lands and tenements given by John Oxonford, £17 15s p.a. Of which, £8 to Sir William ...; 6s 8d (?obit); 6s 8d to the poor; total deductions £8 13s 4d. Clear remainder £9 1s 8d p.a.
[*Priest*]:* [tenements] given by William [Harvye],[3] £12 14s 8d p.a. Of which, £7 to ...,[4] priest; 8s 8d ... ; 6s 4d ... ; total deductions £7 15s. Clear remainder £4 9s 8d p.a.
[*Priest and obit*]:* [tenements] given by Robert [Checheley],[5] £18 10s 4d p.a. Of which, £8 to ... , priest; 8s quitrent to the king; 10s ... ; £2 to the poor; total deductions £10 18s. Clear remainder £7 12s 4d p.a.
[m.4d] [*Priest and obit*]:* lands and tenements given by John Rodynge, £22 12s p.a. Of which, £8 to ... ,[6] priest; £1 quitrent to the king; 6s 8d obit; 13s 4d to the poor; total deductions £10. Clear remainder £12 12s p.a.
Lamp before the high altar: lands and tenements given by Thomas Lincolne for a light of 30 tapers, £8 13s 4d p.a. Of which, 13s 4d quitrent to the churchwardens of St Pancras. Clear remainder £8 p.a., which until 2 years ago was given to the maintenance of the lamp but is now given to the poor.
For the increase of divine service and for the repair of the church: lands and tenements given by Laurence Smythe, £9 14s p.a.
Obit: tenement given by Thomas Kent for his soul, £2 13s 4d p.a.
Priest: £8 p.a. paid by the treasurer of Augmentations, by decree of that court, from land worth £8 p.a. given by John Woode to the prior of St Mary's Spittal to maintain a priest.[7]
Memoranda: Thomas Longlow, rector, receives £18 p.a. and employs a curate in his absence; 400 communicants. From the surplus income 4 conducts and singing men who have no other living are each paid £8: William Stevens, John Grove and Nicholas Abbot.[8]

    1. Cf. (for 1546) LR 2/242 fos 92–100.
    2. Barret (BC).
    3. Supplied from SC 6 and LR 2.

4. Thomas Dale (BC).
5. As n. 3 above.
6. George Strowgar (BC).
7. John Wodde is also the priest's name in BC.
8. Sic. Only 3 men are named. In addition to these, Reginald Smith and Leonard Paret are named in BC. All 5 are merely described as conducts.

17. ST GILES CRIPPLEGATE
Chaplain: lands and tenements given by Richard Chaurye for his soul for ever, £4 p.a.
Augmentation of the same: lands and tenements given by Matthew Ashebye for his soul for ever, £9 7s 8d p.a.
Obit: lands and tenements given by John Sworder: 10s to be spent at the obit and the rest put in the poor box, £3 15s 4d p.a. Of which, 10s obit. Clear remainder £3 5s 4d p.a.
Light before the Sacrament: 7s p.a. rent given by Bartholomew Jecket from a corner tenement in [Grub Street].[1]
Church lands: for which no written evidence survives, £4 13s 4d p.a.
Memoranda: 2,440 communicants. Roger Cobartes, rector, receives £28 p.a. St Giles's brotherhood in the same church described below.

    1. Verified in SC 6.

18. ST GILES CRIPPLEGATE: BROTHERHOOD OF OUR LADY AND ST GILES
*Chaplain and 2 lights:** tenements given by John Ballinger, William Larke and Richard Serle,[1] £13 16s 8d p.a. Of which, £7 13s 10d to Sir Richard Johnson, priest; 12s 4d tenths to the king; 2s 8d lights; 3s 6d to the poor; total deductions £8 12s 4d. Clear remainder £5 4s 4d p.a.
Priest and obit: tenements given by William Grove and Robert Heyworth for their souls for ever, £12 9s 4d p.a. Of which, £7 13s 4d to Sir Philip Reve, priest; 13s 4d quitrent to the king; 2s quitrent to the churchwardens of St Giles; total deductions £7 15s 4d [sic]. Clear remainder £4 0s 8d p.a.
[m.5] *Priest and obit:* lands and tenements given by William Brampton for his soul for ever, £10 18s 2d p.a. Of which, £6 16s to Sir John Barnes, priest; 3s 8d obit; 6s 8d to the poor at St Thomas the Apostle; 7s 4d to poor prisoners; 1s to the sisters at Elsing Spittal; 1s to the wardens of St Thomas the Apostle; total deductions £7 15s 8d. Clear remainder £7 1s [sic] p.a.
Lights and obits: lands and tenements given by Thomas Fisher, William Babe, Richard Coppinge, William Marryner and others, £29 14s 4d p.a. Of which, £1 1s 8d obits; £1 14s to the poor; 14s quitrent to the king; 12s 4d to the churchwardens of St James Garlickhithe; total deductions £4 2s. Clear remainder £25 2s 4d [sic] p.a.
Further lands: given by Walter Stocker, Giles Dockinge, John Frynde, Stephen Linge, Gilbert Prynce and others,[2] £35 8s 8d p.a. Of which, 16s to the churchwardens of St Leonard Foster Lane; 3s 4d to a preacher; £19 2s 1d alms to 16 poor householders;[3] total deductions £20 1s 5d. Clear remainder £14 10s 7d [sic] p.a.

    1. Names supplied from Harley 601; almost illegible here.
    2. Further names are given in SC 6.
    3. BC names 11 poor, but under the heading Corpus Christi brotherhood (m. 10).

19. St Nicholas Cole Abbey[1]

Priest: lands and tenements given by John Sywarde and Thomas Blode, £6 p.a. Of which, £6 13s 4d to Anthony Little, 'priest of the same chantry' aged 50, of mean learning and having no other living. Clear remainder Nil.

Priest and obit: lands and tenements given by John Tripley for his soul for ever, £12 8s 4d p.a. Of which, £6 13s 4d to Ralph Jonson, chantry priest aged ... , very well learned; 5s obit; 16s quitrents to the colleges of Christchurch[2] and Burton Lazars; total deductions £7 14s 4d. Clear remainder £4 13s 8d [sic] p.a.

Priest: lands and tenements in Distaff Lane given by Thomas Barnarde, John Saunderashe and William Cogshale, £7 6s 8d p.a. Of which, £6 13s 4d to Sir William Benson, priest aged 46, a very poor and sickly man having no other living; 3s obit; 2s to the poor; total deductions £6 18s 4d. Clear remainder 8s 4d p.a.

Obit and poor relief: 10s p.a. rent given by Walter Turke for his soul for ever from a tenement, t. Thomas Hare. Of which, 5s 4d obit; 4s 8d to the poor; total deductions 10s. Clear remainder Nil.

Obit: 10s p.a. rent given by William Birde for his soul for ever. Of which, 5s 4d obit; 4s 8d to the poor; total deductions 10s. Clear remainder Nil.

Obit: 10s p.a. rent given by Thomas Padington for his soul for ever. Of which, 5s 4d obit; 4s 8d to the poor; total deductions 10s. Clear remainder Nil.

Lamp before the Sacrament: 8s p.a. rent given by Walter Turke.

Two tapers: 8s p.a. rent given by John Turgolde.

Obit: tenements in Old Fish Street, t. John Wyndeston, given by [blank],[3] £4 13s 4d p.a. Of which, 10s obit; 13s 4d to a chantry priest at St Paul's; total deductions £1 3s 4d. Clear remainder £3 10s p.a.

Memoranda: 180 communicants. Thomas Soudley, rector, receives £18 13s 4d p.a. There are no other priests except his curate.

1. Cf. (for 1546) LR 2/242 fos 120–5.
2. London (LR 2).
3. John Calf and Walter Turke (LR 2).

20. [m.5d] St Dunstan in the West: Brotherhood of Our Lady and St Dunstan

Priest at the altar of St Anne and obit: lands and tenements given by William Chapman for his soul for ever, £11 10s p.a. Of which, £7 4s 4d to Randall Smythe, priest aged 40; 11s quitrent to the king; total deductions £7 15s 4d. Clear remainder £3 14s 8d p.a.

Priest: lands and tenements given by William Marshall for his soul for ever, £22 p.a. Of which, 5s 4d quitrent to the king; £8 to Sir William Neale, priest aged 36; total deductions £8 5s 4d. Clear remainder £13 14s 8d p.a.

Two chaplains: a messuage in the parish t. Henry Eve given by John Westwood, £2 13s 4d p.a. Of which, 5s to St Giles's hospital. Clear remainder £2 8s 4d p.a.

Taper before the Sacrament: a tenement called the Bolt and Tun in the parish, given by William Chapman, £6 p.a.

Obit: 13s 4d p.a. rent given by the same William Chapman for his soul for ever. Of which, 10s 6d obit; 2s 10d to the poor; total deductions 13s 4d. Clear remainder Nil.

Obit: lands and tenements given by Robert Birde for his soul for ever, £5 6s 8d p.a. Of which, 15s obit; 11s 8d to the poor; total deductions £1 6s 8d. Clear remainder £4 p.a.

Obit: a tenement in the parish of St Andrew Holborn, t. John Mylles, given by Richard Dawson for his soul for ever, £1 13s 4d p.a. Of which, 10s obit; 3s 4d to the poor; total deductions 13s 4d. Clear remainder £1 p.a.

Obit: lands and tenements given by Richard Nordon for his soul for ever, £7 6s 8d p.a. Of which, 4s 6d quitrents; 15s 8d obit; 11s to the poor; total deductions £1 11s 2d. Clear remainder £5 15s 6d p.a.

Obit: lands and tenements given by William Parsonne for his soul for ever, £7 6s 8d p.a. Of which, £1 6s 8d quitrents; 10s 10d obit; 9s 2d to the poor; total deductions £2 6s 8d. Clear remainder £5 p.a.

Obit and lamp: a tenement called the Goat given by John Knapp for his soul for ever, £4 p.a. Of which, 3s quitrents; 13s 4d obit; 13s 4d lamp; £2 10s rent to Margaret Kyrkebye during her life; total deductions £3 19s 8d. Clear remainder £4 p.a.

Purpose unknown: lands given by John Ballard and others, £6 17s 4d p.a.

[*Priest*]: an 80 year lease from the bishop of Chichester of several tenements, gardens and some ground where 4 new tenements are being built, yearly rent £2 13s 4d: likely value of the property £26 13s 4d p.a. Of which, £8 to Sir Edmund Elles, priest; £2 13s 4d to the bishop of Chichester; £2 13s 4d to an exhibitioner at Oxford; £8 to Sir John Chelthame [priest][1]; total deductions £21 6s 8d. Clear remainder £5 6s 8d p.a.

Priest: lands in the parish of St Bride given by Robert Hey for ever, £11 19s 8d p.a., but no priest has been provided for the past 20 years, and the money has been devoted to the repair of the church.

Lease: a further lease, with 99 years still to run, from the bishop of Chichester, sub-let at a yearly rent of £19 6s 8d.

[m.6] *Memoranda:* 900 communicants. The king is rector, as the living was formerly appropriated by the abbot of Alnwick and is worth £10 p.a. Richard Lyste has been vicar for 11 years.[2] Jewels and ornaments of the various promotions are in the hands of the churchwardens for the king's use.[3]

Names of poor people relieved in the parish: Alice Hopper £3 0s 8d; Katherine Hedley £3 0s 8d; Katherine Johnson £1 6s 8d; Joan Dean £1 6s 8d; Mother Trynder £1 6s 8d; Thomas Horsham £1 6s 8d; Mother Holmes £1; Mother Gab... £1 6s 8d; Mother Sok... £1; Robert Thompson and his wife £1; [blank] Mayfield £1 6s 8d; total £17 1s 4d.

In view of the number of communicants there is need for a further priest in the parish.

1. In BC, Cheltham is the only priest specifically said to be financed from gild lands: all the others appear to be chantry priests in the parish church, unconnected with the gild. Also named there are John Cotton, organ player and conduct; William Mathew, conduct; John Cotton (probably the same), clerk to the brotherhood, and Robert Wilson, sexton.

2. In the original, the much faded Memoranda appear to read at this point, 'the yearly value of the same parsonage is £10 which the vicar payeth as a pension of the clear yearly value of the said vicarage which over and above the yearly (. . . illegible) £3 10s 11d.'

3. For a later copy of the inventory of goods, see Walters, 639.

21. ST DUNSTAN IN THE EAST

Chantry and obit: founded under royal licence by John Bottesham and Alice Potyn, widow, who originally gave a rent charge of 10 marks p.a. from their 2 tenements to maintain a priest, and subsequently gave the tenements to the parish, on condition that from the profits the priest should be paid 10 marks p.a. and receive a gown worth 10s p.a.; that the priest singing high mass every Sunday should receive 2d; that the chantry priest and parish clerk should both have free lodging in the tenements, and the priest be given bread, wine and candles for his masses. A box was to be kept for the residue of the profits, from which loans could be made to the poor and the costs of maintaining an obit and repairing the tenements could be drawn. Value of the tenements, £17 16s 8d p.a. Of which, 10s quitrent; £7 3s 4d (including the 10s gown) to Robert Neale, chantry priest; £1 3s 8d obit; £1 10s 8d for the clerk's wages; total deductions £10 7s 8d p.a. Clear remainder £6 16s [sic] p.a. for repair of the houses.

Priest at the Jesus altar, and obit: lands and tenements given by Joan Maken and Alice Lynne for their souls for ever, £20 11s 8d p.a. Of which, 3s quitrent to the king; £7 6s 8d to Sir Philip Mathew, chantry priest; 13s 4d quitrent to St Katherine's; 3s 8d alms to the poor; total deductions £8 6s 8d. Clear remainder £12 5s p.a.

Priest and obit: lands and tenements given by Robert Colbrekes and others for ever, £13 3s 4d p.a. Of which, 15s 2d quitrent to the king; £6 1s 8d to Thomas Rock [priest];[1] total deductions £6 16s 10d. Clear remainder £6 6s 6d p.a.

Priest at the Lady altar: lands and tenements given by William Barret for ever, £12 p.a. Of which, £6 13s 4d to Sir John Flude,[2] priest. Clear remainder £5 6s 8d p.a.

Obit: 2 tenements given by persons unknown,[3] one in the parish, t. Thomas Bacon, £3 6s 8d p.a.; the other in the parish of St Mary at Hill, t. Thomas Bradforde, £10 p.a.; total £13 6s 8d p.a. Of which, £7 to John Harforde, priest; 2s 8d to the hospital in Southwark; 3s 4d to the poor; 16s 6½d obit; total deductions £8 2s 6½d. Clear remainder £5 4s 1½d p.a.

Obit: shop in Soper Lane given by Denise Joye for her soul for ever, t. Mrs Stagge, £1 p.a. Of which, 4s obit. Clear remainder 16s p.a.

Obit: tenements given by Sir Bartholomew (?Jay) for his soul for ever, t. Edward Waters, £6 p.a. Of which, £1 14s 4d obit; 6s 8d to the poor; total deductions £2 1s. Clear remainder £3 19s p.a.

[m. 6d] ... :* tenements in Tower Street given by William ... , £6 13s 4d p.a. Of which, £2 ... . Clear remainder £4 13s 4d for the repair of the church.

Light and obit: tenement, t. Henry Hollonde, given by Matthew ... for his soul for ever, £8 p.a., the residue of the profits to be kept in the poor box and lent out on gage. Of which, £1 7s 10d to the poor; £1 light; £1 obit; total deductions £3 7s 10d. Clear remainder £4 12s 2d p.a.

Obit of William Harr(yot?): lands in Thames Street, t. Thomas Blower, Edward Waters and others who are seised in fee in order to maintain the obit, £1 p.a.

Memoranda: 900 communicants. John Pallesgrave, rector, receives £60 p.a. and pays Sir Robert Tyffeng to serve the cure. No other priests.[4] Goods as listed in an inventory[5] handed to the surveyor. Brotherhood as recorded below.

1. BC. He also received a pension of £6 13s 4d from Reading abbey (ibid.).
2. Lloide (BC and E 101).
3. But in BC it is firmly ascribed to William Harriott.
4. But BC has James Rimyger, master of the singing children and organ player, receiving £17 10s p.a. and the following conducts with their several yearly wages: William Andrews £9, Thomas Fyan £8, Edward Paladye £8 and Robert Tynner £7 10s. In addition, James Willet is named as under-sexton at 6s 8d.
5. Walters, 245.

22. St Dunstan in the East: Fraternity of Our Lady

Obit: tenement in Cosin Lane in the parish of All Hallows the Great, given by John Joye to the master and wardens of the fraternity and the wardens of the church on condition of keeping the tenement repaired and maintaining an obit for the brothers and sisters of the fraternity, £1 p.a. Spent accordingly.

23a. St Edmund the King, Lombard Street

Two chaplains and obit for the soul of Richard Jay: lands and tenements given by John Longe for ever, £35 p.a. Of which, £7 to Sir William Myller, priest; £7 to Sir Edmund Hamyn, priest; £2 14s 8d obit; £2 5s to the poor; total deductions £18 19s 8d. Clear remainder £16 0s 4d p.a.

Chaplain, obit and paschal light: lands and tenements given by Thomas Wyllys for the souls of himself, his wife and all Christians, £24 p.a. Of which, £7 to Sir Richard Auncell, priest; £3 6s quitrents to the king; 4s to some preachers; £3 13s 4d obit; total deductions £14 3s 4d. Clear remainder £9 16s 8d p.a.

Lamp, 'Salve', 2 torches and other lights: £3 6s 8d rent, consisting of £1 6s 8d from the brotherhood of St Dunstan's [sic], £1 from the Goldsmiths, £1 from the dean and chapter of St Paul's. All is spent accordingly, save for £1 3s given to the priests and clerks of the church.

Memoranda: 240 communicants. John Person, rector, receives £21 14s 2d p.a., and nobody else helps serve the cure.[1] The plate and goods of the church remain with the churchwardens who have an indenture 'to be answered to the King's Majesty at all times'.[2]

1. BC names Robert Debnam here in addition to those above (cf. **224**), and George Williamson, conduct.
2. For a later copy of the inventory of goods, see Walters, 640.

23b. All Hallows Lombard Street[1]

Priest: £10 6s p.a. rents given by John Buck for his soul for ever from tenements in Bell Alley let to divers people.

Priest and obit: lands and tenements in the parish, given by John Maldon for his soul for ever, £20 3s 4d p.a. Of which, £6 13s 4d to Sir Edward Hollonde, priest; 5s quitrent to the college of Canterbury;[2] 6s 8d to the poor; 14s obit; total deductions £7 19s. Clear remainder £12 3s 4d [sic] p.a.

Chaplain: two tenements in Gracechurch (Gracious) Street given by William Trystor for ever: t. Edmund Cave, £3 3s 4d and t. [blank] Morrell, widow, £2 13s 4d; total £5 16s 8d p.a. No priest has been found for the past 7 years.[3]

Tenements in Gracious Street given by John Buck but with no recorded intention: t. Peter Mynoures, £1 19s 8d; t. Walter Wele, £2; t. Henry Reade, £1 13s 4d; total £5 13s p.a.
Memoranda: 300 communicants. Sir William Jennynes, rector, receives £24 p.a. No other priests except his curate.

> 1. Cf. (for 1546) LR2/242 fos 12–42, which gives texts of founders' wills.
> 2. Christchurch in LR2.
> 3. BC curiously states that Edmund Hamman is the 'incumbent' here, but then records no pension for him.

24. [m.7] Sᴛ Mᴀɢɴᴜs
Chantry at the Lady altar: £6 13s 4d p.a. rent given by Robert Ramsey from a tenement called the Sun in the parish of St Margaret, Bridge Ward. Of which, £9 to Sir Joseph Stepneth, priest. Clear remainder Nil.
Two chaplains at the Lady altar, light and obit: lands and tenements given by Henry Eveley for ever, £12 p.a. Of which, £10 stipends to 2 priests;[1] 16s 8d to the poor; £2 9s 8d obit; total deductions £13 6s 4d. Clear remainder Nil.
Priest: £6 13s 4d p.a. rent given by Andrew Hunte for his soul for ever from 2 tenements called the King's Head in Bridge Street. Of which, £8 to Sir Gilbert Smythe, priest. Clear remainder Nil.
Priest and obit: a tenement called the Castle on the Hoop with 3 adjoining shops, given by Thomas Makinge for his soul for ever, £16 p.a. Of which, £8 to Sir Thomas Parker, priest; 16s quitrent to St Pancras; 3s 4d to the poor; £1 obit; total deductions £9 19s 4d. Clear remainder £6 0s 8d p.a.
Obit: £1 p.a. rent given by John Austen for his soul for ever from a tenement in the parish, called the Dolphin upon the Hoop. Of which, 10s obit; 10s to the poor; total deductions £1. Clear remainder Nil.
Priest and obit: a tenement in Thames Street given by William Brampton for his soul for ever, £9 p.a. Of which, 6s 8d obit; 6s 8d to the poor; total deductions 13s 4d. Clear remainder £8 6s 8d p.a. No priest has been found for the past 20 years.
Obit: a shop in Bridge Street given by Richard Wynter for his soul for ever, £2 13s 4d p.a. Of which, 1s 3d quitrents to the king; 13s 4d to the poor; 11s 8d obit; total deductions £1 6s 3d. Clear remainder £1 7s 1d p.a.
Augmentation of a priest's wages, and obit: £1 rent, given by William Rothinges from a shop in the parish. Of which, 5s to the poor; 8s 4d obit; total deductions 13s 4d. Clear remainder 6s 8d p.a.
Priest: a tenement in the parish, given by Ralph de Grey for his soul for ever, £4 p.a. All spent on the augmentation of the priest's wages.
Other church lands: There are other church lands whose donors and intents are not recorded, but the wardens say they have been used for the past 200 years to maintain the church, repair the tenements, and bear other charges: total £133 13s 4d p.a. Of this, £20 6s 8d was bequeathed by John Bever to maintain 2 priests, but these have not been found since Henry IV's time. Lands worth £81 4s 8d p.a. have been used for the wages of priests and conducts, for anthems, 'Salves', 'and such other like', and the remainder for repair of the lands beside the waterworks, apart from lands worth £6 1s 0½d kept for other charges. They have also bought lands worth

£15 2s 7d p.a. to their common use, and not for priests, lamps etc. Total devoted to lamps, priests etc. £92 13s 4d [sic] p.a.[2] Of which, £9 to Robert Saye, priest; £9 to William Mapperley; £8 to Henry Mudde; £8 to Robert Mornell; £14 13s 4d to Edward Barrye;[3] £5 10s to the sexton; 8s to the keeper of the church doors; total wages of conducts etc. £54 11s 4d; other charges as detailed in a list handed over by the churchwardens, £57 19s 9½d; total expenditure £112 11s [1½d],[4] a deficit of £19 17s 9½d p.a.

[m.7d] *Memoranda:** There are debts due by the church: to Master Turke £39 16s; to the (?painter) for t...ing of the church, £26 13s 4d; to ... , £10; total £76 9s 4d. 535 communicants. Maurice[5] Gruffes, rector, receives £69 5s 5d p.a. There is a brotherhood of Salve Regina as recorded below.

1. William Draper and William Barker (E 101). Only the former in BC.
2. It is unclear how this figure is derived from what precedes.
3. Mapperley *et al.* are presumably the conducts. Barrye, for instance, was employed *ad missam Beate Marie et ad antiphonas* (E 101).
4. Margin defective.
5. Maris in text.

25. ST MAGNUS: FRATERNITY OF SALVE REGINA
Yearly income: £49 16s 8d p.a.[1] from gifts [not detailed] of Andrew Hunte, Thomas Broke, John Wage, John Parnell, Henry Hale and John Potman. Of which, £8 to Sir William Swanne, priest; £8 to William Buntinge, priest;[2] £10 4s 1½d obits, lamps and lights; 15s quitrents to the Bridgehouse; 10s to St Bartholomew's Hospital, Smithfield; £1 0s 8d to the poor; 5½d to the sheriffs of London for socage money; £5 4s to Thomas Atkynson, a brother of the fraternity in prison at Ludgate, at 2s per week; £2 18s 4d to father Woodhouse, a blind brother, at 1s 2d per week for his lifetime; £2 3s 4d to [blank] Kethers, a sister 'fallen in decay and sick of the palsy', at 1s per week for her lifetime; £8 13s 4d to Marchaunt's widow, Dyxover's widow, Swanne's widow and Martyson's wife: sisters 'fallen in poverty and making their suit to them', at 10d per week for their lifetimes, according to the foundation. Total deductions £47 9s 3½d. Clear remainder £2 7s 4½d p.a.

1. 16s 8d scored through and 4s written in, but this does not agree with the totals.
2. BC also names here Edward Bury, conduct.

26. ST ANTHOLIN BUDGE ROW
Priest: £6 13s 4d p.a. rent given by Nicholas Bole for his soul for ever from lands in the parish called "Galles". Of which, £6 13s 4d to Robert Smythe, chantry priest. Clear remainder Nil.
Priest: lands and tenements given by Ralph Sey for a priest to sing divine service in the church and pray for his soul for ever, £7 8s p.a. Of which, £6 3s 4d to [blank],[1] priest; 1 lb pepper as quitrent to the king. Clear remainder £1 4s 8d p.a.
Priest: £7 3s 4d p.a. rent given by William Gregory from lands t. John Fludd in the parish of St Martin in the Vintry. Of which, £6 6s 4d to Sir Edmund Hacket, incumbent. Clear remainder 17s p.a.
Priest: £4 p.a. rent given by John Grauntham from tenements in the parishes of All Hallows the Great[2] and St Pancras, to find a priest[3] singing in the church.

Obit: £1 p.a. rent also given by John Grauntham for his soul for ever, from lands now t. the master of the Savoy. Of which, 5s to the poor; 15s obit; total deductions £1. Clear remainder Nil.

Memoranda: 240 communicants. Sir William Tolwyn, rector, receives £20 p.a. There are no other priests to serve the cure.

1. Roger Thacker (BC).
2. "ad fenum".
3. Perhaps Thomas Sprinte, said in BC to have been supported here by the Grocers, but at a yearly wage of £7 6s 8d.

27. [m.8] ALL HALLOWS THE GREAT, THAMES STREET[1]

Priest: a tenement called "Bewropere" and a tavern then adjoining it were given by William Preston for his soul for ever, £14 16s 8d p.a. Of which, 6s 8d to Stephen Hales for the king; £2 6s 8d quitrents to Mr Haselwoode; £7 14s 8d to a stipendiary priest;[2] 10s to the poor; £1 6s 2d obit; total deductions £12 4s 2d. Clear remainder £2 12s 6d p.a.

Priest: 2 tenements called the Cold Harbour in the parish, given by Nicholas Levon for his soul for ever, £12 6s 8d p.a. Of which, 10s quitrent to St Mary Aldermary for an obit; £8 to a stipendiary priest,[3] including £1 6s 8d for his chamber; 13s 4d obit; total deductions £7 16s 8d.[4] Clear remainder £4 10s p.a.

Priest: £4 p.a. rent given by William Lichefeilde for his soul for ever from 2 tenements in Cousin (Cosyns) Lane; with 2 other tenements in Hay Wharf Lane added to augment this by Thomas Westhawe at £4 16s 8d p.a.; total £8 16s 8d p.a. Of which, £6 13s 4d for a priest's salary;[5] 3s 4d to the rector; total deductions £6 16s 8d. Clear remainder £2 p.a.

Obit: 2 tenements in the parish, given by John West for his soul for ever for 10s to be spent at an obit, £4 6s 8d p.a. Of which, 10s obit. Clear remainder £3 16s 8d p.a.

Anniversary: £9 p.a. rent given by John Brickelles for his soul for ever from a messuage in the parish of St Martin in the Vintry called the Emperor's Head, and also from the lands of the Clothworkers at Hay Wharf.[6] Of which, 13s 4d quitrents; £1 8s 4d obit; total deductions £2 1s 8d. Clear remainder £6 18s 4d p.a.

Lamp before the Sacrament: tenements in Hay Wharf Lane, t. Hans Tutt, given by William Oldwarke, 13s 4d p.a.

Obit: the mayor and sheriffs of London keep an obit for one Raynewell,[7] spending 10s p.a.

Memoranda: 550 communicants. Sir John Wale, rector, receives £46 p.a. and finds a priest under him to serve the cure who is of good and honest conversation.

1. Cf. (for 1546) LR 2/242 fos 1–4.
2. Thomas Ladde (BC).
3. Robert Barrett (BC).
4. The total deducted does not include the payment for the chamber.
5. John Cremor (BC). Richard Prince, conduct, is also listed here.
6. The sum £3 6s 8d has been interlined against each of the two rents.
7. Alderman John Raynewell: see *Husting*, ii, 576n.

28. ST PANCRAS WEST CHEAP

Augmentation of John Causton's priest: tenements given by Simon Ryce,

£13 p.a. Of which, £6 13s 4d to Adrian Arnolde, chantry priest; 4s quitrent; £3 6s 8d annuity to Simon Rige[1] and Lettice his wife for their lives, and then to their heirs for ever; 4s 10d obit; total deductions £10 8s 10d. Clear remainder £2 11s 2d p.a.

Obit: 13s 4d p.a. rent given by John Lagage for his soul for ever from his tenement at the east end of the church. The money is given to the poor.

Obit: 6s 8d p.a. rent given by Robert Burley for his soul for ever from a tenement called the Saracen's Head in the parish of St Mildred Poultry. The money is given to the poor.

Two lamps: tenements given by Simon the Worsted and others,[2] £3 10s p.a. Of which, £1 for 2 lamps; 10s bread and wine; 5s obit; total deductions £1 15s. Clear remainder £1 15s p.a.

Priest: £2 12s 10¾d p.a. rents given by Simon[3] Causton.[4]

Church lands: a void piece of ground given by an unknown donor, 10s p.a.[5]

Priest and obit: £233 6s 8d was left to the Mercers by Margaret Reynolds in her will on condition that they gave the parish £8 13s 4d p.a. rent to maintain a priest and obit. Of which, £6 13s 4d to the priest; £2 obit and to the poor; total deductions £8 13s 4d.[6] Clear remainder Nil.

Memoranda: 146 communicants. Richard Marshe, rector, receives £13 6s 8d p.a. and serves the cure himself.

1. Probably the donor.
2. Simon Worsted and John Barnes (SC 6).
3. ? *recte* John (see above in this section), though SC 6 has William.
4–5. Entries apparently added subsequently.
6. Totals crossed out, most probably because this entry appears under the Mercers' Company, see **194**.

29. [m.8d] St Stephen Walbrook[1]

Priest:[2] lands and tenements in Bucklersbury in this parish, and in the parishes of St Pancras and St Thomas the Apostle, given by Lettice Lee, widow, £14 10s p.a. Of which, £2 18s 3d quitrents. Clear remainder £11 11s 9d p.a.

Priest: £126 13s 4d money given by William Adams for his soul[3] for as long as the money would last at £6 13s 4d p.a. Three years have expired, total spent £20, leaving £106 13s 4d,[4] in the hands of one named Myller of Lynn, Norfolk.

Three obits: 8 tenements t. William Saunders given by Laurence Bere, £4 p.a.

Obit: a tenement in the parish, given by Thomas Oo for his soul for ever, £2 p.a.

Lands: donors and intention unknown, £4 10s p.a.

Memoranda: 250 communicants. Thomas Becon, rector, receives £17 10s p.a., and finds a priest to serve the cure.[5]

1. Cf. (for 1546) LR 2/241 fos 115–19.
2. The text does not specify a priest but refers to 'singing in the church'; nor does it mention a priest's salary. But BC names Richard Wilson, priest.
3. 'for ever' crossed out.
4. A faint attempt has been made to insert 'xx' to turn this total into £126 13s 4d.
5. Henry Fitzwilliam, said to have been supported by the Salters, is named in BC, along with Henry Cockes paid by the Grocers (see **212**).

30. ST MARGARET MOSES

Morrow mass priest: lands and tenements in Friday Street, given by Nicholas Bray, £8 16s 8d p.a. Of which, £7 5s to Sir John Gryffyn, priest aged 46, of virtuous living and small learning, having no other living. Clear remainder £1 11s 8d p.a.

Priest: lands and tenements in Friday Street, given by John Fenne for his soul for ever, £9 10s p.a. Of which, £6 13s 4d to Sir John Brightwyse, priest aged 46, of honest behaviour and indifferently learned and having a further pension of £7; 13s 4d quitrents; £2 2s obit; total deductions £9 8s 8d. Clear remainder 1s 4d p.a.

Priest: a tenement in the parish of St Denis Backchurch, t. William Gonne, £4 p.a., and an annuity from the late monastery of Graces nigh the Tower, £4 p.a., given by Gerrard Dannyell for ever. Of which, 5s to Sir Nicholas Prideoux, priest;[1] £1 obit; 2s 8d 'potations'; total deductions £1 7s 8d. Clear remainder £6 12s 4d p.a.

Lamp before the Blessed Sacrament: a tenement in the parish of St Mildred, t. Robert Sole, given by Thomas le Rous, £2 p.a. Of which, 15s light. Clear remainder £1 5s p.a.

Annuity: £4 p.a., by decree of the court of Augmentations.

Light before the Blessed Sacrament: 6s 8d p.a. rent from a corner tenement in Distaff Lane, given by Simonde de Cockham.

Memoranda: 240 communicants. Robert Johnson, rector, receives £19 0s 5d p.a. and serves the cure himself. There is no other priest.

1. Not named in BC.

31a. ST MICHAEL QUEENHITHE

Two chaplains: lands in the parish, given by Stephen Spilman, £11 16s 8d p.a. Of which, £6 13s 4d to Thomas Gilbert, priest, for his stipend; £1 3s 4d obit; 11s to the poor; 6s 8d quitrents to the chamberlain of London; total deductions £8 14s 4d. Clear remainder £3 2s 4d p.a.

[m.9] *Two chaplains:* lands in the parish, also £1 p.a. rent from a piece of void ground in St Lawrence Lane, and a tenement in the parish, t. Oliver Daubenye, £2 13s 4d p.a., given by Robert Parres, Thomas Eyre and John Clarke for their souls for ever; total £7 13s 4d p.a. Of which, £6 13s 4d to Sir William Bigge, priest, for his stipend; 5s 6d quitrent; 7½d to the sheriffs of London for socage money; total deductions £6 19s 5d.[1] Clear remainder 13s 11d p.a.

Obit: lands and tenements in the parish given by John Parker for his soul for ever, £10 3s 4d p.a. Of which, 3s 4d obit; 6s 8d to the poor; 12s quitrents; total deductions £1 2s. Clear remainder £9 1s 4d p.a.

Priest and obit: lands and tenements given for an unknown purpose by Richard Grey, £5 14s 8d p.a., used as follows: £1 12s quitrents to the hospital in Southwark; 10s to St Nicholas Olave; 5s 7d obit; £1 5s alms to the poor; total deductions £3 12s 7d. Clear remainder £2 2s 1d p.a.

Memoranda: 500 communicants. Sir Philip Bale, rector, receives £20 p.a. There is no other priest besides him and his deputy.[2] Goods and plate as in an inventory held by the churchwardens.

1. ½d disappears in the totals.
2. BC has also Thomas Horner, conduct.

31b. St Leonard East Cheap[1]

Priest: lands and tenements given by William Ivorye for his soul for ever, £6 6s 8d p.a. Of which, £1 13s 4d quitrents to the king; £6 13s 4d to [blank], priest,[2] for his stipend; total deductions £8 6s 8d. Clear remainder Nil.

Priest, light and obit: lands and tenements given by John Bromesburye for his soul for ever, £3 13s 4d p.a. Of which, £8 stipend to a priest; £1 obit; 2s quitrent to the king; total deductions £9 2s. Clear remainder Nil.

Augmentation of the above priest's living: 3 shops in the parish, given by Robert Brickhurst *alias* Bromesburye, £3 10s p.a. Of which, all is spent for this purpose. Clear remainder Nil.

Priest to sing there: tenements and rents in the parish, given by Margery Bodyn, £10 8s p.a. Of which, £7 stipend to a priest. Clear remainder £3 8s p.a.

Priest: lands and tenements given by John Bromesburye and John Aplebye for their souls for ever, £10 p.a. Of which [£2 3s] 4d quitrents; £6 13s 4d stipend to a priest; total deductions £8 16s 8d. Clear remainder £1 3s 4d p.a.

Priest and obit: lands and tenements given by Hugh Browne for his soul for ever, £18 11s p.a. Of which, 6s 8d to the king; 1s 8d to the bishop of Winchester; £3 6s 8d quitrents; £7 to a priest; 10s obit; total deductions £11 5s. Clear remainder £7 6s p.a.

Priest and obit:[3] lands and tenements in the parish given by John Doggett for his soul for ever, £10 p.a. Of which, £2 13s 4d quitrent to St Paul's; 4s 6d to Westminster; £6 13s 4d to a priest; £1 16s obit; total deductions £11 7s 2d. Clear remainder Nil.

[m.9d] *Obit and other charges:*[4] as specified in the will of Thomas Sampson: tenements in the parish and in the parish of St Botolph Billingsgate [£9 10s] p.a. Total deductions £6 3s 6d. Clear remainder £3 6s 6d p.a.

Obit: lands and tenements in the parish and in the parish of St Margaret Bridge Street, given by William (?Levers)eydge, £3 8s p.a. Of which, £1 12s quitrent to Doggett's [priest]; 2s to the poor; 18s 8d obit; total deductions £2 12s 8d. Clear remainder 15s 4d p.a.

Lamp: 6s 8d p.a. rent given by John Bromesburye.

Solemn mass every Friday: a tenement in Bridge Street given by Thomas Champneys for his soul for ever, £4 p.a. Of which, £1 5s for the mass; 14s 8d to the dean of Westminster; total deductions £1 19s 8d. Clear remainder £2 0s 4d p.a.

Memoranda: 260 communicants. Sir John Tornour, rector, receives £25 p.a. and serves the cure himself.

1. Title now largely obscured by parchment overlaid during repair.
2. The priests named here in BC are: John Turnor, William Skipton, John Chatteryse, Stephen Bisseter, Thomas Gallesburgh and John Elliottesson.
3. This entry is very faint. For the will, see *Husting*, ii, 354.
4. This entry is also very faint and partly illegible; partly over-written in a later hand probably to improve legibility. For the will, see PROB 11/2B fo. 53.

32. St Mary Bothaw[1]

Priest: £12 annuity from the court of Augmentations, given by James le Butler for his soul for ever. Of which, £12 to a priest.[2] Clear remainder Nil.

Priest: £6 p.a. rent given by Hugh Fostall from tenements in Butcher Lane. Of which, £6 to a priest[3] for his stipend. Clear remainder Nil.

Priest: a tenement called the Key in Coleman Street, given by John Salesburye for his soul for ever, £7 p.a. Of which, £6 to a priest.[4] Clear remainder £1 p.a.

Augmentation of 2 priests' livings, plus an obit: £2 6s 8d p.a. rent given by William Okeley from tenements in the parish. Of which, £2 6s 8d obit. Clear remainder Nil.

Obit for Elizabeth Bustred and augmentation of a priest's living: a tenement in Aldermary, given by the same William, £3 1s 8d p.a. Of which, 1s 6d to the poor; £1 2s 4d obit; total deductions £1 3s 10d. Clear remainder £1 17s 10d p.a.

Obit for the soul of William Lightwoode, and the augmentation of 2 priests' livings: tenement in the parish of St Martin Orgar, given by Thomas Awdon, £1 6s 8d p.a. Of which, 8d to the poor; 3s 4d obit; total deductions 4s. Clear remainder £1 2s 8d p.a.

Obit: land given by Thomas Huntley to his wife Katherine for her life on condition of maintaining the obit, with remainder to Daulton's heirs on the same condition, 10s p.a.

Memoranda: 182 communicants. Sir William Hogget, rector, receives £10 10s p.a. and serves the cure himself.[5]

1. Cf. (for 1546) LR 2/242 fos. 105–12, which is insistent that there are no chantry priests, only stipendiaries here.
2. William Smythe (BC).
3. Thomas Horde "mortus" (BC).
4. Richard Lawson (BC).
5. Matthew Grenewod, conduct, is also named in BC.

33. [m.10] St Peter Cornhill

Perpetual priest, lamp and obit: lands in the parish, given by William Kingeston for his soul for ever, £47 7s 4d p.a. Of which, £16 to 2 priests[1] who receive £8 each; £1 15s quitrents to the king; 6s 8d to the master of the Bridgehouse; £3 5s 8d obit; 3s 8d to the Chamber of Westminster; £2 13s 4d to the dean of St Paul's; 6s to Mr Bellamy; total deductions £24 10s 4d. Clear remainder £19 17s 0d p.a.

Priest: lands and tenements in the parishes of St Martin and St Peter, given by Dame Alice Bucknell, £12 17s 4d p.a. Of which, £7 10s to James Norres, priest; £1 13s 9d obit; total deductions £9 3s 9d. Clear remainder £3 13s 7d p.a.

Brotherhood of St Giles: lands and tenements given by various people [not named] towards the maintenance of a priest's living, £26 7s 4d p.a. Of which, £16 6s 8d to Richard Carsey and Giles Haukes, priests; 3s 4d quitrent to the Chamber of London; total deductions £16 10s 0d. Clear remainder £9 17s 4d p.a.

Chaplain: lands in the parishes of St Ethelburga (Alborowe) and St Peter, given by [blank][2] Morley, £11 13s 4d p.a. Of which, £7 10s to Roger Hatton, priest; 3s quitrent to the king; 3s to John Birde; 10s obit; 10s to St Bartholomew's hospital; 6s 8d to the church of St Michael le Quern; total deductions £9 2s 8d. Clear remainder £2 10s 8d p.a.

Obit, beam and paschal lights: £1 13s 0d p.a.[3] rent given by Robert Welwike for his soul, from tenements appertaining to the city of London.

Obit: a tenement in the parish, t. Edward Elrington, given by [blank]

21

Wenham for his soul for ever, £3 6s 8d p.a. Of which, 11s 4d to the poor; 8s 8d obit; total deductions £1. Clear remainder £2 6s 8d p.a.
Memoranda: 500 communicants. Dr Taylor,[4] dean of Lincoln, is rector and receives £39 5s 7d. No further priests are found to serve the cure besides the curate.[5]

1. Roger Ponder and Martin Cater (BC).
2. Richard in *Valor*.
3. Possibly altered from £1 16s 0d.
4. John Taylor.
5. BC also names Nicholas Jackeson (see **212**) and Robert Stokes (see **211**), with Thomas Assheton, conduct.

34. St Martin Orgar[1]
Chaplain: lands in the parishes of 'St Swithin and St Olave nigh Crooked Lane', given by William Cromar, £30 15s 4d p.a. Of which, 15s 4d quitrent to the king; £6 13s 4d to John Carre, priest;[2] 13s 4d to St Paul's; 10s 8d to the poor; £3 17s 4d obit; total deductions £12 10s. Clear remainder £18 5s 4d p.a.
Augmentation of the Lady mass 'to be sung by note': tenements in the parish, given by John Weston, £12 18s 8d p.a. Of which, £1 7s 4d quitrents; £1 16s 8d obit; total deductions £3 4s. Clear remainder £9 14s 8d p.a.
Two chaplains: lands and tenements given by William Creswike for his soul for ever, £13 5s p.a. Of which, £16 to Sir Charles and Sir Ralph,[3] priests; 2s to the poor; 7s obit; total deductions £16 9s. Clear remainder Nil.
Prayers: tenement given by P[blank][4] Picarde 'to be prayed for', £2 13s 4d p.a. Of which, 6s 8d quitrent; 6s 8d to the poor; total deductions 13s 4d. Clear remainder £2 p.a.
Prayers: tenement in the parish of St Clement, given by Leonard Johnson 'to be prayed for', £4 13s 4d p.a. Of which, 9s quitrents to the king; 6s 8d obit; £1 6s 8d poor; total deductions £2 2s 4d. Clear remainder £2 11s p.a.
[m.10d] *Anniversary:* lands in the parish, given by Dame Margaret Mathew for her soul for ever, £3 6s 8d p.a. Of which, 5s 8d obit; 7s 8d to the poor; total deductions 13s 4d. Clear remainder £2 13s 4d p.a.
Three lamps and a paschal light: 15s p.a. rent given by [blank] from a tenement in the parish. 'Witholden these 7 years'.[5]
Obit: £3 6s 8d money given by Mr Cosen to keep an obit 'during a certain time'. Of which, 13s 4d obit. Clear remainder £2 13s 4d p.a.
Memoranda: 280 communicants. Sir Thomas Wethers, rector, receives £19 19s 8d. There are no priests besides those named above,[6] who all help serve the cure.

1. Cf. (for 1546) LR 2/241 fos 84–100.
2. In addition to Carre, BC also has Jervys Linche here, but he should probably be one of Cresswick's priests in the following entry.
3. BC has only Ralph Collier here.
4. LR 2 has William.
5. '6 years' crossed out.
6. BC has also James Sharpulles, conduct.

35. St Michael Crooked Lane
Five chaplains: lands and tenements given by William Walworthe for his soul and all Christian souls, £20 13s 4d p.a. Of which, £7 4s to Sir William

Birte, priest; £7 to Sir Thomas Harper, priest; £8 to Sir William Hale, priest; £7 4s to Sir William Clayton, priest; £7 4s to Sir John Nesehame, priest; £4 0s 4d to the king for their tenths; total deductions £40 12s 4d. Clear remainder Nil.

Chaplain to sing divine service: lands and tenements given by John Rothinge, £6 p.a. Spent towards Walworth's chaplains.

Chaplain: a tenement called the Boar's Head in East Cheap, given by Walter Wordon for his soul for ever, £4 p.a. Spent towards Walworth's chaplains.

Divine service and prayers: lands and tenements given by William de Burgo for his soul for ever, £6 13s 4d p.a. Of which, 14s quitrent to the king. Clear remainder £5 19s 4d p.a.

Chaplain: lands and tenements given by Roger Sterre for his soul for ever, £8 8s p.a. Spent towards Walworth's chaplains.

Chaplain: lands and tenements given by William Jordan for his soul for ever, £5 16s 8d p.a. Spent towards Walworth's chaplains.

Morrow mass priest: lands and tenements given by John Abell for ever, £2 13s 4d. Spent towards Walworth's chaplains.

Chaplain: £6 13s 4d p.a. rents given by John at Lee for his soul for ever, as follows: £3 6s 8d rent from St Leonard East Cheap; £1 6s 8d rent from the church of All Hallows the Great; £2 from a tenement in Distaff Lane formerly belonging to the Crutched Friars. Spent towards Walworth's chaplains.

Augmentation of a priest's living, and obit: £6 6s 8d p.a. rent given by Robert Sprotborough for his soul for ever from divers tenements in London. Of which, 16s 4d obit. Clear remainder £5 10s 4d p.a.

Priest and obit: tenements in the parish, given by Robert Brocket for his soul for ever, £7 p.a.[1]

Obit: 10s p.a. rent given by John Longe from a tenement owned by the Lady Forman.

Memoranda: 354 communicants. Sir John Ponnet, DD, rector, receives £13 6s 8d p.a. There are no priests besides the rector, his curate and the above.

1. In addition to the priests named above, BC has Thomas Tailor and Philip Duly here (cf. **222**), and John Frankelyng, conduct, who may have been Brocket's priest.

36. [m.11] St Mary Woolchurch[1]

Priest: lands and tenements given by Anne Cawoode for her soul for ever, £8 p.a. Of which, £1 quitrents; £6 16s 8d to Henry Cockes, priest; 2s 8d obit; 4s to the poor; total deductions £8 3s 4d. Clear remainder Nil.

Priest: a tenement in the parish of St Michael Cornhill, given by Roger Barlow for his soul for ever, £3 6s 8d p.a. Spent towards Cawoode's priest.

Priest: £3 6s 8d p.a. rent given by Walter Wenlock, Bennet Cornewall, Margaret Cornewall and William Wyken from an entry in the parish of St Mary Woolnoth; also a tenement in the same parish, £2 13s 4d p.a. and a shop there, £3 6s 8d p.a.; a tenement in the parish of St Michael Cornhill, £2 6s 8d p.a.; total £15 13s 4d [sic] p.a. Of which, £6 13s 4d to Sir Lawrence Hay, priest; 2s 8d obit; 10s 8d to the poor; total deductions £7 6s 8d. Clear remainder £8 6s 8d p.a. which is put towards the repair of the tenements.

Lamp: 9s p.a. rent given by Edward Culpeper from various tenements in the parish. Not paid for the past 8 years.

Obit for the soul of Christian Maulen, and poor relief: 13s 4d p.a. paid by the masters of the Bridgehouse in London, 'and to the poor 6s 8d'.[2]

Obit: 10s p.a. paid by William Swayne, 'and to the poor 6s 8d'.[3]

Memoranda: 360 communicants. Sir Griffith Jones, rector, receives £18 13s 4d p.a. and hires Nicholas Audley to serve the cure with him.[4]

1. Cf. (for 1546) LR 2/243 fos 77–83, where there is a note that at Easter 'all the priests we have do not suffice'.
2–3. It is unclear whether these gifts to the poor are included in the figures first stated.
4. BC records that Thomas Well, priest, serves here, paid by the Drapers from Maud at Vine's land; but cf. **224** where a different allocation of resources is indicated. BC also has Henry Barker, conduct, here.

37. ST MARY ALDERMARY[1]

Priest: 4 tenements in Aldermary, given by John Ipport for his soul and all Christian souls for ever, £19 6s 8d p.a. The priest[2] 'taketh the whole lands for his salary by the will'.

Priest and obit: £7 3s 4d p.a. rent given by Robert FitzRobert from tenements in the parish of St Botolph Billingsgate. Of which, £7 6s 8d to Sir Roger Lamb,[3] priest; 10s obit; 5s to the poor; total deductions £8 1s 8d. Clear remainder Nil.

Priest: £4 13s 4d p.a. rent from the court of Augmentations, given by Thomas Romayn. Of which, £7 to Sir Edmund Laurence, priest. Clear remainder Nil.

Conduct,[4] and prayers from the pulpit: tenements in the parish, given by Henry Barton, £9 p.a. Of which, £2 rent to the Skinners' Company. Clear remainder £7 p.a.

Payment towards a priest: a tenement in a street called the Old Royal in the parish of St Michael, given by Richard Cancer, £2 10s p.a. Of which, £1 5s rent to St Michael's[5] church. Clear remainder £1 5s p.a.

Priest: tenements in Golding Lane in the parish of St Giles Cripplegate, given by Hugh Mosse, £1 5s p.a. Of which, 1s 3d quitrent to the manor of Finsbury. Clear remainder £1 3s 9d p.a.

Repair of the church: a tenement in the parish, t. Robert Dove, given by William Darbye, £3 6s 8d p.a.

Lamp: 6s 8d p.a. rent from a brewhouse in Phillip Lane given by Gilbert de la Bas.

Memoranda: 400 communicants. Edward Crome, rector, receives £41 p.a. No other priests besides his curate.[6]

1. Cf. (for 1546) LR 2/243 fos 113–20.
2. William Bowthe (BC).
3. Robert West in BC.
4. In BC this is described as Henry Barton's chantry, but there is no priest here, only Peter Tippe, conduct.
5. Querne crossed out. In LR 2 it is St Michael Paternoster.
6. BC also lists Thomas Artes (see **212**), Richard Abbot and Thomas **Garnet** supported by the Skinners (see **192** where Nicholas Dunston is named instead of Abbot).

38. [m.11d] St Margaret Bridge Street
Two chaplains at St Peter's altar, obit and light: lands and tenements given by John Coggeshall for his soul for ever, £13 10s p.a. Of which, £7 13s 4d to Sir Richard Bee, chantry priest; 3s 4d obit; 3s 4d to the poor; total deductions £8. Clear remainder £5 10s p.a.
Priest and 2 tapers: 2 shops in the parish, given by John Rous, £5 p.a. Of which, £6 13s 4d to Sir John Redde, priest; 8s quitrents to the king; total deductions £7 1s 4d. Clear remainder Nil.
Obit: a shop in the parish, given by Hugh Ryebreade for his soul for ever, £4 p.a. Of which, 6s 8d obit; 3s 4d to the poor; total deductions 10s. Clear remainder £3 10s p.a.
Priest: lands and tenements given by Thomas Dursley for his soul for ever, £4 p.a. Of which, £5 6s 8d to a conduct;[1] 6s 8d obit; total deductions £5 13s 4d. Clear remainder Nil.
Anniversary: lands and tenements given by William West for his soul for ever, to spend £2 yearly: £10 p.a. Of which, £1 6s 8d obit; 13s 4d to the poor; total deductions £2. Clear remainder £8 p.a.
Priest: tenements in the parish of St Leonard, given by Robert Whaplode for his soul for ever, £2 p.a. Of which, £1 to augment a priest's living; 6s 8d obit; 13s 4d to the poor; total deductions £2. Clear remainder Nil.
Two yearly commemorations: a tenement in Crooked Lane, given by Thomas Badbye for his soul for ever, £1 6s 8d p.a. Of which, 16s 8d obit;[2] 10s to the poor; total deductions £1 6s 8d. Clear remainder Nil.
Anniversary: 6s 8d p.a. rent given by [blank] for his soul for ever from a tenement and shop in the parish. Of which, 3s 4d obit; 3s 4d to the poor; total deductions 6s 8d. Clear remainder Nil.
Church lands: worth £2 6s 8d p.a.
Torch: 6s 8d p.a. rent given by Robert a Mockinge from a tenement belonging to Roger Paddye.
Purpose unknown: £2 2s 4d quitrents given by Jeffrey Badcock from divers tenements in London.
Memoranda: 200 communicants. Richard Archar, rector, receives £31 10s 6d p.a.

1. Richard Clerke, conduct (BC).
2. £1 6s 8d altered.

39. St Mary Aldermanbury[1]
Chaplain and anniversary: tenements in Aldermary, given by Dennis Towres for his soul for ever, £5 19s 4d p.a. Of which, £3 12s to Sir John Mordock, morrow mass priest; 7s 6d quitrents; 13s obit; 1s to the poor; total deductions £4 13s 6d. Clear remainder £1 5s 10d p.a.
Maintenance of the beam light for 300 years: a tenement in the parish, given by Robert Draycote, £2 p.a.
Church lands: lands in the parish given by the late alderman Bury of London and others, £17 15s 8d p.a. Of which, £1 2s 4d quitrents to the king; £6 16s 10½d 'for priests' wages and other'; total deductions £6 19s 2½d [sic]. Clear remainder £9 16s 5½d p.a.
Memoranda: 371 communicants. John Remes, rector, receives £18 p.a.[2]

1. Cf. (for 1546) LR 2/243 fos 70–6.

2. BC names 2 further priests here: John Mede and Richard Ungle, at the chantry of Sir William Estfelde; but cf. **194**.

40. [m.12] St Mary Woolnoth
Two chantry priests: tenements given by Thomas Nocket, £13 6s 8d p.a. Of which, £6 13s 4d to Sir William Wentors, chantry priest; £6 13s 4d to Sir Richard Browne,[1] chantry priest; total deductions £13 6s 8d. Clear remainder Nil.
Priest: lands given by Sir Hugh Brige, kt., for ever, including a rent charge of 8s 4d[2] p.a. from a capital messuage in Lombard Street, t. Sir Martin Bowes, £13 13s 4d p.a. Of which, £6 13s 4d to John Meres, priest; 13s 4d tenths to the king; 2s quitrent to the king; total deductions £7 8s 8d. Clear remainder £6 4s 8d p.a.
Obit and clerk: a tenement in Sherborne Lane given by Thomas Wymounde (after the death of his wife Elizabeth, now deceased), £2 p.a. Of which, 5s obit; £1 15s to the clerk; total deductions £2 p.a. Clear remainder Nil.
Obit: £1 p.a. rent given by Dame Elizabeth Brice for ever.
Five tapers: 2 tenements given by Dame Emma Meger for ever, £1 9s 4d p.a.
Memoranda: 300 communicants. Sir John Shether, rector, receives £26 p.a. No other priests[3] besides his deputy.

1. Richard Harbert in BC.
2. Or possibly "liii s iiij d".
3. But John Palmer, Thomas Somerton and John Fyssher were maintained here by the Merchant Taylors: see **211**; and Hugh Jones, conduct, received £6 15s p.a. for his service and for teaching singing children (BC).

41. St Swithin London Stone
Chaplain: lands and tenements given by William Newe, £17 8s 4d p.a. Of which, £6 13s 4d to Sir John Hudson, priest; £3 quitrents to the parson of the Tower; total deductions £9 13s 4d. Clear remainder £7 15s p.a.
Poor relief: lands, £2 [p.a.][1] given by John Tryston.
Priest and obit: lands given by Geoffrey Chittock for his soul for ever, £13 6s 8d p.a. Of which, £6 13s 4d to Sir Roger Butte, priest; 12s obit; total deductions £7 5s 4d. Clear remainder £6 1s 4d p.a.
Priest and obit: lands in the parish, given by John Betson for his soul for ever, £13 15s 8d p.a. Of which, £6 13s 4d to Richard Hudson, priest; 17s 4d obit and poor relief; total deductions £7 10s 8d. Clear remainder £6 5s p.a.
Priest: £5 6s 8d p.a. rent from the mayor and commonalty of London in fulfilment of the will of Roger Depham.[2]
Obit: a shop in East Cheap given by John Bull for his soul for ever, 15s p.a.
Memoranda: 320 communicants. Sir Richard Chaterton, rector, receives £15 p.a. No other priest. An old red velvet vestment, another vestment of thread and a mass book, together valued at 13s 4d, belonging to these promotions, are in the hands of the churchwardens to the king's use.

1. Not specified.
2. See *Husting*, ii, 7. John Williams, priest (BC).

42. St Margaret Lothbury[1]
Priest and obit: lands and tenements given by John Julyan for his soul for

ever, £7 4s p.a. Of which, £6 13s 4d to John Badye, priest; 2s 6d quitrents; 2s 4d obit; 2s to the poor; total deductions £7 0s 2d. Clear remainder 3s 10d p.a.

Priest: a tenement in the parish, given by John Iforde, £6 13s 4d p.a. Of which, £6 13s 4d to Sir Patrick Faber, priest. Clear remainder Nil.

Obit: £1 13s 4d p.a. rent given by Richard Oldcastell for his soul for ever and received from the wardens of St Martin's.[2] Of which, 10s to the poor; 11s 4d obit; total deductions £1 1s 4d. Clear remainder 12s p.a.

Paschal light and obit: a tenement given by Richard Haukes for his soul for ever, £2 p.a. Of which, 7s obit; 13s 9d paschal light; total deductions £1 0s 9d. Clear remainder 19s 3d p.a.

Obit: lands and tenements given by William Pastley for his soul for ever, £4 p.a. Of which, 13s 9d quitrents; 4s 4d obit; total deductions 18s 1d. Clear remainder £3 1s 11d p.a.

*Memoranda:** 279 communicants. Sir William Reade, rector, receives £13 6s (?8)d p.a. No other priest.

1. Cf. (for 1546) LR 2/243 fos 65–69a.
2. Ludgate (LR 2).

43. St Lawrence Jewry[1]

*Priest:** tenements given by Simon Benyngton[2] for his soul for ever, £22 13s 4d p.a. Of which, [£6 13s 4d p.a.] to Thomas Sylvestre, priest. Clear remainder £16 p.a.

[m.12d] *Priest:** a tenement in the parish, given by Simon Bartlet[3] for his soul for ever, £7 4s 8d. Of which, £8 to Sir Thomas Bullocke, priest; 6s obit; total deductions £8 6s. Clear remainder Nil.

Beam light: tenements in Cateaton Street (Catten Lane) given by the same Simon, £7 10s p.a.

Two priests: a tenement in the parish of St Mary le Bow, given by John Gossenham for his soul for ever, £13 6s 8d p.a. Of which, £13 6s 8d to Thomas Reyley and Thomas Whorleston, priests;[4] £1 13s 8d quitrents to the king; total deductions £15 0s 4d. Clear remainder Nil.

Priest at the Lady altar: a tenement in St Lawrence Lane, given by Thomas Wytton, £8 3s 4d p.a. Of which, £8 to Thomas Sandlond,[5] priest; 1s quitrents to the king; total deductions £8 1s 0d. Clear remainder Nil [sic].

Singing man at the Lady altar, and obit: £7 6s 8d p.a. rent given by William Myldreth from 6 tenements in Milk Street and Lad Lane. Of which, £11 to Roland Robynsonne, priest. Clear remainder Nil.

Thirty priests: lands in Grub Street,[6] St Laurence Queenhithe,[7] and St Mary Somerset, given by Thomas Burgoyne for 30 'Diriges' and 30 masses, £10 16s 8d p.a. Of which, £1 to the 30 priests. Clear remainder £9 16s 8d p.a.

Morrow mass priest:[8] £7 13s 4d p.a. paid by Robert Charsey 'but for what time, or what lands be charged therewith it is unknown'.

Repairs, anniversary, lights and chaplain for the brotherhood of the Holy Rood: a corner house in St Lawrence Lane, given to the vicar and the keepers of the Rood light and St Anne's light, by the will of John Lane, £4 13s 4d p.a.

Obit: £1 6s 8d p.a. rent given by Richard Messenger from a great tenement in Milk Street, and 1s 8d to the poor.

Obit: £1 p. a. rent from a tenement in Soper Lane given by John Chickham.

Priest: lands given by John Marshall for ever, £6 13s 4d p.a.

Obit: lands given by Joan, widow of John Chigham, £2 3s 4d p.a.

Memoranda: 548 communicants. Robert Cosen, vicar, receives £8 0s 5d p.a. and finds no other priest except his curate in his absence.

1. The first 2 entries are now largely illegible, but have been compared with E 101 and Hennessy, 265.
2. Will in *Husting*, ii, 121.
3. Will in *Husting*, ii, 446.
4. Reyley is not named in BC and Whorleston appears only as a conduct.
5. John Kirkeby is the priest named here in BC, and Sandelonde is only named as a conduct.
6. Parish of St Giles Cripplegate (SC 6).
7. Parish of St Michael Queenhithe (SC 6).
8. Perhaps Henry Alred, conduct, who is also named here in BC.

44. ST JOHN WALBROOK

Chaplain: lands in Walbrook, given by Thomas Suffolke and Robert Parson[1] for his soul for ever, £8 1s 4d[2] p.a. Of which, £6 13s 4d to John Fennymore, priest. Clear remainder £1 7s 4d p.a.

Priest: tenements in the parish, given by Robert P ...[3] for his soul for ever, £11 18s 8d p.a. Of which, £7 6s 8d to William Bryan, priest; 16s 4d obit; £1 to the poor; total deductions £9 3s. Clear remainder £2 15s 8d p.a.

Two chaplains and obit: tenements in Finch (Finkes) Lane, given by William Comberton for his soul for ever, £14 3s 4d p.a. Of which, £6 13s 4d to Henry Smythe, priest; £6 13s 4d to the poor; £1 4s quitrents to the king; 10s obit; total deductions £15 0s 8d. Clear remainder Nil.

Augmentation of a priest's living, and prayers: 'John Newburye gave unto the same parson and churchwardens towards the augmentation of a priest's living, and after Thomas Barnard being sole seised gave unto the same parson to have him in remembrance amongst the solemnities of their masses and that they should suffer the church to take the residue of the profits to bestow upon the reparations of the body of the church, all those his lands in Budge Row',[4] £9 10s.

Memoranda: 375 communicants. Richard Wolley, rector, receives £16 p.a. and finds a priest to serve the cure.[5]

1. 'and Robert Parson' is interlined.
2. Altered from £8 0s 8d.
3. Erased; Penne in Harley 601.
4. This rather complex formula is explained by reference to *Husting*, i, 404, where it is clear that Newburye gave the lands in reversion to St John's.
5. Others named in BC are Ralph Shepard and Richard Straunge, priests (cf. **192**), and John More, organ player and conduct.

45. ST MICHAEL HOGEN LANE

Two priests: tenements in St Lawrence Jewry, given by William de Basingstoke for his soul for ever, £13 2s 8d p.a. Of which, £6 7s to Thomas Gaspole, priest, for his stipend. Clear remainder £6 15s 8d p.a.

Priest: a tenement in Wood Street, given by Henry Bane for his soul for ever,[1] £4 1s 4d p.a. Of which, £1 10s quitrents. Clear remainder £2 11s 4d p.a.

Priest: a tenement in Wood Street, given by Robert Bright, £3 6s 8d p.a.

Lamp: tenements in the parish, given by Thomas Hatfeild, £5 7s 4d p.a.

Obit: 6s 8d p.a. spent, but unknown for whom.[2]

Two torches: £1 rent, given by John Currounde from certain houses in Wood Street, paid by the dean of St Paul's.

Memoranda: 317 communicants. Thomas Jennyns, rector, receives £18 13s 4d. There is no other priest.

    1. An interlineation reads '. . . but yet answerable'.
    2. SC 6 has John Walshe.

46. [m.13] ALL HALLOWS BARKING[1]

Chantry priest: lands in Barking, bequeathed by Thomas Pilkes, £27 1s p.a. The present incumbent of the chantry is John Rudde, a man of good learning, who receives all the profits.

Perpetual chaplain and obit: lands in the parish, given by John Croke for his soul for ever, £9 p.a. Of which, £7 to John Batman, priest; 5s obit; 5s to the poor; total deductions £7 10s. Clear remainder £1 10s p.a.

Obit: tenements in the parish of St Michael Queenhithe, given by William Kyrfote for his soul for ever, £5 17s 4d p.a. Of which, £1 quitrents; 16s 8d obit; £1 to the poor; total deductions £2 16s 8d. Clear remainder £3 0s 8d p.a.

Church works: a tenement in the parish, given by Isabel Hurar, £1 p.a. Of which, 5s quitrent to the king. Clear remainder 15s p.a.

Church lands: in Sidon (Sydinge) Lane, donor and intention unknown, owned by the parish since time out of mind, £4 6s 8d p.a.

Memoranda: 800 communicants. William Dowes, vicar, receives £32 13s 4d p.a. No other priest.[2]

    1. An original declaration concerning these chantries, made by the commissioners and bearing the clearly erroneous date 1 January, 1 Edward VI, is bound into the back of an annotated copy of Joseph Maskell, *Berkyngechirche iuxta Turrim* (1864) in the British Library. I am indebted for this reference to Revd Philip Blewett.
    2. William Cresmore, conduct, appears in BC: cf. **47** n. 2.

47. [ST MARY'S] CHAPEL, BARKING: BROTHERHOOD[1]

Two chantries and chaplains: the manor of Tooting Bec (Totenbecke), Surrey, given by King Edward IV for his and other souls for ever, to the master and wardens of the fraternity, £24 3s 2d p.a. Of which, £10 to Sir John Alen, M.A., priest; £8 to John Wysdayle [priest]; £4 2s 8d quitrents to the king; total deductions £22 2s 8d. Clear remainder £2 0s 6d p.a.

Chaplain: tenements in the parishes of St Christopher and St Bartholomew the Less, given by Sir John Rysley, kt., for his soul for ever, £17 2s p.a. Of which, £8 to Sir John Arley, priest; 10s obit; £7 wages of conducts and other charges; total deductions £15 10s. Clear remainder £2 p.a.

Chaplain and obit: lands given by Robert Tate for his soul for ever, £22 10s 8d p.a. Of which, £8 to Richard Davyers, priest; £4 11s 8d obit; 15s to the poor; 8s quitrents; total deductions £13 14s 8d. Clear remainder £8 16s p.a.

Lands and tenements called Chichele's rents, £14 2s 4d p.a. Of which,

£9 13s 8d 'in ordinary deductions yearly'.[2] Clear remainder £4 8s 8d p.a.
Goods: various goods of the fraternity remain with the master and wardens
to the king's use by inventory indented.[3]

> 1. 'The brotherhood or chapel of Barking within London'.
> 2. BC names Robert Smythe, priest, here. In addition John Spence helped the first 2
> chaplains at mass. John Fotehedde sang a daily anthem. William Smith and William
> Cresmore sang the Lady mass and a further conduct was Henry Forster.
> 3. For a later copy of the inventory, see Walters, 633–5.

48. St Botolph Aldersgate[1]

Chaplain: a tenement in the parish, given by John Bathe for his soul for
ever, £3 p.a.

Obit: 2 tenements in Fenchurch Street, given by Thomas Clarke for his and
other souls, £1 13s 4d p.a. Of which, 3s 4d obit; 3s 4d to the poor; total
deductions 6s 8d. Clear remainder £1 6s 8d p.a.

Obit for Thomas Lillingston: £1 p.a. rent given by Andrew Newport for ever
from a tenement in Cornhill.

Obit for Alice Cobwell: tenements and rents at Charing Cross, given by
John Bedford for ever, £2 6s 8d p.a. Of which, 8s 11d obit; 5s 6d to the poor;
total deductions 14s 5d. Clear remainder £1 12s 3d p.a.

Obit: a tenement in Aldersgate Street, given by Alan Johnson for his soul
for ever, £2 13s 4d p.a. Of which, 4s 4d to the poor; 5s 8d obit; total deductions 10s. Clear remainder £2 13s 4d p.a.

Obit: a tenement in Aldersgate Street, given by Philip at Phyn for his soul
for ever, £2 p.a. Of which, 10s obit. Clear remainder £1 10s p.a.

Brotherhood of the Trinity:[2] lands and tenements, £17 16s p.a. Of which,
£6 13s 4d to Sir Oliver [blank],[3] priest; 6s 8d quitrents; £2 17s to the poor;
£4 13s 10d other charges; total deductions £14 10s 10d. Clear remainder
£3 5s 2d p.a.

*Memoranda:** 1,100 communicants. William Benson, dean of Westminster,
rector, receives £12 ... p.a. Goods and further sums of money belonging to
the church are in the hands of ... to the king's use, as appears by an
inventory.

> 1. Cf. (for 1546) LR 2/241 fos 120–8.
> 2. A full return for this brotherhood in 1546 is in LR 2/241 fos 68–81.
> 3. BC has Lingard; in addition Robert Gregorye, priest and Richard Harres, conduct.

49. [m.13d] St Mary Abchurch[1]

[*Priest and obit:* lands and tenements given by John Lyttle]ton,[2]
[£11 19s 4d p.a.]. Of which, £6 ... 4d to Sir Thomas Watson, priest;
[other deductions illegible]; total deductions £9 8s. Clear remainder
£2 11s 4d p.a.

Chantry: tenements in the parish, given by Simon de Wynchcombe for his
soul for ever, £[19] 17s 4d p.a.[3] Of which, £6 13s 4d to Sir Richard Base,
chantry priest; £1 6s 8d quitrents; £1 4s 4d to the poor; total deductions
£9 4s 4d. Clear remainder £9 8s p.a.

Memoranda: 368 communicants. Sir John Arker, rector, receives £22 p.a.
No other priests serve the cure.[4]

> 1. The first 2 entries on the membrane are both faded and damaged.

2. Cf. *Husting*, ii, 532.
3. The pounds figure has been altered from £18, but still does not tally with the deductions.
4. But see also **211**.

50. St Nicholas Acon[1]

Chaplain: lands given by Solomon Oxney for his soul for ever, £14 p.a. Of which, £7 14s to Sir Thomas Sawter, chantry priest aged 68, who has in addition a pension of £5 p.a.; 10s obit; total deductions £8 4s. Clear remainder £5 16s p.a.

Chaplain: £7 annuity for 20 years given by Sir John Bridge, kt., for his soul; paid by the court of Augmentations.

Light: 3s p.a. quitrent given by Sir Gilbert Chapleyne from a tenement in Abchurch Lane in the parish, t. Baptist Boreham.

Lights and torches: 6s 11d p.a. rents given by Maurice Goldesmythe, Gilbert Chepstede and Geoffrey Buttrell.

Rents received by the church: 2s 8d from Baptist Boran and 3s from George Taylor for back doors from their houses into the churchyard, and 6s 8d from Sir Thomas Sauter for a chamber in the churchyard; total 12s 4d.

Memoranda: 154 communicants. Sir Maurice ap Gryffyth, rector, receives £13 6s p.a. No other priests besides his curate.[2]

1. Cf. (for 1546) LR 2/241 fos 82–3.
2. BC and E 101 also record one William Kynton here.

51. St Anne and St Agnes Aldersgate

Priest and obit: lands and tenements in the parish, given by William Gregorye, £19 17s 4d p.a. Of which, £8 to a priest; 10s obit; 13s 4d 'to the gatherers of the rent'; 6s 8d repairs to the church; 6s 8d to the auditor; 3s 4d for making accounts; 4s bread, wine and wax; 6s 8d quitrents to the king; total deductions £10 8s [sic]. Clear remainder £9 9s 4d p.a.

Obit and other charges: lands and tenements given by John Werke, £6 13s 4d p.a. Of which, 6s 8d quitrents to the king; 13s 10d obit; 6s 8d in coal to the poor; 1s 8d to a preacher; 4s to the wardens of the Goldsmiths; 6s 8d to John Colloy during his life; total deductions £1 19s 6d. Clear remainder £4 13s 10d p.a.

Obit: lands in Greenwich Lane, given by Edward Redknapp to Lewis Sutton and Agnes his wife, for his soul for ever, £1 p.a.

Memoranda: 300 communicants. John Hopton, DD, rector, receives £8 p.a. and finds a priest to serve the cure.

52. All Hallows Honey Lane[1]

Chaplain: lands and tenements given by Alexander Sprat for his soul for ever, £6 16s 8d p.a. Of which, £7 6s 8d to Sir William Emringale, priest; 10s quitrent to the king; total deductions £7 16s 8d. Clear remainder Nil.

Chaplain and obit: lands and tenements given by Thomas Trompington, John Downe and Henry Edelmeton, £24 13s 4d p.a. Of which, 13s 4d tenths to the king for the chaplain's stipend, though there is no chaplain found;[2] 10s obit; £9 8s quitrents to the king; total deductions £10 11s 4d. Clear remainder £14 2s p.a.

Memoranda: 150 communicants. Sir Thomas Pannell, rector, receives

£19 10s 8d p.a. There is no other priest besides himself, and his deputy in his absence.

1. Cf. (for 1546) LR 2/243 fos. 27–9.
2. Though Miles Sandes is named in E 101 and BC.

53. [m.14] ST MARY MAGDALENE OLD FISH STREET
Chaplain: lands and tenements bequeathed by John Lytington after the death of his wife and children, for his soul for ever, £10 7s 4d p.a. Of which, £6 13s 4d to Sir John Hanby, aged 64, of small learning and having no other living. Clear remainder £3 14s p.a.
Chaplain and obit: lands and tenements bequeathed by Robert Coldam for his and other souls for ever, £9 4s p.a. Of which, £6 13s 4d to Sir Martin Clipisham, aged 32, sufficiently learned and having also a pension of £5 6s 8d; 13s 4d obit; £2 2s quitrents to the king; total deductions £9 8s 8d. Clear remainder Nil.
Priest: lands and tenements bequeathed by William Edwarde for his soul for ever, £9 p.a. Of which, £6 13s 4d to Sir William Honylande, aged 52, meanly learned and having no other living; £1 2s to the rector 'for the tithe Boar's Head and the Peter Key'; total deductions £7 15s 4d. Clear remainder £1 4s 8d p.a.
Obit: lands and tenements bequeathed by Richard Weston for his soul for ever, £2 p.a. Of which, £1 spent at the obit and in alms to the poor. Clear remainder £1 for the church repairs.
Purpose unknown: lands and tenements given by William Buterfelde and John Carpenter, £11 17s 8d p.a. Of which, 6s 8d quitrents; 16s 8d to Aldermary parish for a chamber given to the rector rent free; 6s 8d for a chamber given to John Clutton; total deductions £1 10s. Clear remainder £10 7s 8d p.a.
Lamp: 8s p.a. rent given by John Abraham, late rector of the church, from a tenement in the Old Change, t. William Kendall waxchandler, and owned in fee simple by John Worseley, Esq.
Memoranda: 360 communicants. Sir Thomas Chipping, rector, receives £18 14s p.a. There are no other priests besides the above chantry priests.

54. ST MARTIN VINTRY
Priest and obit: 2 tenements given by William Clovyle, John Cornewalles and Gilbert Admershe for ever, £8 p.a. Of which, £6 13s 4d to Sir Jeffrey Davy singing for them, aged 53 and having no other promotion; 8s 4d obit; £1 quitrent to the king; 3s 4d to the parish of St John Walbrook; total deductions £8 5s. Clear remainder [blank].
Poor relief: 6s 8d p.a. given among the poor on the day before the feast of St Michael the Archangel each year by Whittington college.
Memoranda: 460 communicants. Sir Edward Saunders, rector, receives £18 13s 4d p.a. and serves the cure himself. No other priests.[1]

1. But cf. **193**: Thomas More.

55. ST BENET FINK[1]
Priest and obit: lands and tenements bequeathed by William Bealle, including 2s 8d for a storehouse, £24 16s p.a. Of which, £7 6s 8d to the stipendiary priest,[2] aged 50, meanly learned; 13s 4d obit, including money

32

for the poor; £4 6s 8d quitrent to a priest singing at St Mary Somerset, Queenhithe Ward; total deductions £12 6s 8d. Clear remainder for the repair of the tenements £12 9s 4d p.a.

Memoranda: Over 300 communicants. The dean and chapter of the college of Windsor are rectors and receive £16 p.a. One priest is found to serve the cure, 'very unable to serve the same'.

Grammar school: The free school called St Anthony's, of which the school-master is Master Edmund Johnson, paid by the steward of St Anthony's, but amount unknown.

    1. Cf. (for 1546) LR 2/243 fos 40–1.
    2. John Blomer morrow mass priest (BC).

56. [m.14d] St Martin Pomery
Chantry, and torch to burn at obit time: £4 3s 4d p.a. rent from the Swan Inn, Bishopsgate and £2 16s 8d p.a. rent from the former land of Robert Brockett, given by Henry att Rothe and Robert Brocket, and paid by the White Bakers, total £7 p.a. Of which, nothing is paid to any chantry priest, the post being vacant since last Easter; 13s 4d tenths to the king. Clear remainder £6 6s 8d p.a.

Five wax candles: a shop in Iremonger Lane, given by William Wylehale for ever, 6s 8d p.a.

Chapel annexed to the church for the ease of poor people: now leased by Ambrose Barker, 13s 4d p.a.

Memoranda: 120 communicants. Sir Richard Quene, rector, receives £12 13s 4d p.a. and serves the cure himself.

57. St Alban Wood Street
Priest for the soul of John Wodcocke, and obit:[1] lands and tenements bequeathed by John Shadworthe for his and other souls for ever, £7 16s 8d p.a. Of which, 6s obit; 3s 4d quitrent to the king; total deductions 9s 4d. Clear remainder £7 7s 6d [sic] p.a.

Priest for the soul of Thomas Chulton, and obit:[2] lands and tenements bequeathed by John Andrewes for his and other Christian souls, £13 2s 8d p.a. Of which, £6 13s 4d to Sir Robert Jackeson,[3] stipendiary priest; £1 0s 8d obit; total deductions £7 1s 2d [sic]. Clear remainder £5 10s 8d p.a.

Priest and obit: lands and tenements given by Sir Richard Illyngworth, kt., for his soul for ever, £17 p.a. Of which, £6 13s 4d to the stipendiary priest; 13s 4d 'to the said Sir Robert Jakelyng by his will'; £1 0s 8d obit; total deductions £8 7s 4d. Clear remainder £8 12s 8d p.a.

Lamp, torch and anthem: a tenement in the parish, t. Thomas Dodyngton, tenant at will, bequeathed by Henry Payn to provide a lamp burning day and night before the rood, a torch on Corpus Christi Day, an anthem before the rood in Lent, and 6s 8d for the churchwardens to see these dues performed, £2 p.a.

Memoranda: 300 communicants. Master William Catericke, BD, rector, receives £16 8s 4d p.a. No priest is found by him to serve the cure.

    1–2. The dedication of the obit is obscured by the form of words chosen; it was probably for the donor.
    3. *Recte* 'Jackelyng' (as below and E 101), or Jacklyn (BC).

58. Sᴛ Aɴᴅʀᴇᴡ UɴᴅᴇʀsʜᴀFᴛ

Obit: a tenement bequeathed by John Felde for his soul for ever, £1 10s p.a. Of which, 6s 8d to priests and poor at the obit. Clear remainder £1 3s 4d p.a.
Obit: 10s annuity from the gild of St John Baptist at York, given by Sir John Savage, clerk. Of which, 6s 8d obit. Clear remainder 3s 4d p.a.
Church tenements: 'builded of the church goods', adjacent to the parsonage, for the maintenance of the clerk and sexton, £4 9s 4d p.a.
Obit: tenements, cottages and chambers given by Thomas Stokes, £4 10s 4d p.a. Of which, 6s 8d to the poor at the obit. Clear remainder £4 3s 4d p.a.
Obit and poor relief: 10s annuity bequeathed by John Goodwyn and paid by the Haberdashers' Company.[1]
Obit and poor relief: 13s 4d annuity bequeathed by Sir John Raynwell, kt., and paid by the chamberlain of London.
Memoranda: 373 communicants. Sir John Standysche, clerk, DD, rector. receives £19 12s 0½d[2] p.a. No other priests besides the curate.

1. See **220.**
2. The parchment has been torn and fitted together incorrectly; this is the most likely reading.

59. Sᴛ Eᴛʜᴇʟʙᴜʀɢᴀ Bɪsʜᴏᴘsɢᴀᴛᴇ

Priest: £1 13s 4d p.a. quitrent from a tenement called the Angel in this parish, paid by the masters of the Bridgehouse.
Intent unknown: £2 p.a. rent bequeathed by William Assell from the Swan Inn in the parish, now t. Thomas Nixson.
Priest: £2 p.a. rent bequeathed by the same Thomas Nixson.
Memoranda: 180 communicants. Sir John Day, rector, receives £11 12s p.a. and serves the cure himself.

60. [m.15] Sᴛ Pᴇᴛᴇʀ 'ᴛʜᴇ Lɪᴛᴛʟᴇ ᴀɴᴅ ᴛʜᴇ Pᴏᴏʀ'[1]

Priest: £4 6s 8d p.a. quitrent bequeathed by William Barnarde for his soul for ever from a tenement in the parish.[2]
Priest: lands and tenements bequeathed by Walter Kent for his soul for ever, £7 4s p.a. Of which, £6 6s 8d to Sir Thomas Potter, chantry priest. Clear remainder 17s 4d p.a.
Memoranda: 200 communicants. Sir John Hollonde, rector, receives £9 3s 2d p.a. and serves the cure himself with the help of the above chantry priests.
Obit: 4 small tenements bequeathed by Thomas Johnson for his soul for ever, £4 7s p.a. Of which, 17s 8d obit, including 3s 4d to the poor. Clear remainder £3 9s 4d p.a.
Memoranda: 160 communicants. Sir John Dalton, rector, receives £8 10s p.a. and serves the cure himself.

1. The 2 parishes are described together in one entry. The first 3 headings refer to St Peter Paul's Wharf and the last 2 to St Peter the Poor.
2. Augmented by a donation from the Armourers, see **215**: James Payn, priest. For the original return with detailed information on foundations and property, see Guildhall MS. 12140/3.

61. ST KATHERINE CREE
Chaplain and obit: lands and tenements bequeathed by Alice Cressewycke for her soul, the chaplain to celebrate daily, £10 13s 4d p.a. Of which, £6 13s 4d to Sir Richard Patteson,[1] priest; 7s 2d obit; 18s 4d to Sir Ralph Sadler for quitrent; 3s 4d to the churchwardens for their pains; total deductions £8 2s 2d. Clear remainder £2 11s 2d p.a.
Obit and lamp: £1 p.a. rent from lands of one Rusche, paid by the church-wardens of St Michael Cornhill. Of which, 3s for Russe's obit; 12s lamp; total deductions 15s. Clear remainder 5s p.a.
Memoranda: 542 communicants. The master and fellows of Magdalene college, Cambridge are rectors and receive £21 p.a. A curate serves the cure.

1. But called Parkenson in BC and E 101. In 1550 he said he was 54 years old (PRO, Chancery Town Depositions, C 24/23 Bright v. Lytlecote and Lambert).

62. ST OLAVE SILVER STREET
Rent: 7s p.a. paid by New college, Oxford 'without any intent'.
Obit: 'William Tattorne gave to the brotherhood of 60 priests one tenement wherein they dwell to the intent that they should keep an obit in the said church: of the yearly rent of £3'. Of which, £1 0s 2d obit including 16s 8d to the poor. Clear remainder £1 19s 10d p.a.
Memoranda: 180 communicants. Sir William Assheton, rector, receives £9 12s 9½d and serves the cure himself without any help.

63. [m15d] ST JOHN ZACHARY
Stipendiary priest singing daily for the soul of Bartholomew Seyman: £6 13s 4d p.a. paid by Giles Bridges to Sir Robert Clynebeckke, priest[1] aged 70, impotent.
Obit for the same Seyman: 6s 8d p.a. from Seyman's lands, paid by the same Giles Bridges, including 4s to the poor and 2s 8d to the priests and clerks.
Obit for the soul of William Duffelde: 13s 4d p.a. rent from a tenement called the Lion in the Barbican, paid by John Andrewe. The foundation was for 80 years, of which 17 have passed as shown by an indenture.
Prayers: 4 tenements in Gutter (Gooderon) Lane given by William Hope for prayers for ever for his soul and those of Henry Eveley, Dame Agnes Redyng, Richard Parker and Agnes his wife, and to maintain the tenements, the church and the ornaments, £4 p.a. Of which, £1 quitrent to the king in the right of the late hospital of St John. Clear remainder £3 p.a.
Memoranda: 240 communicants. Sir Ralph Bentley, rector, receives £12 p.a. 'and is not resident upon the same but a French priest not able to serve the cure'.

1. BC names also John Fissher, stipendiary and William Tofte, chantry priest, maintained here by the Goldsmiths. See also **222**.

64. ST BOTOLPH BISHOPSGATE[1]
Chantry: £6 13s 4d p.a. paid by the court of Augmentations to maintain a priest formerly paid by St Mary Spittal under the will of Walter Delamore. The priest is Sir Thomas Fyldust,[2] aged 26, meanly learned.

Lamp: 8s p.a. rent given by Thomas Marowe from his tenements in the parish.

Memoranda: 650 communicants. Hugh Weston, rector, receives £22 p.a. No other priests serve the cure besides his curate.

> 1. Cf. (for 1546) LR 2/241 fos 108–14 which also records a brotherhood of St George here.
> 2. In BC and E 101 the priest named here is John Bowyer. See also **214**: Richard Nelson.

65. ST LEONARD FOSTER LANE[1]

Priest: £1 p.a. quitrent bequeathed by Roger of Northall from a tenement in Cordwainer (Corvester) Street in Aldermary parish.

Priest: £2 4s p.a. quitrents bequeathed by Henry Edelmenton from 2 tenements in Fleet Street in the parish of St Bride: £1 14s and 10s p.a. respectively.

Priest: 8s p.a. quitrent given by Isabel, daughter of Garell Bate, from a tenement in the parish of St Peter, Broad Street.

Priest and anniversary: 6s 8d p.a. quitrent bequeathed by John Moreslonde, former rector of St Leonard's, from a tenement in the parish of St Botolph Aldersgate.

Chaplain, tapers and obit: £4 15s 4d p.a. quitrents bequeathed by William de Wyndesor: £3 13s 4d from a tenement in Nicholas Lane, Candlewick Street, in the parish of St Nicholas Acon for the chaplain; £1 2s from tenements without Cripplegate in the parish of St Giles for 6 tapers and an obit at which 9s 8d is for the poor, and 4d for ringing.

'*Anniversary by note with light and other things*': £1 p.a. quitrent given by William Cressewycke for the soul of Robert Cressewycke from a tenement in Moor (More) Lane next Grub Street.

Thomas Exteme's bequest:[2] 2 shops in the parish (less 3s 4d p.a. quitrent), £1 15s 4d p.a. 'to find an anniversary, to discharge the parishioners of candle silver on Easter Day and to find a Paschal, and for a wax taper of 10 lb to burn in the church at the sepulchre, and to be prayed for solemnly in the pulpit'. Of which, 13s 4d quitrent to the king; 6s 4d anniversary; total deductions 19s 4d. Clear remainder 15s 8d p.a.

Memoranda: 452 communicants. Sir Robert Crome, rector, receives 40 marks p.a. and serves the cure with the help of a stipendiary priest found by the parishioners 'of devotion and good will at their own charges'.

> 1. Despite all these bequests for priests, note that no payments are recorded, and no pension was paid afterwards (E 101).
> 2. Exton (*Husting*, ii, 447).

66. [m.16] ST BARTHOLOMEW [EXCHANGE][1]

Priest and obit: a tenement in the parish of St Michael Crooked Lane, t. John Johnson, bequeathed by James Willforde for his and other souls for ever, £16 p.a. Of which, £7 6s 8d to Nicholas Willes, chantry priest; £2 9s 6d obit, including 3s 4d to the poor; 15s 6d for wax at the obit and for 4 tapers through the year; 1s to the preachers of the Spittal; 3s 4d for washing the linen belonging to the priest and chantry; £1 11s 4½d for other charges, including 19s 0½d subsidy; total deductions £12 7s 4½d. Clear remainder £3 12s 7½d p.a.

Perpetual chantry and obit ('*Frayes chantry*')*:* the manor of Collingham Hall (Collyngamhalle), Suffolk and £1 16s 2½d p.a. rent from Cavendish (Candische) and Glemsford (Glemforde), Suffolk, given by John Clopton Esq., under licence from Edward IV to Thomas Colwell the then chantry priest and his successors; total £16 p.a.[2]

Obit: a tenement in the parish bequeathed by Richard Tofte, £3 p.a. Of which, 10s obit, including 7s to the poor. Clear remainder £2 10s p.a.

Obit for the soul of Sir William Capell, kt.: maintained by the Lord St John, Lord Great Master, but amount spent unknown.

Memoranda: 392 communicants. Sir George Nevell, rector, aged 40, receives £18 p.a. 'who keepeth the country', and finds Sir Michael West, aged 60, to serve the cure.

Jewels and ornaments of Willforde's chantry: as by a schedule[3] annexed to the certificate, are in the custody of Nicholas Crofton, one of the church-wardens.

Vestment of blue velvet for Fraye's chantry, worth 10s; in the hands of the incumbent.

1. 'Little St Bartholomew'. Cf. (for 1546) LR 2/242 fos 66–71.
2. Richard Stocketon, priest (BC).
3. The inventory is given in LR 2, and printed in Walters, 636.

67. ALL HALLOWS LONDON WALL[1]

Obit and lamp: a tenement near London Wall called the Rose, given by Robert Farbras, £4 11s 4d p.a. Of which, 3s quitrent to the king. Clear remainder £4 7s 4d [sic] p.a.

Memoranda: 217 communicants. John Robardes, rector, receives £8 7s 1d p.a. and serves the cure himself.

Goods belonging to the 'said' priests or brotherhood of Pappey[2] are as in an inventory annexed.

1. Cf. (for 1546) LR 2/242 fos 7–8.
2. The Papey is not otherwise mentioned here; see **105.**

68. ST MILDRED BREAD STREET[1]

Priest and obit: lands and tenements bequeathed by Stephen Bugge for ever, £6 6s 8d p.a. Of which, £6 6s 8d to the stipendiary priest.[2] Clear remainder Nil.

Priest and obit: lands and tenements given by John Frary for ever, £6 16s 8d p.a. Of which, £1 13s 4d to the stipendiary priest to augment his wages; 19s 2d expenses at the obit; 6s 6d quitrent to St Paul's and to the college of Westminster; total deductions £2 19s. Clear remainder £3 17s 8d p.a.

Priest: lands and tenements given by Margaret de Wyborne for ever, £4 p.a. Of which, £2 to the stipendiary priest.[3] Clear remainder £2 p.a.

Priest: lands and tenements given by William Palmer for ever, £10 16s 8d p.a. Of which, £4 to the stipendiary priest; 2s to the rector 'according to the will'; total deductions £4 2s. Clear remainder £6 14s 8d p.a.

Chaplain: £3 10s p.a. rent given by William Aldern[4] for his soul for ever. Of which, £1 to the stipendiary priest. Clear remainder £2 10s p.a.

Priest: 16s p.a. quitrent given by deed of William Ardern for his and his 'said' father's souls for ever.

[m. 16d] *Obit:* 13s 4d p.a. rent given by a deed of John Shadworthe from a tenement called the Rose in Smithfield.

Lamp: 10s p.a. quitrent bequeathed by John Cliff from the Inn called the Pie upon Smithfield.

Memoranda: 216 communicants. Sir William Bell, rector, receives £19 8s 7d p.a. and serves the cure with the help of the other priests.[5]

1. Cf. (for 1546) LR 2/242 fos 115–18.
2. Thomas Shapire (BC). His income seems to have been augmented from the endowment following.
3. Robert Haddowe (BC). All the augmentations following appear to have gone to him.
4. *Recte* Ardern as in the next entry.
5. BC also names here Stephen Busshopp, conduct.

69. St Matthew Friday Street[1]

Priest: lands and tenements given by John Martyn for ever, £10 p.a. Of which, £6 13s 4d to Sir Henry Coldewell, chantry priest aged 70, meanly learned. Clear remainder £3 6s 8d p.a.

Obit: a tenement given by one[2] Walpole for his soul for ever, £3 8s 4d p.a. Of which, 6s 8d obit; 7s quitrent to the college of Westminster; 5s quitrent to the house of Burton Lazars; total deductions 18s 8d. Clear remainder £2 9s 8d p.a.

Memoranda: 200 communicants. Sir Walter Morewell, rector, receives £25 15s 4d p.a. There is no other priest, but 'for a small sum he hireth one of the said priests to serve for him'.[3]

1. Cf. (for 1546) LR 2/243 fos 84–7.
2. Peter (LR 2).
3. BC has 2 further priests here, William Dean (? see **222**) and John Smythe (see **191**).

70. St John the Evangelist Watling Street[1]

Perpetual chaplain: lands and tenements given by William de Aungree for prayers for ever, £8 13s 4d p.a. Of which, £7 to Sir John Taylor, stipendiary priest aged 50; 13s 4d quitrent to the king; total deductions £7 13s 4d. Clear remainder £1 p.a.

Memoranda: 100 communicants. Sir John Gray, rector, receives £15 19s 7d p.a. No other priest has been found to serve the cure than the stipendiary.

1. Cf. (for 1546) LR 2/242 fos 102–3.

71. College of St Lawrence Pountney

College lands: £113 18s 8d[1] p.a. [not detailed]. Of which, £7 19s 9½d tenths to the king; £3 14s 6d quitrents to the king; £1 pension to the king; £1 12s expenses at the obits; 13s 4d farm rent to a chantry priest in St Paul's; £35 8s 4d stipends and other necessary charges and fees;[2] £2 3s repairs, alms and 'necessaries'; total deductions £52 10s 11½d. Clear remainder £56 7s 0½d [sic] p.a.

Memoranda: 270 communicants. William Latymer, aged 49, rector, receives £16 p.a. and at his own cost finds a curate and a morrow mass priest besides himself.

1. Original figure erased, which probably explains why the totals do not balance.
2. Not detailed. E 101 has Richard Dowtye, Christopher Rowche and John Plough, fellows; and John Blacket, William Moises, James Amyson and Thomas Blackden, 'ministers'. BC describes the 4 latter as conducts, but their respective incomes (£2, £1 10s, £1 6s 8d and £1) suggest they were lesser officials.

72. FRATERNITY OF THE SIXTY PRIESTS
Obits and poor relief: lands and tenements, £7 10s p.a. Of which, 2s 7½d quitrent to the king; £1 14s 8d at 2 obits, with 19s 8d to the poor; £1 for singing 60 masses; 10s to the registrar of the fraternity; 10s to the beadle; £1 6s 8d to the common cook; total deductions £5 3s 11½d.
Memoranda: jewels, plate, money and ornaments as in a schedule annexed.[1]

1. Not included in the certificate.

73. ALL HALLOWS THE LESS[1]
Priest: six tenements given by James Andrew, £8 9s 4d p.a., but no priest has been found since last Michaelmas.
Obit and poor relief: 6s 8d p.a. rent given by Ralph Markhame. Of which, 2s 8d obit; 4s to the poor; total deductions 6s 8d. Clear remainder Nil.
Obit for John Chamberlayn: kept in the church by Bernard Jennyns, skinner, but amount spent not stated.
Memoranda: 200 communicants. William Latymer, rector, receives £17 p.a. and finds no priest but his curate.

1. Cf. (for 1546) LR 2/241 fos 23–4.

74. [m.17] ST MICHAEL BASSISHAW[1]
Priest: a tenement called the Bell on the Hoop in the parish, bequeathed by John Asche, £3 6s 8d p.a.[2]
Two chaplains:[3] in fulfilment of the will of Sir James Yardeforde, his widow Lady Yardeforde pays 2 priests to sing for him; after her death the Mercers 'shall have the same lands' to continue the endowment: £16 p.a.[4]
Obit: a tenement or brewhouse called the Cock on the Hoop, bequeathed by John Asche as above, £5 p.a. Of which, 6s 8d to the rector of St John Walbrook; 6s 8d obit; total deductions 13s 4d. Clear remainder £4 6s 8d p.a.
Lights: a tenement called the Talbot, in the parish of St John Walbrook, bequeathed by Richard Osborne for 'a light upon the common beam before the crucifix' and other lights 'at the anthem time', £2 p.a.
Memoranda: 500 communicants. Sir John Anderton, rector, receives £17 p.a. and gives £8 p.a. to a resident priest to serve his cure.

1. Cf. (for 1546) the original return in E 301/89.
2. E 301/89 makes clear that this endowment was for the morrow mass, and that there were other church lands from which the stipend was supplemented, making a total of £7 6s 8d p.a. Henry Unwin is named as the priest in BC.
3. Charles Wentworth and Richard Smithe (BC).

4. BC also records that Yardeforde left a further bequest to the Mercers' Company to find a further conduct and a clerk; they each received pensions and are named respectively as John Cockes and Robert Risbie; cf. E 101.

75. ST ANDREW HOLBORN[1]

Priest: lands and tenements bequeathed by Amy Edyman and John Rowell, £13 7s 8d p.a. Of which, £6 13s 4d to the stipendiary priest.[2] Clear remainder £6 14s 4d p.a.

Obit and priest: a messuage given by William Forman to the fraternity of St Sythe in the parish, £1 17s 4d p.a. Of which, 6s 8d obit. Clear remainder £1 10s 8d p.a.

Lamp before the sacrament: an acre of land in Gray's Inn Field, given by Roger Horlyn, 6s 8d p.a.

Church works only: 4 tenements bequeathed by John Tavy, £4 6s 8d p.a. Of which, 9s 10d quitrent to Westminster. Clear remainder £3 16s 10d p.a.

Lamp: a gate room in Gray's Inn Lane, given for 79 years beginning at Christmas 33 Henry VIII, 1s 8d p.a.

Memoranda: 1,000 communicants. Sir Nicholas Burton, rector, receives £16 p.a. No other priests, save the chantry priest, to whom he gives £2 p.a.

    1. Cf. (for 1546) LR 2/243 fos 34–9.
    2. William Vincent and Richard Conigrave are named in BC.

76. ST CHRISTOPHER LE STOCKS

Chantry and anniversary: lands and tenements given by Margaret de Norforde, William de Berghe and Christian Vugham, widow, for ever, £10 4s p.a. Of which, £6 13s 4d to the stipendiary priest;[1] 18s quitrents to the king; 8s 8d at the two obits; 13s 4d tenths to the king; total deductions £8 13s 4d. Clear remainder £1 10s 8d p.a.

Priest and anniversary: lands and tenements bequeathed by John Plonkett, sherman, for ever, £13 17s 8d p.a. Of which, £6 13s 4d to the chantry priest; 16s 1d obit; 16s 5d for coal and other relief to the poor; total deductions £8 5s 10d. Clear remainder £5 11s 10d p.a.

Priest and anniversary: lands and tenements bequeathed by John Watles, mercer, for ever, £10 13s 4d p.a. Of which, £6 13s 4d to the priest; £1 rent charge to Lady Nerforde's priest; 16s 7d for 2 wax tapers at the obit; £1 3s 4d quitrent and tenths to the king; total deductions £9 13s 3d. Clear remainder £1 0s 1d p.a.

Priest, obit and poor relief: lands and tenements bequeathed by Benedict Harlewyn for his soul for ever, £5 13s 4d p.a. Of which, £1 6s 8d tenths to the king; 3s 4d to the Drapers for the poor; 13s 4d obit; total deductions £2 3s 4d. Clear remainder £3 10s p.a.

[m.17d] *Obit:* Richard Sheryngton bequeathed a rent charge of £2 16s 8d p.a. for ever, but the parish now owns the lands, which yield £2 13s 4d p.a. Of which, 13s 4d quitrent to the king; 4s 3d obit; total deductions 17s 7d. Clear remainder £1 15s 9d p.a.

Obit: a tenement given by Joan Ball for ever, £3 6s 8d p.a.

Memoranda: 221 communicants. Sir Robert Stanney, rector, receives £18 2s p.a.

    1. Priests named in BC are Thomas Winstanley, Nicholas Rose, Edmund Frevell and William Leake; with Robert Merchaunt, conduct.

77. St Mary le Bow[1]

Priest and obit: lands and tenements bequeathed by Henry Frowycke for ever, £15 10s p.a. Of which, £8 to the stipendiary priest;[2] 10s quitrent to the king; 4s 2d to Sir Ralph Sadler; 6s to Sir Richard Leigh; 8s obit; total deductions £11 8s 2d [sic]. Clear remainder £4 1s 10d p.a.

Chantry priest: lands and tenements bequeathed by John de Holleghe for ever, £7 p.a. Of which, £6 16s to the stipendiary priest;[3] 4s quitrent to Austin Hynde; total deductions £7. Clear remainder Nil.

Beam light and ringing of Bow bell: a tenement given by John Donne, mercer, £4 p.a. Of which, £1 13s 4d for the light; 4s for the bell; 1s 'to a priest for exhorting to pray for the said Donne'; total deductions £1 18s 4d. Clear remainder £2 1s 8d p.a.

Obit: a piece of ground formerly a garden and now a churchyard bequeathed by John Rothame, 6s 8d p.a.

Priest: £4 annuity or rent given by Dame Eleanor, former prioress of Winchester, and her convent.

Augmentation of a morrow mass priest: £1 15s p.a. annuity or rent bequeathed by John Donne for certain lands 'in Bow church'.[4]

Morrow mass priest: £2 5s annuity or rent bequeathed by John Norman from lands 'in Bow church'.[5]

Church lands held by the rector and churchwardens for some time without any specified intent, £7 p.a.

Poor relief: Thomas Baldry gave £44 to the prioress of Elsing Spittal to pay an annuity of £1 2s for poor relief in the parish, which has been paid accordingly, £1 2s p.a.

Two torches before the Sacrament at the elevation: 6s 8d p.a. annuity or rent, given by Robert Mompleres from a tenement called the Beads in West Cheap.

Memoranda: 300 communicants. Sir John Joseph, BD, rector, receives £30 p.a. No other priest besides his curate.

1. Cf. (for 1546) LR 2/242 fos 82–90.
2. Henry Warden (BC).
3. BC names no chantry priests here other than Warden as above, but the following conducts are listed: Walter Tempest, William Squier, Jasper Rolf, John Walker and Robert Walker.
4–5. i.e. in the churchyard (LR 2).

78. St Martin Ludgate[1]

Priests:[2] lands and tenements given by Roger Payne, William Powe, Simon Newell and Thomas Froddeshame for ever, £16 16s 8d p.a. Of which, 4d to the parish church of St Bride; 3s to the bishop of Salisbury; 3s 4d to the king; total deductions 6s 8d. Clear remainder £16 10s p.a.

Priest at Thingdon, Northants; priest at Dronfield, Derb., and obit here: lands and tenements bequeathed by William Alstone, £23 16s 8d p.a. Of which, £9 6s 8d to the 2 priests. Clear remainder £14 10s p.a.

[m.18] *Priest:* £3 6s 8d p.a. annuity given by William Sevenocke from a tenement called the Cup and Hoop, for ever.

Obit: 8s p.a. quitrent, given by William Wilschere for ever from tenements in the parish of St Clement Candlewick Street.

A lamp to burn before the High Cross: 7s p.a. rent given by Adam Hagete from a tenement called the Welshman on the Hoop in Old Bailey.

Church lands: further lands certified by the rector and churchwardens, £12 13s 4d p.a. Of which, £1 13s 4d quitrent to the parish church of St Margaret Lothbury; 13s 4d quitrent to St Michael le Querne; total deductions £2 6s 8d. Clear remainder £10 6s 8d p.a.

Memoranda: 476 communicants. Sir Barnard Sandeforde, rector, receives £33 6s 8d p.a.

> 1. Cf. (for 1546) LR 2/241 fos 101–7.
> 2. Priests named in BC are Henry Woodhouse, James Rowe and Thomas Graye, with Roger Markes and William Monday, conducts.

79. ST OLAVE JEWRY[1]

Perpetual chantry: lands and tenements bequeathed by Sir John Bryan, priest, late rector of the church, to Sir Reynold Bryan, chaplain 'to make, sustain and celebrate one perpetual chantry', for his soul for ever, £13 1s 4d p.a.[2]

Light and obit: tenement and 4 chambers bequeathed by Thomas Musted, £2 10s p.a. Of which, 4s for the 'waste and repair' of tapers; 4s quitrent to the king; 2s 1d to the choir at the obit; 6s 8d to the poor; total deductions 16s 9d. Clear remainder £1 13s 3d p.a.

Memoranda: 198 communicants. Sir Clement Erington, vicar, receives £13 6s 8d p.a.

> 1. Cf. (for 1546) LR 2/243 fos 88–90.
> 2. Humphrey Sheffelde, priest (BC).

80. ST MARY AXE

Memoranda: 100 communicants. Sir Peter Toller, rector, receives £5 p.a. and serves the cure himself without any help.

81. ST OLAVE HART STREET[1]

Three obits or anniversaries: 2 tenements given by Robert Lawrence and Thomas Faux, £2 13s 4d p.a. Of which, 14s 8d to the king for 2 quitrents. Clear remainder £1 18s 8d p.a.

Memoranda: 435 communicants. Sir John Johnson, rector, receives £21 and serves the cure himself without any help.[2]

Poor relief: Sir John Alleyn, kt. deceased, appointed Thomas Pyke to receive £60, of which £50 was to be shared among the poor at the rate of 10s per week and £10 given for poor maidens' marriages: of which Pyke has not yet spent over £10.

> 1. 'Tower Street'.
> 2. BC and E 101 name Thomas Tyckle, priest, here (see **194**).

82. ALL HALLOWS STAINING

Chantry and priest's salary: £3 6s 8d p.a. paid by the court of Augmentations for the salary of a chantry priest, the king having taken into his hands the lands devoted to this purpose by William Palmer.[1]

Anniversary for John Cosyn: 14s 4d p.a. is spent by Thomas Jenkynson of the city of Norwich, according to Cosyn's will.

Poor relief: the same Thomas distributes yearly among poor householders of the parish 100 qrs of coal.
Memoranda: 424 communicants. The king is rector and receives £22 14s 10d p.a. The curate and the chantry priest serve the cure.

> 1. Stephen Fountayn, priest (BC).

83. St Alphege[1]
Chaplain: lands and tenements bequeathed by John Graunte for ever, £15 10s 8d p.a. Of which, £6 13s 4d to the stipendiary priest.[2] Clear remainder £8 17s 4d p.a.
Memoranda: 345 communicants. The benefice is void, but worth £8 p.a. in the king's books, 'and the parishioners of the profits of the same benefice among the parishioners levied find a priest to serve the cure'.

> 1. Cf. (for 1546) LR 2/243 fos 30–3.
> 2. Lewis (Lodovicus) Pestyll, priest (E 101); Lewes Pestell (BC).

84. [m.18d] St Botolph Aldgate
Chaplain to sing divine service: lands and tenements given by Thomas Weston for his soul for ever, £5 6s 8d p.a. Of which, 12s 10d for 2 quitrents to the king; £4 13s 10d to the stipendiary priest;[1] total deductions £5 6s 8d. Clear remainder Nil.
Perpetual chaplain and obit: lands and tenements bequeathed by Alexander Sprot and John Grace for ever, £22 15s 4d p.a. Of which, £1 8s 2d quitrents to the king; 2s 4d quitrent to Sir John Gates; £7 3s 4d to Sir John Lovell, stipendiary priest; £2 9s 6d to Sir William Grene[2] in augmentation of his wages; 7s 6d obit; £1 1s 8d to the rent gatherer;[3] £1 to the sexton;[4] total deductions £14 5s 10d. Clear remainder £8 9s 6d p..a
Memoranda: 1,130 communicants. The king is rector and receives £48 p.a.[5]

> 1. William Grene (BC).
> 2. See above, n. 1.
> 3. Thomas Rutter (BC).
> 4. John White (BC).
> 5. John William, priest, is also named here in BC (see **209**).

85. Holy Trinity [the Less]
Priest and obit: rents and tenements given by the king under the seal of the court of Augmentations, and by Thomas Cosyn's will for ever, £8 18s 8d p.a. Of which, 13s 4d tenths to the king; £6 13s 4d to the priest;[1] 6s obit; 8s for 3 wax tapers; total deductions £8 0s 8d. Clear remainder 18s p.a.
Priest: lands and tenements bequeathed by John Bryan for ever, £13 1s 3d p.a. Of which, £6 13s 4d to the stipendiary priest; 13s 4d tenths to the king; £1 quitrents to the king 'as to the late house of Westminster'; total deductions £8 15s. Clear remainder £4 6s 3d p.a.
Memoranda: 170 communicants. Sir John Dorell, bachelor of law, rector, receives £8 6s p.a. He gives 16s and a chamber yearly to one of the stipendiary priests to help him minister.

> 1. Priests named in BC are Edward Ravensdayle and Richard Jenkinson.

86. Sᴛ Fᴀɪᴛʜ

Memoranda: 400 communicants. John Denman, DD, rector, receives £23 17s p.a. He is not resident, but finds a curate.

87. Sᴛ Aɴᴅʀᴇᴡ Hᴜʙʙᴀʀᴅ[1]

Obit: a tenement, t. John Wentforde, mercer, given by Julian Fayrehedde, widow, £4 p.a. Of which, 8s quitrent to the king; 12s obit, including 2s 6d to the poor; total deductions £1. Clear remainder £3 p.a.

Memoranda: 282 communicants. Sir William Swifte, rector, receives £19 19s 4d p.a. 'and cometh not past once in 2 years to his cure, but findeth his curate to serve it'.

    1. 'St Andrew, East Cheap'.

88. Sᴛ Mᴀʀɢᴀʀᴇᴛ Pᴀᴛᴛᴇɴs

Priest, 'Dirige' and requiem: £4 6s 8d p.a. rent from certain tenements in the parish, bequeathed by Andrew at Vyne for ever. Of which, £4 6s 8d to Sir Henry Fynkell, stipendiary priest. Clear remainder Nil.

Augmentation of a priest's salary, obit and anniversary: lands and tenements bequeathed by Ralph Hollonde for ever, £3 17s 8d p.a. Of which, £2 in augmentation; 6s 8d obit, including 5s to the poor; total deductions £2 6s 8d p.a. Clear remainder £1 11s p.a.

Anniversary: lands and tenements bequeathed by William Twrnor, £4 p.a. Of which, 2s quitrent to the king; 1s 5d obit; total deductions 3s 5d. Clear remainder £3 16s 7d p.a.

Obit or anniversary: a tenement bequeathed by Davy Turbervyle for his soul, £1 13s 4d p.a. Of which, 10s obit, including 5s to the poor. Clear remainder £1 3s 4d p.a.

Obit: 13s 4d is received yearly by the rector and churchwardens from the tenement where Sir John Champnenys lives.

Memoranda: 223 communicants. Sir William Brady, rector, receives £9 19s 10½d p.a. The cure is served by him and the stipendiary priest.

89. [m.19] Sᴛ Mᴀʀʏ Sᴛᴀɪɴɪɴɢ

Memoranda: 98 communicants. Sir William Jackeson, rector, receives £7 4s 7d p.a. and serves the cure himself.

90. Aʟʟ Hᴀʟʟᴏᴡs Bʀᴇᴀᴅ Sᴛʀᴇᴇᴛ[1]

Priest: £6 13s 4d p.a. salary paid by Sir Henry Hubthorne, kt., to Sir Henry Haynes, priest, to sing daily there.

Chaplain: £6 13s 4d p.a. salary paid by the Lady Pargetor to Sir Robert Shawe.

Obit: William Harper keeps a yearly obit for one Stokes, value unknown.

Obit or anniversary for Master Farrefax: kept by John Packyngton, value unknown.

Memoranda: 300 communicants. Sir William Soplande, rector, receives £37 p.a. 'who serveth the cure by his deputy that farmeth the parsonage'.[2]

    1. Cf. (for 1546) LR 2/243 fos 23–6.
    2. BC has in addition John Cornysshe, John Stote and Gilbert Cade, all said to be paid by the Mercers and Henry Dent by the Goldsmiths. But Cornysshe and Cade were paid by the Salters (see **191**).

91. ST MARTIN OUTWICH
Chaplain, taper and St Michael's lights: £4 3s 4d rents now received from the court of Augmentations by letters patent; originally bequeathed by John de Bredstreate from 8 shops in Watling Street under one roof, for the following purposes: £3 13s 4d for an honest chaplain;[1] 6s 8d for a wax taper; 3s 4d for St Michael's lights.
Rood light and prayers: lands and tenements given by Edmund Moundevill, £3 6s 8d p.a. Of which, 4s 8d quitrents to St Bartholomew's; 4d to St Giles church; total deductions 5s. Clear remainder £3 1s 8d p.a.
Cash for purchase of 'the said' lands: £40 given by one Rawson.
Anniversary or obit: 15s 3d p.a. spent by the master and fellows of St Catherine's hall, Cambridge, 'out of their possessions'.
Obit: 13s 4d p.a. rent given by Katherine Carpenter from a tenement on Oyster Hill near London Bridge.
Obit and poor relief: £200 cash was bequeathed by John Kyddermester senior to buy property worth £10 p.a. to maintain an obit of £5 6s 8d p.a. including £2 11s 8d to the poor. The property has not been bought, and his son John still has the money, but the obit has been kept.
Memoranda: 227 communicants. Dr Nicholas Wilson, rector, receives £17 p.a. but is never resident and did not find a curate until last Michaelmas.

1. But all those named in BC are said to have been supported by the Merchant Taylors: John Turnour, George Sharpe (see **211**), John Willyamson (cf. Wilkenson, **211**) and Richard Palmer.

92. THE LATE GUILDHALL COLLEGE
Lands and tenements[1] amount to £51 8s 4d p.a. Of which, £8 13s 4d to the master of the college;[2] £20 to 3 priests fellows there; £3 6s 8d quitrent to the king; 4s quitrent to St Paul's; 3s 4d to the vicar of St Lawrence for oblations; 3s 4d to the lord mayor; 6s 8d to the chamberlain; 3s 4d to the clerk of the Chamber; 6s 8d to the tenants for potation; £2 16s 8d tenths to the king for the stipends; 12s tenths to the king for the college; 4s 8d for tithes to the rector of St Michael Bassishaw; total deductions £37 0s 8d. Clear remainder £14 7s 8d p.a.

1. Not detailed here, but SC 6 gives a good idea of the lands. See also Caroline M. Barron, *The Medieval Guildhall of London* (1974), 40–2 and 53–5.
2. Priests named in BC are Roger Asshe, Robert Rogers, John Richardson; and Robert Foxe (see **192**).

93. [m.19d] ST MARY COLECHURCH[1]
Brotherhood, gild or fraternity of St Katherine: lands to maintain a priest, founded by letters patent of Henry VI to John Tenterden and others, £9 p.a. Of which, £6 to Sir Robert Evans, stipendiary priest. Clear remainder £3 p.a.
Priest for 20 years:[2] £140 cash given to her executors by Agnes Fenne in her will dated 28 March 1541.
Memoranda: 220 communicants. The wardens of the Mercers' Company are rectors and receive £24 p.a. There is no priest besides the curate.

1. Cf. (for 1546) LR 2/241 fos 25–6, which includes an inventory of goods.
2. BC also has Robert Sandewiche (cf. **210**).

94. ST MICHAEL LE QUERNE

Priest: lands and tenements given by Robert Newcombe and John Combe for ever, £10 16s 8d p.a. Of which, £7 6s 8d to Sir John [blank],[1] stipendiary. Clear remainder £2 13s 4d p.a.

Priest for 7 years: £7 p.a.[2] rent bequeathed by John Lydyat on 23 June 1545 for his soul from 4 tenements in the parish.

[*Intent unspecified*]: 6s 8d p.a. quitrent given to the church by Thomas Poetowe from a tenement in Leadenhall called the Bell.

Obit: 6s 8d p.a. quitrent bequeathed to the church by William Herwode, and now paid by the Chamber of London.

Obit: 10s p.a. rent from 2 houses owned by the late Edmund Shawe and bequeathed by him to his wife who married George Gyfford.

Obit for 18 years: 13s 4d p.a. rent bequeathed by Alice Baillie, widow, on 30 January 1543 for her soul; 10s to be given to the poor.

Fraternity: a tenement given by Richard Verney and others, £1 6s 8d p.a. Of which, 10s 2¾d to the churchwardens of St Pancras. Clear remainder 16s 5¼d p.a.

Memoranda: 350 communicants. Sir Thomas Whitmore, rector, receives £25 10s p.a. There is no priest besides the curate.

> 1. Pokesson (BC).
> 2. 10d crossed out after £7. BC has Thomas White here.

95. ST THOMAS THE APOSTLE

Chaplain: £3 13s 4d p.a. quitrent given by Roger at Vyne for ever, from tenements, houses and shops in the parish; now paid 'out of the late dissolved house of Acon'.

Chaplain to sing daily: £5 6s 8d p.a. rent given by William Champenes for ever from tenements in the parish.

Priest: lands and tenements given to the Salters by Richard Chawry for his soul for ever, £6 13s 4d p.a. Of which, £6 13s 4d to Sir George Walpole,[1] incumbent. Clear remainder Nil.

Priest: lands and tenements given to the brotherhood of St Giles Cripplegate, by William Brampton for his soul for ever for a priest to sing here, £6 13s 4d p.a. Of which, £6 13s 4d to Sir John Barnes, incumbent. Clear remainder Nil.

Anniversary: 4s 4d p.a. rent given by Roger at Vyne for ever from his lands and tenements.

Chaplain: £4 p.a. paid by the master and brethren of St Bartholomew's hospital by deed enrolled in the Hustings.

Anniversary or obit: a shop bequeathed by William Brampton, £2 6s 8d p.a., including 6s to the choir; 3s 4d to the masters of the fraternity of St Nicholas 'holden by the clerks'; 2s to prisoners at King's Bench, 1s at the Marshalsea, 3s 4d at the Counters, 2s at Newgate, 1s 8d among clerks convict at Westminster, 1s at the Fleet; 1s 8d to the poor sisters at Elsing Spittal.

Obit: Anne Gasconne willed that her executors should buy lands in the city of London to the clear yearly value of £8 to maintain an obit 'by note', spending £2 p.a., with £3 6s 8d p.a. in money to the poor. No lands have been purchased, but Martin Gowse, scrivener, maintains the obit and spends £2 p.a.

[m.20] *Two obits and poor relief:* lands and tenements given by William Bromewell for his soul, £4 16s 8d p.a. Of which, £2 15s obit, including £1 to the poor; 2s for 4 lb of wax; total deductions £2 17s. Clear remainder £1 19s 8d p.a.

Memoranda: 298 communicants. Sir Richard Deane, rector, receives £12 p.a. The curate serves the cure with the help of the chantry priest.

> 1. BC and E 101 mention only a 'Thomas' Walpole here (see **191**). This, and the use of the singular ('priest') in the Memoranda, suggest that other endowments had lapsed.

96. WHITTINGTON COLLEGE IN ST MICHAEL PATERNOSTER ROYAL[1]

Money paid yearly by the Mercers: £63. Of which, £6 13s 4d to Dr Smythe,[2] master; £29 6s 8d to 4 fellows at £7 each [sic];[3] £5 6s 8d to the senior conduct; £13 6s 8d to the choristers; £5 to the 2 conducts; total deductions £59 13s 4d. Clear remainder £3 6s 8d p.a.

Mansion house: rented yearly, £4 6s 8d.

Two obits: 3s 5d p.a. rent from chambers let in the mansion house.

Obit for the souls of John Carpenter and Katherine his wife: 17s 4d p.a. paid by the wardens of the fraternity of Our Lady, Barking, including 8s 2d to the masters, 7s to 13 bedesmen of the college and 1s 1d to the poor.

Obit: a tenement in Little East Cheap in the parish of St Leonard, given by Sir Steven Guyns for his soul, £2 13s 4d p.a.

Preacher to keep a yearly obit: a tenement in the parish of St Leonard, given by Master Gilbert Haydecke, sometime master of the college, £6 13s 4d p.a.

Obit: £4 p.a. annuity given by John Millet, sometime clerk of the Signet, from his lands and tenements at the Three Cranes in the Vintry.

Memoranda: 213 communicants. Dr Smythe, rector, receives £7 p.a.

> 1. Cf. (for 1546) LR 2/243 fos 91–2.
> 2. Richard Smythe STP (E 101). Doctor of Divinity in BC.
> 3. Six fellows are named in BC: Richard Pitte, Thomas Tudball, Richard Tailor, Christopher Nelson, Richard Fawconer and William Wheteley; and 4 choristers: William Gowghe, Henry Bridde, Francis Welber and Henry Cholmeley. Richard Knight, conduct, is also listed in E 101.

97. ST CLEMENT CANDLEWICK STREET[1]

Parish lands: lands and quitrents given by unknown donors for bread, wine, oil, wax and repairs, £5 13s 4d p.a.

Perpetual chantry: lands and tenements given by John Cartneney, £11 13s 4d p.a. Of which, 2s for a taper; 5s to 2 priests for a breakfast; 5s to the poor on Good Friday; total deductions 12s. Clear remainder £11 1s 4d p.a., 'to the use of the said chantry priests'.[2]

Two priests: lands and tenements given by William Ivorne for ever, £20 2s 4d p.a. Of which, £6 13s 4d to Sir Reynolde Gawlty; £6 13s 4d to Sir John Adocke every other year; 13s 4d tenths to the king; 10s to the churchwardens for overseeing the lands; total deductions £14 10s. Clear remainder £5 12s 4d p.a.

Morrow mass priest and obit: lands given by Robert Halyday for prayers, and 8s to the morrow mass priest,[3] £14 10s p.a. Of which, 5s 8d obit; £1 coal for the poor; 8s to the morrow mass priest; 5s for a dinner on "Sher-thursday";[4] 6s 8d for overseeing the lands; 10s quitrents to the king; total deductions £2 15s 4d. Clear remainder £11 13s 4d p.a.

Obit 'and other godly intents': lands and tenements given by Thomas Daglas for his soul, £1 10s p.a. Of which, 2s 4d obit; 5s for the maintenance of charity; 6s 8d to the poor on Good Friday; total deductions 14s. Clear remainder 16s p.a.

Prayers and three tapers: a garden given by Hugh Johnson, £1 p.a. Of which, 3s to the rector for tapers. Clear remainder 17s p.a.

[m.20d] *Obit:** 9 chambers given by Sir John ... , £2 4s p.a. Of which, 2s 4d obit; 1s to the poor; total deductions 3s 4d. Clear remainder £2 0s 8d p.a.

Church lands: lands, tenements and quitrents, £5 4s 4d p.a.

Memoranda: 266 communicants. Sir Laurence Taylor, non-resident, is rector and receives £15 16s p.a. Sir William Thole his deputy 'and the said priest' serve the cure.

1. Cf. (for 1546) LR 2/243 fos 60–4.
2. Perhaps those who follow, though BC has John Lewes as priest here.
3. Not named in any of the sources.
4. Thursday in Holy week, see *Husting*, ii, p. xiii.

98. ST GABRIEL FENCHURCH

Rectory:[1] mansion given by Helmyng Legget, Esq., (a tenement, curtilage and appurtenances), now t. Richard Caryngton, merchant tailor, 'for certain years', £2 p.a. over and above 4d in quitrent to the king and 13s 4d paid yearly to the rector by Caryngton.

Daily 'Salve Regina', and a churchyard: a tenement now in decay but used as a garden was given by the same Helmyng for a 'Salve Regina' every evening; a further garden with an alley leading into it was given for a churchyard, value unknown.

Priest to say mass every Sunday and holy day: a tenement given by John Gambon and Helen his wife for prayers, the priest to receive 4d, 5d or 6d for each mass. Total yearly rent £1 13s 4d.

Memoranda: 200 communicants. Sir Thomas Osmonde, rector, receives £16 p.a. No other priest.

1. 'It appertaineth to the parson' entered in the margin in another hand.

99. ST PETER WOOD STREET[1]

Chantry priest and obit: lands and tenements given by one[2] Farrendon, £29 3s 4d p.a. Of which, £6 13s 4d to Sir William Alee, chantry priest; 10s quitrent to the king; 10s quitrent to Burton Lazars; 6s 8d to Canterbury cathedral; £2 13s obit; total deductions £10 13s. Clear remainder £19 0s 4d p.a.

Chaplain: £3 6s 8d p.a. rent from a tenement in the parish given to St Mary's hospital Bishopsgate in pure alms by Simon Parys.

Memoranda: 360 communicants. Master John Gwynnythe, rector, receives £26 6s 8d p.a. No other priest besides his curate.[3]

1. Cf. (for 1546) E 301/120 which includes detailed rentals and gives information which in some respects conflicts with that given here: for example in naming the donors of Farrendon's chantry as John Foster and Thomas Polle.

2. Nicholas de Farrendon (*Husting*, ii, 19).
3. Other priests named in BC are Christopher Reynoldes (see **209**), Richard Mery and Robert Paternoster, said to be at Robert Butler's chantry maintained by the Goldsmiths; with Edward Lutwick and Reginald Churcheman, conducts. Cf. **222**.

100. ST MILDRED POULTRY
Two chaplains: a tenement in the parish, now divided into 4 tenements, bequeathed by Solomon Lausare to John Lausare for his soul, with a clause of distress to the churchwardens for the non-payment of the chaplains, £7 p.a.[1]
Priest and obit: 3 tenements bequeathed by Hugh Game, poulter, £10 13s 4d p.a. Of which, £6 13s 4d to John Move, chantry priest; 9s 4d obit; total deductions £7 2s 8d. Clear remainder £3 11s 8d [sic] p.a.
Anniversary: a messuage called the Red Cock bequeathed by John Hylday, poulter, with 6s 8d for the anniversary and £4 6s 8d p.a. to the heirs of Cockeham, total £4 13s 4d p.a.
Two tapers and a torch to burn daily: 13s 4d p.a. rent from a tenement in the parish, given by Solomon Lausare.
Priest to sing for 6 years: £40 cash bequeathed by William Brothers.
Corpus Christi brotherhood: lands and tenements given by John Mymmes under licence from King Richard II, £10 8s 8d p.a. Of which, £7 to John Wotton, chantry priest; 6s 6d obit 'and otherwise'; 2s 6d quitrent to the Lady Leyghe; £1 3s 4d quitrent to the king; 2s to the Skinners; total deductions £8 14s 4d. Clear remainder £1 14s 4d p.a.
A little chapel:[2] in the parish, valued at £3.
Memoranda: 277 communicants. John Neale, rector, receives £20 p.a. and serves the cure himself. Ornaments of the chapel are with the surveyor, as in an inventory.

1. In addition to John Mole [sic] in the next entry, BC records only one other priest here, John Wulton, in a chantry founded by William Pinchbecke, a former rector.
2. Corpus Christi chapel (SC 6).

101. ST HELEN
Two chantry priests:[1] £13 13s 4d p.a. paid by the king from Augmentations.
Memoranda: 220 communicants. The king is rector, 'and no vicar there but a parish priest'.[2]

1. Thomas Wynston (Winstanley in E 101) and Thomas Robson in BC.
2. No value of benefice given.

102. [m.21] ST MARY SOMERSET
Chantry: £4 6s 8d p.a. quitrents from tenements, t. parishioners of St Benet Fink, given by John Goldesburgh by licence of King Edward III. Of which, £4 6s 8d to Sir John Bordell,[1] incumbent. Clear remainder Nil.
Chantry: lands and tenements given by Thomas Wilforde for ever by licence of King Henry IV, £3 7s 4d p.a. Of which, £3 7s 4d to Sir John Meryall, incumbent. Clear remainder Nil.
Obit and augmentation of the priests' salaries: lands and tenements given by Johan Fraunces, widow, for her soul, £4 5s p.a. Of which, 6s 8d obit; 3s 4d to the poor; total deductions 10s. Clear remainder £3 15s p.a.

Obit: lands and tenements in the parish of St Dunstan in the East, bequeathed to Roger Hale, fishmonger, and Johan his wife in survivorship by Elizabeth Wilforde, to keep an obit for her soul: 10s 10d to be spent at the obit; 9s 2d to be given to the poor: total £1 p.a.

Lamp before the image of Our Lady: 4s p.a. quitrent bequeathed by John Sywarde from tenements in Broken Wharf.

Memoranda: 300 communicants. Sir Thomas Balam, rector, receives £12 10s p.a. and serves the cure himself.

    1. BC has John Meriell.

103. ST STEPHEN COLEMAN STREET

Priest and obit: lands and tenements given by King Edward IV who also 'incorporated the vicar and churchwardens',[1] £50 5s 4d p.a.[2] Of which, £6 13s 4d to the stipendiary priest;[3] 16s 8d obit; 1s 8d taper; total deductions £7 11s 8d. Clear remainder £43 0s 8d p.a.

Obit for the soul of William Kyng, cooper: 10s p.a. spent by the Lady Longe, widow.

Obit for Richard Allexaunder: maintained by the Curriers,[4] but it is unknown how much they spend.

Obit for John Tylney: Sir Robert Lee, rector of Little [blank], Suffolk, should maintain this, 'which hath long continued until now within one year last past'.

Memoranda: 880 communicants. Richard Kettell, vicar, receives £11 p.a. and serves the cure without any help.

    1. This was previously a chapel in the parish of St Olave Jewry (J. Stow, *Survey of London*, ed. C. L. Kingsford, 2 vols. (Oxford, 1908), i, 283).
    2. The shillings figure has been altered.
    3. Priests named in BC are Robert Biggen (see **194**) and James Whitebury.
    4. See **199**.

104. ST GEORGE BOTOLPH LANE

Priest formerly in St Mary Spittal: £6 p.a. paid by the king from the court of Augmentations from land given to St Mary's by Roger de la Vere.

Priests and obits: lands and tenements given by Robert Pyckeman, William Kyngeston and Thomas Bonde for ever, £15 10s p.a. Of which, 13s 10d for obits, viz.: 2s 6d Thomas Bonde, 2s 4d Master Combes, 9s William Kyngeston 'and a torch yearly for the same'; £13 6s 8d to Sir John Parker 'and another'[1] singing for Kyngeston and Pyckeman; 16s quitrent to the king; 14s to the house of Rochester; total deductions £15 10s 6d. Clear remainder Nil.

Obit and other deeds of charity: a tenement in the parish, given by James Monforde, £5 p.a. Now t. Richard Closse who should therefore maintain the charity, giving 4 cart loads of coal to the poor in alms, but he refuses.

Memoranda: 123 communicants. Sir Richard Bromeley, rector, receives £8 p.a. and serves the cure himself.

    1. William Rilande (BC).

105. [m.21d] BROTHERHOOD OF THE PAPEY

Lands, tenements and possessions [not detailed]: £15 4s 8d[1] p.a. Of which,

9s quitrent to Sir Thomas Pope; 4s quitrent to Austin Hynde; total deductions 13s. Clear remainder £14 11s 8d p.a.[2]

1. Total damaged by gall.
2. The master of the Papey, Robert Fox, received a pension, along with Richard Bee and George Strowger, wardens; and Richard Byrehall, John Barrett and John Mordock, poor men (E 101). For an inventory of the goods of the brotherhood, see Walters, 644. BC styles the institution 'the house of priests called the Pappey'. For the history of the brotherhood see T. Hugo, 'The Hospital of Le Papey in the City of London' in *Trans. London and Midd. Arch. Soc.*, v (1877), 183. The BC entry is there printed in full (p. 216).

106. FRATERNITY OF JESUS UNDER ST PAUL'S
*Lands, tenements and possessions:** [not detailed] £3 15s p.a. Of which, 6s 8d including 2s 9d to the poor, spent at John Hall's obit; 5s 4d to 4 almsmen that keep (?the altars) yearly within the Shrouds;[1] total deductions 12s. Clear remainder £3 3s p.a.

1. For the statutes and accounts (for 1534) of the fraternity of Jesus in the Crowds (or Shrouds, as the crypt was called), see *Registrum Statutorum Sancti Pauli*, ed. W. Sparrow Simpson (1873), pp. lxv–lxvii, 441–62.

107. ST BRIDE FLEET STREET[1]
Chantry priest: lands and tenements given by John Ugley and William Evisham, £6 10s p.a. Of which, 10s quitrent to the churchwardens of St Leonard, London. Clear remainder £6 p.a.
Chantry priest, obit and light: lands and tenements given by John Ulstrope for his soul, £10 13s 4d p.a. Of which, £6 13s 4d to Sir Robert Walker for his salary; £3 for a perpetual taper to burn before the Sacrament; 10s obit; 11s 6d quitrent to the bishop of Salisbury; 5s quitrent to St Giles's; total deductions £10 19s 10d p.a. Clear remainder Nil.
Chantry priest, obit and light: lands and tenements bequeathed by John Wygan and John Hill for ever, £15 14s 7d p.a. Of which, 8s quitrent to the warden of the Fleet; 8s quitrent to St Giles [in the Fields];[2] 10s at Hill's obit including 5s 6d to the poor; total deductions £1 6s. Clear remainder £13 18s 8d p.a.
[Brotherhood of Our Lady]:[3]
    Two chantry priests: lands and tenements given by Simon at Nax for his soul for ever, £15 14s 4d p.a. Of which, £13 6s 8d to Sir John Mathew and Sir Philip Dey, incumbents; 15s quitrent to the warden of the Fleet; 6s quitrent to the dean of Worcester; £1 6s 8d tenths to the king for the 2 priests; total deductions £15 14s 4d. Clear remainder Nil.
    Obit: 2 tenements given by Agnes Lres[4] for her soul for ever, £2 6s 8d p.a. Of which, 14s obit; 3s quitrent to the bishop of Salisbury; total deductions 17s. Clear remainder £1 9s 8d p.a.
    Obit, alms and light: lands and tenements given by William Broke, £5 3s p.a. Of which, £2 13s 8d to the rector of Bisley, Surrey 'according to the will'; 8s 10d obit, including 1s 1d to the poor; 5s for a lantern at Fleet Jakes, 'a common house'; total deductions £3 7s 6d. Clear remainder £1 15s 6d p.a.
    Obit: a tenement given by Johan Cressey, £1 13s 4d p.a. Of which, 10s obit. Clear remainder £1 3s 4d p.a.

Anniversary: a tenement given by George Gay for his soul, £1 10s p.a. Of which, £1 obit. Clear remainder 10s p.a.

Lands and tenements given without condition by Richard Hawkeshede, John Spanyshebue and others, £15 19s 4d p.a.

Parish tenement: t. John Grey, £2 p.a. Of which, 3s quitrent to the bishop of Salisbury. Clear remainder £1 17s p.a.

Repair of the church: 2 tenements given by John Ulstrope, £4 p.a. Of which, 19s quitrents to the king; 6s quitrents to St Giles's; total deductions £1 5s. Clear remainder £2 15s p.a.

[m.22] *Obit:* a tenement given by John Carter, £1 3s 4d p.a. Of which, 1s 6d to the bishop of Salisbury. Clear remainder £1 1s 10d p.a.

Chantry priest: 2 tenements given by Nicholas Benblott, £3 13s 4d p.a. Of which, 4s quitrent to St Giles in the Fields. Clear remainder £3 9s 4d p.a.

Church works: 12s p.a. rent from a tenement in the parish called "Master Poksattes Place", t. Robert Smythe, who has witheld it for the past 3 years.

Rent: 7s p.a. from a tenement in the parish called the church backhouse, unpaid since anno 22 Henry VIII.

Rent: 1s 4d p.a. from a tenement in the parish called "Master Mownslowes Place", unpaid since anno 29 Henry VIII.

Church works: 2d p.a. rent from the "Belsavage" in the parish, unpaid since anno 25 Henry VIII.

Church works: 1s p.a. rent from tenements in Shoe (Show) Lane belonging to the Goldsmiths.

Rent: 7s 4d p.a. from a tenement in the parish, t. Arthur Watkynson, paid.

Rent: 4d p.a. from a tenement in Bride Lane belonging to St Martin's church, Ludgate.

Memoranda: 1,400 communicants. The benefice is impropriated to the dean and chapter of Westminster. Sir John Taylor *alias* Cardemaker, resident vicar, receives £16 p.a. No other priests help him except the chantry priests.[5]

Poor persons relieved by the fraternity of Our Lady: Johan Marlowe, widow, £1 p.a.; Margaret Jakes, widow, £1 p.a.; Edmund Briges, £2 p.a.; Harry Maxwell, £2 p.a.; Ellen Griffiths, 10s p.a.; Margaret Brokefelde, £1 p.a.; Alice Temple, 10s p.a.; total £8 p.a.

Obit: £36 cash was bequeathed to the church 12 years ago by Wynkyn de Worde for an obit for his soul for ever.

Goods of the fraternity are as in an inventory[6] submitted.

1. Cf. (for 1546) LR 2/243 fos 45–59.
2. LR 2.
3. No separate heading is given, but the brotherhood is mentioned in the inset entries.
4. Sic. The same spelling is given in LR 2.
5. E 101 has Robert Goldar, 'minister', in addition to those above.
6. The inventory of all the goods and plate appears in LR 2/243 fos 56–9.

108. ST PAUL'S CATHEDRAL: CHANTRIES

Chantry of[1] *Thomas Stowe for priest, obit and other charges:* lands, £15 6s 8d p.a. Of which, £8 to Sir Thomas Walle including 16s for tenths; £2 obit; £2 5s 8d to the king in right of St Helen's; 10s to the king in right of

Merton abbey; 10s to Simon Coston, collector of the rents; total deductions £13 5s 8d. Clear remainder £2 1s p.a.

Chantry of Ralph Baldocke for 2 priests, obit and other charges: lands, £45 13s 4d p.a. Of which, £16 to Sir Henry Saunderson and Sir Walter Preston; £2 6s 8d quitrent to the Master of the Rolls; 12s 4d quitrent to the king; 2s quitrent to the church of St John the Evangelist; £6 obit and potation including 10s to the poor; £1 6s 8d for the rent collector; £1 10s to 2 poor chorister students towards their exhibition; total deductions £27 17s [8d].² Clear remainder £17 [15s 8d] p.a.

[m.22d] *Chantry of John Powlteney for 3 chaplains, obit and other charges:* lands, £47 9s 8d p.a. Of which, £14 to the 3 chaplains;³ £13 6s 8d p.a. rent to the master and chaplains of 'Corpus Christi of St Lawrence's', London; £5 9s 2d obit; £1 6s 8d quitrent to the king in right of Halywell; 10s quitrent to the master of St Giles in the Fields; £1 18s quitrent to St Edmund Lombard Street; £1 to the choristers of St Paul's for their livery; £1 16s 8d to poor⁴ prisoners in Newgate and 16s to those in the Fleet (total £2 12s 8d); total deductions £4[0] 3s 2d. Clear remainder £7 6s 6d p.a.

Chantry of Robert Munden, John Lovell, William Milworthe⁵ and Richard Plesses for 3 priests⁶ singing daily, obit and other charges: lands, £16 6s 8d p.a. Of which, £5 4s 8d to Sir Fulk Whitney including 18s for tenths; 13s 4d quitrent to Sir Thomas Pope, kt.; £2 13s 4d to the choristers of St Paul's; £1 6s 8d obit; £4 2s 8d to Sir Richard Blosse including £1 6s for tenths; £4 18s to Sir John Richardson including 18s for tenths; total deductions £18 18s 8d. Clear remainder Nil.

Chantry of Roger Waltham⁷ for 2 priests, obit and other charges: lands, £29 16s p.a. Of which, £13 6s 8d to Sir Thomas Waryngton⁸ and Sir Anthony Mason; £2 obit; 13s 4d quitrents to the heirs of Thomas Nevell; £1 quitrent to the churchwardens of St Michael's;⁹ £1 6s 8d quitrent to the king; 6s 8d for bread, wine and wax; total deductions £18 13s.¹⁰ Clear remainder £11 3s p.a.

Chantry of Roger Holme for 4 chantry priests and other charges: lands, £46 12s p.a. Of which, 15s 4d quitrent to the king; 8s to the dean and chapter for the 4 priests' mansions;¹¹ 6d quitrent to St Botolph Aldgate;¹² 13s 4d to 2 collectors; 10s to 2 auditors; £4 3s 2d tenths to the king; 13s 4d for bread, wine and wax; total deductions £7 3s 8d. Clear remainder £38 8s 4d p.a.¹³

Chantry of John Hiltofte for a priest, obit and other charges: lands, £10 p.a. Of which, £6 13s 4d to Sir Lancelot Burrell; £3 6s 8d obit; total deductions £10. Clear remainder Nil.

Chantry of Gilbert de Bruera for a chaplain, 2 obits and other charges: lands, £18 8s 8d p.a. Of which, £6 13s 4d to Sir Thomas Barnard singing for the said Gilbert; £4 to Sir John Basse singing for 'the said Richard Wendover';¹⁴ £3 18s 4d obits; 6s 8d to the almoner of St Paul's; 3s 4d for bread, wine and wax; 10s quitrent to the Chamber of London; total deductions £15 11s 8d. Clear remainder £2 7s p.a.¹⁵

Chantry of Richard Fitzjames, sometime bishop of London,¹⁶ for a priest, obit and other charges: lands, £14 6s 8d p.a. Of which, £8 to Sir John Hill; £3 6s 8d obit; £1 for bread, wine and wax and other necessaries;¹⁷ £1 to the lord mayor and others coming to the obit; 16s 8d to the ministers of the church at the obit; 3s 4d to the chamberlain of London; total deductions £14 6s 8d. Clear remainder Nil.

1. In this and similar subsequent entries, 'of' may not always mean 'for'; see introduction p. xvi.
2. Torn away; supplied from Dugdale, 381.
3. The original return in the archives of St Paul's cathedral (WD 26) explains that the three chaplains recorded in the subsequent entry (*Chantry of Robert Munden . . .*) were priests of Powlteney's chantry. The endowments had become insufficient, so 3 other chantries were annexed to provide them with sufficient income: Whitney received Munden's endowment, Richardson that of Mylforth and Plessis, and Blosse that of Lovell, each in addition to his share of the Powlteney endowment.
4. 'Poor' does not appear in the original return (WD 26 fo. 3).
5. Mylforth in WD 26: William Melford, archdeacon of Colchester, d. 1336.
6. See above, n. 3.
7. *Recte* Walden, see WD 26: Roger de Walden, bishop, d. 1406. Roger Waltham's chantry is recorded separately in **110** below.
8. Warmyngton in WD 26 fo. 5. He was priest of this chantry in St Paul's but Mason was attached to another of Walden's foundations at Tottenham.
9. Wood Street (WD 26).
10. *Recte* £18 13s 4d.
11. Holmes college, see **113**.
12. Aldersgate in WD 26.
13. £39 8s 4d (correctly) in WD 26 fo. 7v. The priests are named there as Henry Rawlyns, William Stryckett, Thomas Maynarde and John Parker. BC has their gross income as £10 each.
14. WD 26 fo. 8 explains that a separate endowment had been made for Wendover. The scribe has telescoped the entry. Omitted from BC.
15. *Recte* £2 17s.
16. 1506–22.
17. Maintenance of chalice, books, vestments 'and all other ornaments' (WD 26 fo. 9).

109. [m.23] St Paul's Cathedral: Chantries (cont.)[1]

Chantry of John Dowman for 2 chaplains and one obit: lands, £22 p.a. Of which, £16 to Sir John Tompson and Sir Richard Syll; £6 obit; total deductions £22. Clear remainder Nil.

Chantry of Beatrice de Rosse for a chaplain for her soul: lands, £8 p.a. Of which, £8[2] to Sir Thurstan Hickemans. Clear remainder Nil.

Chantry of John Wythers for 2 chaplains for his soul and other charges: lands, £21 1s 8d p.a. Of which, £16 to Sir Henry Buckell and Sir William Hough; £1 1s 4d to the same for their chambers in the priests' house; £3 17s obit, including 4s to 12 poor men or women; 3s 4d bread, wine and wax; total deductions £21 1s 8d. Clear remainder Nil.

Chantry of William Say for a priest for his soul for ever and other charges: lands, £15 p.a. Of which, £9 to Sir Thomas Smythe; £4 obit; 10s to the rent gatherer; 6s 8d bread, wine and wax; total deductions £13 16s 8d. Clear remainder £1 3s 4d p.a.

Chantry of Godfrey de Acra for a priest for his soul for ever and other charges: £13 2s 8d p.a. Of which, £2 2s for 2 obits;[3] 8s quitrent to the king; 5s to the dean of St Paul's for wax to burn before the high altar; £2 2s 3¾d tenths to the king;[4] total deductions £4 17s 3¾d. Clear remainder £8 5s 4¼d p.a.

Chantry of Thomas Ever for a chaplain for his soul for ever, obit and other charges: lands, £16 p.a. Of which, 3s quitrent to the king; £2 quitrent to St Matthew's church;[5] £6 13s 4d to Sir Richard Walton; 16s 8d to 2 collectors, according to the foundation; £1 18s 4d obit; 2s to the poor; 3s 4d bread, wine and wax; £1 10s to the choristers[6] of St Paul's for their exhibition; total deductions £13 6s 8d. Clear remainder £2 13s 4d p.a.

Chantry of Walter Sheryngton for 2 chaplains for his soul for ever and other charges: lands, £20 p.a. Of which, £17 to Sir Thomas Bateman[7] and Sir John Wylmy; 10s to the dean and chapter for bread, wine and wax and other charges; 10s to the rent gatherer; total deductions £18. Clear remainder £2 p.a.

Chantry of James Frisell and John Romayn for a chaplain for their souls for ever, obit and other charges: lands, £11 p.a. Of which, £2 6s 8d quitrent to the House of Ely; 13s 4d obit; 16s tenths to the king;[8] total deductions £3 17s.[9] Clear remainder £7 4s p.a.

Chantry of the Duke of Lancaster[10] *for 2 chaplains for his soul for ever and other charges:* lands, £20 p.a. Of which, £16 to Sir Richard Smythe and Sir George Charleton; 6s 8d bread, wine and wax; total deductions £16 6s 8d. Clear remainder £3 13s 4d p.a.

1. The division of the entry for St Paul's into sections **108–11** is the work of a later indexer, purely for convenience, largely coinciding with the changes of membrane. It does not represent any subdivision of the original return in WD 26.
2. WD 26 fo. 9v notes that this sum includes 2s 6d distributed to the poor each Good Friday.
3. One for the founder and one for Godfrey Wysenham (WD 26 fo. 11).
4. Richard Martyndale, priest (idem).
5. Friday Street (ibid. fo. 12).
6. Poor choristers (idem).
7. Batmanson (ibid. fo. 13). See also **113**.
8. John Heytor is priest in BC. In WD 26 fo. 13v 'Robert Hudson' crossed out in favour of 'Hyetor'.
9. £3 16s (correctly) in WD 26.
10. John of Gaunt d. 1399. See also Lancaster college in **113**.

110. [m.23d] St Paul's Cathedral: Chantries (cont.)[1]

Chantry of Nicholas [Wokyndon] for a priest for ever [and other charges: lands, £8 2s 10d p.a. Of which, 10s wax;[2] 16s 3d tenths to the king;[3] total deductions £1 6s 3d. Clear remainder £6 16s 6d p.a.]

Chantry of Eustace Faconberge, William [Haverhull and John Grantham] for a priest for ever and other charges: [lands, £8 17s 4d p.a. Of which, 17s 8½d tenths to the king.[4] Clear remainder £7 19s 7½d p.a.]

Chantry of Martin Patteshall for a chaplain for his soul for ever: lands, £12 p.a. Of which, 10s quitrent to the king; £2 obit; 6s 8d bread, wine and wax; £1 0s 4d tenths to the king;[5] total deductions £3 17s. Clear remainder £8 3s p.a.

Chantry of William Everdon and Ralph Doungeon for a priest for ever and other charges: lands, £8 12s 8d p.a. Of which, 18s 8d tenths to the king.[6] Clear remainder £7 14s p.a.

Chantry of Walter Thorpe for a priest for ever and other charges: lands, £11 16s p.a. Of which, 14s 3½d tenths to the king;[7] 14s 8d quitrents to the king; 8s quitrent to the Bridgehouse; 3s 10d quitrent to the Fleet; 4s to the collectors of St Martin le Grand; £2 obit; total deductions £4 4s 9½d. Clear remainder £7 11s 3½d p.a.

Chantry of Reginald Brandon for a priest and other charges: lands, £12 p.a.

Of which, 16s 8d quitrent to the king; £1 2s 3d tenths to the king;[8] 3s 4d bread, wine and wax; total deductions £2 2s 3d. Clear remainder £9 17s 9d p.a.

Chantry of Fulk Lovell and John Braynford for a priest for ever and other charges: lands, £17 2s 8d p.a. Of which, £1 8s 10½d tenths to the king;[9] 8s quitrent to St Andrew Holborn; 8s 4d quitrent to the prebend of Portpool; 3s quitrent to the prebend of Holborn; 3s 4d bread, wine and wax; total deductions £3 1s 6½d. Clear remainder £14 1s 1½d p.a.

Chantry of Roger Waltham for a priest and other charges: lands, £9 19s 4d p.a., to which the dean and chapter have added further lands worth £3 6s 8d p.a.; originally for the augmentation of Fulk Basset's priest:[10] total £13 6s p.a. Of which, £1 obit; 10s quitrent to St Paul's; £2 1s 8d to the poor;[11] 16s to the ministers of St Paul's; £1 4s 10d tenths to the king;[12] total deductions £5 12s 6d. Clear remainder £7 13s 6d p.a.

Chantry of Philip Basset[13] *for a priest for ever and other charges:* lands, £6 12s 4d p.a. Of which, 6s 8d to the poor; 3s 4d bread, wine and wax; 13s 4d tenths to the king;[14] total deductions £1 3s 4d. Clear remainder £5 9s p.a.[15]

1. Much of the top of this membrane is illegible, and may well have been so at the time of Caley's transcript used in Dugdale, 384. The figures for Wokyndon's chantry have been supplied from WD 26; all the other information in square brackets is from Dugdale, checked in SC 6. BC gives the priests' gross incomes used for calculating pensions.
2. Including the 'wages of the lighter thereof' (WD 26 fo. 14).
3. Robert Sewter, priest (idem).
4. Robert Hay (ibid. fo. 15); Hayes (E 101); Haies (BC).
5. Christopher Bricket, priest (BC).
6. Thomas Banester, priest (BC). WD 26 has slightly different figures including a deduction of 6s 8d for bread, wine and wax, but the totals there do not balance.
7. Richard Nelson, priest (BC). WD 26 has a further deduction of £1 quitrent to Master Curteaux, with a corresponding £1 less in the clear remainder.
8. John Basse, priest (BC). See Bruera's chantry in **108**.
9. Alexander Smyth, priest (BC).
10. See next entry.
11. A hundred starlings to the poor on 10 days each year (WD 26 fo. 18v).
12. Tristram Sparkman, priest (BC).
13. Fulk Basset in WD 26. In fact a chantry for the brothers Philip and Fulk.
14. William Pyrryn, priest (BC).
15. Both WD 26 and Dugdale have income £6 13s 4d and remainder £5 10s.

111. [m.24] St Paul's Cathedral: Chantries (cont.)
Chantry of Thomas More for 4 chaplains and an obit for his soul: lands and tenements, £67 6s p.a. Of which, £5 9s 1¼d tenths to the king; £36 13s to Sir Richard Gates, Sir Robert Garret, Sir Maurice Griffith and Sir William Bucke; £1 3s 4d to the dean and chapter for the rent of the priests' chambers; £3 0s 6d quitrent to the king; £1 to the proctors of the priest house; 13s 4d quitrent to the churchwardens of St Martin's;[1] 4s quitrent to Windsor college; 5s 4½d quitrent to the master of Burton Lazars; 2s quitrent to the master of St Giles;[2] 13s 4d to the choristers of St Paul's; 1s quitrent to Sir Thomas Pope, kt.; £2 obit; 5s to 3 preachers at St Mary's Spittal; 13s 4d to the chamberlain of St Paul's for keeping the accounts and surveying; £1 6s 8d to the rent collector; 10s to the launderer for repairing

the ornaments;[3] £1 6s 8d bread, wine and wax and lights; total deductions £56 9s 7½d.[4] Clear remainder £10 16s 4½d p.a.

Chantry of William, bishop of London;[5] *Gerrard Braynbroke, kt.; Edmund Hampden; John Boyes Esq.; and Roger Albrighton, clerk, for a chaplain for their souls for ever:* lands, £12 17s 8d p.a. Of which, £1 8s 3½d tenths to the king.[6] Clear remainder £11 9s 4½d p.a.

Chantry of Walter Blockley and William Shalteshunte[7] *for a priest and obit for ever:* lands, £10 8s 8d p.a. Of which, £8 8s 8d to Sir Thomas Acrigge, including 16s 10¾d for his tenths; £1 19s obit; total deductions £10 7s 8d. Clear remainder 1s p.a.

Chantry of Henry Gulforde for a chaplain for his soul for ever and other charges: lands, £14 5s p.a. Of which, £6 13s 4d to Sir Thomas Abbott; 3s 4d bread, wine and wax; £1 to the chamberlain of London; total deductions £7 16s 8d. Clear remainder £6 9s p.a.

Chantry of John Beauchampe, kt., for a priest for his soul for ever and other charges: lands, £12 8s 8d p.a. Of which, £6 13s 4d to Sir Richard Stringe;[8] £2 10s obit; 3s 4d bread, wine and wax; total deductions £9 6s 8d. Clear remainder £3 2s p.a.

Chantry of Geoffrey Eton and Geoffrey Lucy for a chaplain, 2 obits and other charges: lands which, with £3 6s 8d given in augmentation by the dean and chapter, amount to £10 6s 8d p.a. Of which, £6 13s 4d to Sir Edward Gregory; £3 13s 4d obits; 2s bread, wine and wax; total deductions £10 8s 8d. Clear remainder Nil.

Chantry of John Fabell and Roger de la Lay for a priest, 2 obits and other charges: lands, £19 p.a. Of which, £1 8s tenths to the king;[9] 13s 4d [quit-rents to the Taylors];[10] £3 obits; total deductions £5 1s 4d. Clear remainder £3 18s 8d p.a.

Chantry of Michael Norborowghe[11] *and [Henry Idesworthe]*[12] *for a priest for ever:* lands, £8 6s 8d p.a. Of which, 17s 8d [tenths to the king];[13] 3s 4d [bread, wine and wax]; 10s [quitrent to the bishop of London]; total deductions £1 11s. Clear remainder £6 15s 8d p.a.

Augmentation of a chantry: lands at Much Thackeston, Essex, in the possession of John Thurston, given by Thomas Kempe to the dean and chapter, £4 13s [4d] p.a.

1. Ludgate (WD 26).
2. in the Fields (idem).
3. i.e. vestments.
4. The totals are incorrect. WD 26 has total £55 0s 6¾d, and £12 5s 0¼d clear.
5. William de Ste-Mère Eglise, 1199–1221, appears in obits in Sparrow Simpson, 201.
6. Robert Wyllampton, priest (WD 26).
7. Chateshunt in WD 26 fo. 23.
8. Straunge in ibid. fo. 25v.
9. John Andrew, priest (WD 26).
10. Dugdale, 387. WD 26 has Taylors' Hall.
11. Northburgh, bishop, 1354–61.
12. SC 6.
13. Edward Turner, priest (WD 26). Items in brackets supplied from Dugdale.

112. [m.24d] ST PAUL'S CATHEDRAL: OBITS[1]

[William de Melford	£2	0s	0d
Harvey de Borham	£10	0s	0d

Ralph Dungeon	£1	6s	8d
Thomas Lysars[2]	£1	6s	8d
William Brewster	£2	13s	4d
Cincius Romanus[3]	£1	6s	8d
Roger Chapelyn[4]	£2	13s	4d
Progenitors of St Roger[5]		13s	4d]
Richard de Gravesend	£2	0s	0d
Robert Fitzwalter		8s	0d
William Purley	£1	0s	0d
Thomas Northflete	£1	0s	0d
John Romayn	£2	0s	0d
John Bel ...[6]	£2	0s	0d
Peter de Durhame	£1	8s	10d
John Bulmer	£2	13s	4d
William Everdon	£1	5s	8d
Richard Follyott		7s	0d
Duke of Lancaster[7]	£3	5s	8d
John de Sylvester	£2	0s	0d
Roger de Wygornia[8]		13s	4d
Peter Newporte	£1	8s	0d
Richard Elye	£1	1s	8d
Henry de Cornhill		13s	4d
Stephen de Gravesende	£2	0s	0d
Peter Treasorer[9] and others		13s	4d
Richard Jennyns	£1	6s	8d
Thomas Vestibulo		10s	8d
Fulk Bassett	£2	0s	0d
Richard de Stratforde		13s	4d
John Lovell		13s	4d
John Penbroke	£1	6s	8d
King Henry II	£3	6s	8d
William de Ryssyng	£1	0s	0d
John de Braynforde	£2	12s	8d
Henry de Wenhame	£4	5s	0d
Thomas Asshewey	£14	0s	0d
Martin Ellis		18s	0d
Adam Scotus		12s	0d
William Lychefelde		13s	4d
Progenitors of same		13s	4d
Walter Neale and Alice, his wife		13s	4d
John de Venghame	£1	6s	8d
John de Sancto Laurencio	£2	0s	0d
Richard Newporte	£2	0s	0d
James Abyngworthe		10s	0d
Dean Alard[10]		13s	4d
"Richard iii" bishop of London[11]	£4	0s	0d
Blanche, countess of Lancaster	£3	5s	8d
Nicholas Husband	£1	10s	0d
Henry de Sandewyco[12]	£2	0s	0d

King Henry VII and Dame Elizabeth his wife £6 13s 4d
Thomas Kempe   £3 4s 8d
Lady Barton   £2 0s 0d

1. The top of the membrane is badly faded. Caley's reading in Dugdale, 387 is also suspect and has been compared with SC 6. No indication is given of the provenance of the revenue here recorded but SC 6 m. 92 records the lands and rents in question. Particulars of the higher clergy mentioned in the text and in the notes below may be found in J. Le Neve, *Fasti 1066–1300*, i, *St Paul's*, ed. D. E. Greenway (1968) and *1300–1541*, v, *St Paul's*, ed. J. M. Horn (1963).
2. Lisieux, dean d. 1456.
3. Caley has Cincine Romayne (Dugdale, 387); Cincius Romanus in SC 6; Cinthius the Roman, prebendary of Rugmere in Le Neve, i, 75.
4. Roger the Chaplain, prebendary of Oxgate, 1192 (Sparrow Simpson, 200).
5. Roger Niger, bishop 1229–41 (Dugdale, 8).
6. Probably Belemeyn (Sparrow Simpson, 195): Belemains, prebendary of Chiswick in Le Neve, i, 42.
7. John of Gaunt.
8. Roger of Worcester, canon until *c*.1229.
9. Peter of Ste-Mère Eglise, treasurer, d. *c*. 1228.
10. Alard de Burnham, dean, d. 1216.
11. Ricardus Tertius succeeded Foliot (Dugdale, 402); i.e. Richard FitzNeal, bishop, 1189–98.
12. Henry of Sandwich, bishop, 1263–73.

113. CHAPELS WITHIN THE PRECINCT OF ST PAUL'S
Charnel chapel and shed: £2 p.a. rent.
Peter college:[1] £6 p.a. rent. Of which, £1 13s 4d to the dean. Clear remainder £5 16s 8d p.a.
Sherington chapel:[2] 6s 8d p.a. rent.
Lancaster college:[3] £1 10s p.a. rent. Of which, 10s quitrent to the bishop of London. Clear remainder £1 p.a.
Holmes college:[4] £2 p.a.

1. The priests' house, owned by the dean and chapter.
2. Walter Sheryngton's chantry, see **109.**
3. Residence for the priests of the Lancaster chantry, see **109.**
4. Residence for the priests of Holmes's chantry, see **108.**

114. [m.25] ST DIONIS BACKCHURCH
Two priests and obit: lands and tenements bequeathed by John Darby, alderman, for his soul for ever, £13 p.a. Of which, £7 6s 8d to James Sewcaunt, priest; £1 10s 4d obit; 16s 8d to the wardens at the obit; £1 6s 8d quitrent to the Lady Ferres; total deductions £11 0s 4d. Clear remainder £1 19s 8d p.a.
Priest and obit: lands and tenements given by Maud Bromeholme, £5 7s 4d p.a. Of which, 1s obit. Clear remainder £5 6s 4d p.a.
Two priests: lands and tenements given by John Wrotham, £15 7s 4d p.a. Of which, £8 14s 4d to Nicholas Metcalfe,[1] priest; 1s 11d obit; 10s quitrent to the king; total deductions £9 6s 3d. Clear remainder £6 1s 1d p.a.
Obit: 10s p.a. rent given by Thomas Bonamitie from a tenement in the parish called the Star on the Hoop.
Obit: 16s 8d p.a. rent given by Thomas Hodson and John Hudson [sic]

for their souls for ever. Of which, 2s quitrent to the king. Clear remainder 14s 8d p.a.

Lamp: a tenement given by Giles Kelsey for ever, £2 p.a.

Memoranda: 405 communicants. Thomas Barsore, rector, receives £25 p.a. and serves the cure himself, finding no other priest 'but in time of necessity'.

> 1. Metcalfe and Sewcaunt (Shewcant) are the only 2 priests mentioned in E 101 and BC.

115. St Benet Gracechurch (Grasschurch)[1]

Perpetual chantry: lands and tenements given under the king's licence by Dame Johan Rose, £14 3s 4d p.a. Of which, £1 9s 2½d quitrents to divers people [not itemised]; £7 to the chantry priest;[2] total deductions £8 9s 2½d. Clear remainder £5 14s 1½d p.a.

Obit for the soul of Henry Smythe: 5s p.a. spent by Johan, wife of Robert Crowell.

Memoranda: 223 communicants. John Bryckenden, rector, receives £19 18s 5d p.a. There are no other priests besides the rector and chantry priest. An inventory of goods is with the surveyor.[3]

> 1. Cf. (for 1546) LR 2/242 fos 76–9.
> 2. John Bacter (BC).
> 3. Inventory included in LR 2.

116. St Mary Magdalene Milk Street

Priest: lands and tenements in the parish of St Michael Bassishaw, given by John Offam for ever, £14 9s 6d p.a. Of which, £6 13s 4d to Sir William Baker, priest.[1] Clear remainder £7 16s 2d p.a.

Augmentation of the priest's living: £3 14s 8d p.a. rent given by Robert Kelsey from a tenement in West Cheap called the Cow Face. Of which, £3 6s 8d in augmentation; 8s quitrent to the king; total deductions £3 14s 8d. Clear remainder Nil.

Priest: lands worth £12 13s 4d given by Thomas Kelsey to yield 4 marks p.a. to a priest.

Memoranda: 220 communicants. Sir Jeffrey Page, clerk, rector, receives £19 17s 6d p.a. and has always served the cure himself.

> 1. Edward Grene is also named here in BC. Richard Inglesby was supported by the Mercers (see **194**). See also **212**.

116a. Sum total of all the lands within the city of London: £4,589 0s 5¾d

Communicants: 41,664

[Signed]: Roger Chulmley; Nich Hare; John Godsalve; Wymounde Carew; Rico Goodrick; Richard Moryson; John Carrell; Hugh Losse.

[m.25d blank]

[MIDDLESEX]

117. [m.26] South Mimms (Southmymes)

Lamp: a cow bequeathed by John Hardon, kept by Robert Nicholl in Watling Street who pays 1s 4d p.a.

Obits and poor relief: various cows bequeathed and kept as follows: 4 bequeathed by Richard Hunt, of which 2 kept by Thomas Bowman and 2 by Edward Dell, 5s 4d p.a.; 4 bequeathed by one Pettyt, kept by William Johnson, 5s 4d p.a.; 3 bequeathed by John Hartiswell, of which 2 kept by John Shere and 1 by Thomas Hartiswell, 4s p.a.; 3 bequeathed by John Birt, of which 2 kept by Hugh Mylwarde and 1 by Thomas Hartiswell, 4s p.a.; 3 bequeathed by William Nicholl, of which 2 kept by Robert Hayly and 1 by Thomas Mathewe, 4s p.a.

Purposes unspecified: further cows bequeathed and kept as follows: 2 bequeathed by Robert Bird and kept by Thomas Bird, 2s 8d p.a.; 2 bequeathed by Anne Cufflay[1] and kept by Richard Parson, 2s 8d p.a.; 2 bequeathed by John Fraunces[2] and kept by Thomas Bowman, 2s 8d p.a.

Purpose unknown: 12 acres of land worth 8s p.a.

Memoranda: 340 communicants. The bishop of Exeter, rector, receives £20 p.a.; Sir William Spenser, vicar, £12 13s 4d p.a. No other priests.

1–2. 'for the said intents'; presumably obits and poor relief as above.

118. WEST BRENTFORD (West Brayntford)

Priest to minister the sacraments, and obit: lands and tenements in the parish, given by Johan Redman, £4 17s 4d p.a. Of which, 5s 1d quitrent to Master Rowseley; 8d quitrent for 4 acres of land; 6s 8d obit; 1s 6d to the churchwardens for their pains; £3 9s 4d towards a priest's salary, 'according to the will';[1] total deductions £4 2s 10d [sic]. Clear remainder 14s 8d p.a.

A "Crendell"[2] of wax to burn before the altar: one cow, also given by Johan Redman. Sold 2 years ago to Henry Davyes of the town for £1, not yet paid.

Memoranda: 120 communicants. Sir Thomas Cheney is rector.

1. No priest is named here in E 101 or BC, but the latter notes that 1s 4d per week is paid by the parish to a priest.
2. Presumably 'trendell': a recognised, though uncertain quantity: see R. E. Zupko, *Dictionary of English Weights and Measures* (Madison, 1968).

119. UXBRIDGE (Woxbridge)[1]

Chantry lands and chapel: £11 4s 4d p.a. including 16s for a house 'having stalls under it, for the maintenance of a chapel builded and erected by the parishioners'. Of which, 5s 2d quitrents to the earl of Derby; 10s to George Stockes; 1s to Thomas Burbage; 1 lb pepper to John Myles; 3s quitrent from the house and stalls; total deductions 19s 2d. Clear remainder £10 5s 2d p.a.[2]

Brotherhood of Our Lady: lands, £10 14s p.a. Of which, 11s 7d quitrent to the sub-bailiff of Uxbridge; 2s to the earl of Derby; 6s to the manor of Cowley (Coueley) Hall; 6d to [blank] Saunderson; 4d to Christopher Pope; 8d to John Le ... ; 8d to George Riche; total deductions £1 1s 9d. Clear remainder £9 12s 3d p.a. The brotherhood also has a tenement called "Wakefeldes" held rent-free by John Horsey, a poor blind man; the tenement is always used in alms or charity.

Memoranda: Sir Richard Turner, vicar, receives £8 p.a.[3]

1. Hennessy has this entry, wrongly, under Hillingdon.

2. The totals ignore payments to priests; those in BC are Thomas Bartholomewe and William Murfell.
3. Number of communicants not given.

120. [m.26d] BEDFONT[1]
Unknown purpose and donor: one acre of land, 2s …d.[2]
Memoranda: 80 communicants. Sir Richard …lyng, vicar, receives £6 13s 4d p.a.

  1. A repair covers the title, but a comparison with SC 6 shows it to be Bedfont.
  2. Pence torn away.

121. ISLINGTON (Iseldon)[1]
Obit and Jesus Brotherhood: a close of 12 acres, bequeathed by Richard Clowdesley and now t. Walter Coyny, £7 p.a. Of which, £1 obit, including 6s 8d to the poor; £1 6s 8d to the brotherhood singing masses for the same Clowdesley; total deductions £2 6s 8d. Clear remainder £5 13s 4d p.a.
Obit and honest priest: a close in the parish, bequeathed by John Englande and t. Robert Walter, £4 6s 8d p.a. Of which, 2s 9¾d quitrent to Thomas Fowler, gent. Clear remainder £4 5s 10¼d [sic] p.a.
Memoranda: 440 communicants. Sir James Robynson, vicar, receives £30 p.a.

  1. Much of this entry is stained with gall. Despite the references below, no priest is mentioned in E 101.

122. BROMLEY
Memorandum: 140 communicants.

123. MONKEN HADLEY (Hadley)
Obit: 4 cows given by Thomas Hall for his soul.
Obit: 5s p.a. rent given by John Twrnor from a tenement in the parish.
Memoranda: 180 communicants.

124. SHEPPERTON (Sheperdon)
Maintenance and furniture of the parish church: 2 acres of land t. Richard Harte, 2s p.a.
Memoranda: 133 communicants. The rectory is worth £40 p.a.
Lamp:[1] an acre of land bequeathed for a yearly lamp, 2s p.a.

  1. This item is bracketed to neither **124** nor **125** and could form a part of either.

125. STAINES (Stanes)
Fraternity: lands, including 6s 8d for the chantry priest's chamber, £11 17s 6d p.a. Of which, 15s 4d quitrent to the king; 3s quitrent to the lord of the manor of Grove Barns; 1s 7½d to the manor or farm of Yeoveney (Iveney) Court; £2 5s 4d to the poor; 6s 8d for a sermon yearly; total deductions £3 11s 11½d. Clear remainder £8 5s 6½d p.a.
Memoranda: 400 communicants. Sir Humphrey Perkyns, vicar, receives £12 3s 4d p.a. In his absence he finds a priest to serve the cure. Goods and plate belonging to the fraternity as listed in the inventory [not detailed here].

126. St Leonard Shoreditch
Morrow mass priest: lands, tenements and hereditaments given by Sir John Eldrington, kt., £8 2s 8d p.a. Of which, 7s 9¾d quitrent to the king; 15s quitrent to Master Wates; 2s quitrent to John But; 2s quitrent to William Bull; £7 4s to Sir James Stocton, priest,[1] including 4s for his chamber; total deductions £8 10s 9½d [sic]. Clear remainder Nil.
Poor relief: lands and tenements given by Angel Johns, £5 19s 8d p.a. to discharge the poor of various dues: Easter; the 4 offering days; the housling; the paschal light; the rood loft 'and such like'.
Memoranda: 800 communicants. The archdeacon of London is rector and receives £12 p.a. Sir Griffith Willyams, vicar, receives £16 p.a. Only the vicar serves the cure.[2]

  1. Thomas Stowghton in BC.
  2. Haliwell chapel was also in this parish (see **212**).

127. [m.27] Little Stanmore (Stanmer Parva)
The church house, t. William Style, 5s p.a.
Memoranda: 127 communicants. Sir John Stile, vicar, receives [blank]. Christopher Tompson, curate, serves the cure.

128. Hillingdon
Rabbes chantry: lands, £5 3s 6d p.a., now occupied by Sir Nicholas Wever, incumbent, 'who enjoys the same as his living'.
Perpetual anniversary or obit: lands and tenements given by Sir William Knyghtoote, £1 3s p.a. Of which, 3s 4d quitrent to Master Burbage; 4d quitrent to the bishop of Westminster; 19s 4d obit including 3d to the poor; total deductions £1 3s. Clear remainder Nil.
Memoranda: 320 communicants. The rectory is impropriated to the bishop of Worcester, who receives £33 6s 8d p.a. The vicar receives £16 p.a.

129. Hornsey (Hornessey)
Obit: one acre of customary land held of the manor of Hornsey and worth 3s 4d p.a. was given. For 5 years the money has been given to the poor and lately spent on the highways.
Church repair and poor relief: a close of 5 acres, 13s 4d p.a.
Memoranda: 160 communicants. Sir Richard Ewer, rector, receives £30 p.a. He finds 'but one priest' to serve the cure besides himself.

130. Harefield
Memoranda: 200 communicants. The rector receives £20 p.a. and pays a curate £6 13s 4d p.a.

131. Hampton [on Thames]
Church maintenance and poor relief: the church house and 2½ acres of copyhold land held of the honour of Hampton Court, now t. Thomas Younge, Richard Balden and Roger Belson, 16s p.a.
Lamp: a cow price 12s was bequeathed by John Newman.
Memoranda: 230 communicants. Robert Newman, vicar, receives £10 p.a. and serves the cure himself.

132. STANWELL[1]

Lamp: 10 acres of land on the East side of the parish church, given for ever and long used for this purpose, t. Philip Hewlet, 10s p.a.

Obit: 2½ acres of land called "Londons Hanysshe" for an obit for the souls of John London, Johan his wife and Robert Moryng, now t. Robert Asteway, 2s 8d p.a.

Memoranda: 240 communicants. The king is rector and receives £30 p.a.

    1. Title now obscured with gall, but confirmed in SC 6 and Harley 601.

133. [m.27d] STRATFORD AT BOW

Chapel:[1] King Edward III gave land 10 perches long and 2½ perches broad on the common highway to found a chapel with a churchyard for the maintenance of divine service with sacraments and sacramentals. [Value blank].

Priest and anniversary: lands and tenements bequeathed by Helen Hillarde 'to be continually prayed for', £2 10s p.a. Of which, 4s 4d quitrent to the king. Clear remainder £2 5s 8d p.a.

Priest's wages[2] *and other charges of the chapel:* lands and tenements given by divers persons, £13 6s 8d p.a. Of which, 4d to the bishop of London; 2s 6d to the dean of St Paul's; 2s to Sir Ralph Sadler; 1s 10d to Sir Peter Mewtes; £1 4s to the churchwardens of Stepney (Stebunhethe); total deductions £1 10s 8d. Clear remainder £11 16s p.a.

Memoranda: 360 communicants. 'There is no parson but a curate who hath for his salary £8.'

    1. In the parish of Stepney (BC).
    2. No priests are recorded in E 101. BC has Edward [blank].

134. ST MARTIN IN THE FIELDS

Obit for 20 years: Christian Norrice gave 'the yearly value of 10s'.

Memoranda: 700 communicants. Sir Robert Beaste is vicar.[1]

Morrow mass priest: £1 6s 8d p.a. was given yearly to the church by Humphrey Coke, 'but detained and witholden by Master Bassell'.

    1. No value is given.

135. HAMPSTEAD

Obit: 6s 8d p.a. given by Edward Wesby: 6d for the priest and clerk, and 6s 2d for the poor, 'which sum was delivered unto the churchwardens by Master Lynton'.

Light on the high altar: 2s 4d p.a. kept by one Slanyng by composition with the master and brethren of Eton college.

Obit and poor relief: 10s p.a. distributed by George Kempe every Good Friday: 6s 8d bread to the poor; 5d to the poorest of the parish; 1s 1d to the poorest householders; 1s 10d for an obit; total 10s: under the terms of his mother Margaret Kempe's will, in return for 11 beasts she bequeathed him.

Memoranda: 147 communicants. The bishop of Westminster is rector and receives £10 p.a. 'which he giveth to serve the cure'.

136. ST PANCRAS
Obit: 4 acres of meadow called "Kylborne" croft, given by John Morrant, 16s p.a. Of which, 1s at the obit to the priest and clerk; 15s to the poor 'in recreation'; total deductions 16s. Clear remainder Nil.
Memoranda: 140 communicants. The dean and chapter of St Paul's are rectors and receive £13 6s 8d p.a. Sir William Greveson, vicar, receives £9 p.a. and serves the cure without help.

137. FRIERN BARNET (Frearing Barnet)
Lamp: 4 cows given by John Doggett, John Pratt, William Longe and Thomas Tyrrey for ever: 2 kept by Gilbert Rosse, 1 by John Day and 1 by William Moggyn, paying yearly [blank].
Memoranda: 81 communicants. Sir Thomas Shipsid, vicar, receives £6 p.a.

138. [m.28] ASHFORD
Lamp: an acre of land in Stanwell parish t. John Bechampe, 1s 4d p.a.
Church maintenance: another acre of land t. John Beauchampe, 1s p.a.
Memoranda: 77 communicants. Sir Roger Griffyn, vicar, receives £8 p.a. and serves the cure himself.

139. ST MARGARET WESTMINSTER
Priest and clerk: £8 p.a. paid by the court of Augmentations from the revenue of the late brotherhood of Ronceval. Of which, £6 13s 4d p.a. to Sir Richard Kylgo, priest; £1 6s 8d p.a. to Henry Elwoode, clerk.
Fraternity of Our Lady: lands, tenements and hereditaments [not detailed],[1] £55 10s 4d p.a. Of which, £1 2s 2d quitrent to the dean and chapter of Westminster; 2s quitrent to Eton college; 5s quitrent to the Mercers' Company; 1s quitrent to 'the Lady of Oxford'; 8s quitrent to Henry Burton; 1s 8d quitrent to the Merchants of the Staple; £8 to Sir Richard Hall, £8 to Sir John Hickley, £9 to Sir Edward Story, £8 to Sir William Langborne (chaplains of the fraternity); £3 4s 2d obits throughout the year excluding poor relief; £2 15s 8d poor relief at the obits; £1 6s 8d each for the maintenance of 4 poor persons in alms for their lives: Richard Tomlyns, Agnes Wattes, Agnes May and Alice Baker (total £5 6s 8d); £4 for the salary of a conduct;[2] £2 13s 4d to Robert Wattes beadle of the fraternity for his wages; £1 18s torches, tapers and a lamp; total deductions £54 17s 8d. Clear remainder 12s 8d p.a.
Memoranda: 2,500 communicants. The dean and chapter of Westminster are rectors and receive £26 13s 4d p.a. The cure is served by a curate provided by the rectors, and by the brotherhood priests. Goods, plate and jewels of the fraternity are entered in an inventory with the Surveyor.

1. For details see SC 6.
2. John Elles (BC).

140. HENDON
Priest: £8 p.a. from the profits of houses and land bequeathed by Alan Braynt to his wife Joan for his soul for 20 years.[1]
Obit: 13s 4d p.a. from the profits of a tenement and 3 closes in Hendon

bequeathed by Richard Braynt and now t. John Braynt, the money being for priest and poor at the obit.
Memoranda: 400 communicants. The bishop of Westminster is rector [value blank]. 'No priest is found by the parson or vicar, but a curate by the vicar's farmer'.

1. No priest recorded here in E 101.

141. [m.28d] SUNBURY (Sondebury)
Church repair:* lands including Halford Field, the profits of which are used to repair the church, 1s 6d p.a. Of which, 10d to the king; 4d to ... ; total deductions 1s 2d. Clear remainder 4d p.a.
Memoranda: 174 communicants. The dean of St Paul's is rector and receives £13 6s 8d p.a. [Blank], vicar, receives £13 6s 8d and finds no other priest to serve the cure.

142. PINNER
Obit: a tenement in Harrow, given by William Streate, now t. John Wokes of Aldenham, 12s p.a. Of which, 1s 4d quitrent to John Clercke. Clear remainder 10s 8d p.a.
Unknown purpose: 2 tenements in Pinner churchyard, now t. William Tompson and Isabell [blank]: 8s p.a. Of which, 10d quitrent to William Newman. Clear remainder 7s 2d p.a.
Memoranda: 300 communicants. The rector receives £18 p.a. and the vicar £13 6s 8d, and the vicar finds a curate to serve the cure.

143. CHISWICK (Ceswicke)
Poor relief: 2 small tenements and 2 acres of land belonging thereto, t. Edward Kyng and Hugh Edwyn, 13s 8d p.a. Of which, 2s 4d quitrent to the dean and chapter of St Paul's. Clear remainder 11s 4d p.a.
Poor relief: a cow given by John Morecocke, and kept by [blank], 2s p.a.
Memoranda: 120 communicants. The dean and chapter of St Paul's are rectors and receive £40 p.a. William Wharton, vicar, receives £10 p.a.

144. TEDDINGTON (Tuttington)
Obit: 'three half acres' of arable land and 1 rood of meadow, given by William Gose and now t. Henry Bundell, 5s 6d p.a. Of which, 5d quitrent to the manor of Gayles. Clear remainder 5s 1d p.a.
Church repair: 'three half acres' of arable land, given by William Wocetor and now t. Robert Chirte, 1s 6d p.a.
Obit: 7s 8d p.a. rent out of the land called Gayles, given by John Wyther and now t. Hugh Mannyng.
Memoranda: 72 communicants. The rectory and vicarage are impropriate to the king, and now let to George Gates at £7 6s 8d p.a. Only one priest serves the cure.

145. ISLEWORTH
Obit: a tenement in Hounslow, given by Edmund Askewe and now t. Robert

Grene, £2 p.a. Of which, 6s 8d at the obit for the choir and the poor. Clear remainder £1 13s 4d p.a.
Memoranda: 400 communicants. The rector receives £35 p.a. and the vicar £18 p.a.

146. [m.29] Norwood
Church lands: now t. William Thomas, £1 p.a. Of which, 4s 8d quitrent. Clear remainder 15s 4d p.a.
Lamp: 4 acres of land are held by Henry Harwode to maintain a lamp, which he has done for 6 years but now denies, 4s 6d p.a.
Obit and lights: 12 acres of customary land given by Alice Hyat to William Twrnor for this purpose, 12s p.a.
Obit: copyhold lands called Hill House given by Robert Cheseman; 12 poor women to be given £1 2s at the obit; if the lands do not yield enough the balance is to be met from Henry Cartor's land within 6 days of Hallowmass, or the churchwardens to distrain, £1 2s p.a.
Memoranda: 140 communicants. Dr Worham, rector, receives £30 p.a. Sir Ralph Wakefelde, vicar, receives £20 p.a.

147. Harmondsworth (Harmanworth)
Memoranda: 245 communicants. Sir Richard Kyte, vicar, receives £12 p.a. and serves the cure himself.

148. St Giles in the Fields
Memoranda: 305 communicants. Sir William Rowlandson, vicar, receives £8 p.a. and serves the cure himself.

149. Cranford (Craneforde)
Repair of the church: 3 acres of arable land, now t. churchwardens, 5s p.a. Of which, 1s 4d quitrent to Lord Windsor; 4d quitrent to John Coke; total deductions 1s 8d. Clear remainder 3s 4d p.a.
Maintenance of the church: 4 sheep and 2 lambs kept by the wardens, worth 10s.
Memorandum: 60 communicants.

150. Cowley
Memoranda: 36 communicants. Sir Adrian Carowe, rector, receives £11 p.a.

151. Hackney
Chaplain for the fraternity of the Holy Trinity and St Mary the Virgin: a tenement in St Nicholas Shambles, London, bequeathed by Sir Bartholomew James, kt., for his soul for ever, and now t. Robert Egleston, butcher, £8 p.a. Of which, £6 13s 4d to Sir Richard Bucklerst, incumbent.[1] Clear remainder £1 6s 8d p.a.
Obit: 1½ acres of land in Hackney Marsh, t. Christopher Pate, given by John Godyng, 5s p.a. Of which, 3s 4d obit. Clear remainder 1s 8d p.a.
Obit: 3 acres of land in "Southemylfelde" in the parish, given by John Warryn and now t. Thomas Chatcher, 7s 4d p.a. Of which, 4s obit. Clear remainder 3s 4d p.a.
[m.29d] *Two obits:* 7 acres of land at "Pawrnehill", given by Thomas

Clifforde for his soul, now t. John Roberts, £1 6s 8d p.a. Of which, £1 6s 8d obits. Clear remainder Nil.

Obit: a field of 3½ acres called "Welfelde", in Hackney, given by Robert Lawrence for his soul and now t. Katherine Axe and Richard [blank], 18s p.a. Of which, 8s obit. Clear remainder 10s p.a.

Obit: William Lowthe bequeathed to Robert Latham, goldsmith, money to purchase lands from which Latham maintains the obit, with 6s 8d to the poor: £1 6s 8d p.a.

Lazar house with 1½ acres of arable land: 10s p.a.

Lamp: 2 acres of customary land in Hackney Marsh, t. John Nonne, 8s p.a. Of which, 1s 4d to the bishop of London. Clear remainder 6s 8d p.a.

Church repair: a copyhold cottage and garden in [blank], t. Richard Rippyn, 13s² p.a. Of which, 1s quitrent to the king; 4d quitrent to the bishop of London; total deductions 1s 4d. Clear remainder 11s 8d p.a.

Ornaments and church repair: 3 roods of customary lands t. Johan Maxfelde; ½ acre t. Johan Hude; 1 rood t. Mistress Lymsay; 1 rood t. Robert Rowe: total 7s p.a. Of which, 1s 2d quitrent to the bishop of London. Clear remainder 5s 10d p.a.

Church house built by the parishioners: 'that they might meet together and common of matters as well for the king's business as for the church and parish', worth £1 p.a. to let.

Memoranda: 600 communicants. Master John Spendlowe, rector, receives £21 p.a. [Blank] Moreton, vicar, receives £20 p.a.

1. Richard Nicholles is named as an additional priest here in BC (see **209**), with John Pillyn, conduct.
2. Originally 13s 4d but the pence scored through.

152. St Clement Danes

Morrow mass priest and 5d poor relief in honour of the Five Wounds: 3 tenements in the parish, leased by Thomas Newburghe to William Beckingham by indenture 5 November 1488 for 80 years. Beckingham bequeathed the tenements to his wife Alice for life, and after her death to the parish church, £4 p.a. Of which, 3s 4d quitrent to the king; £1 16s 8d to Newburghe's heirs; 5d to the poor; £1 19s 7d to the morrow mass priest;[1] total deductions £4. Clear remainder Nil.

Morrow mass priest: 2 tenements built by Roger Bowle, a former priest of the church, on a void piece of ground adjoining the churchyard, given by King Henry VI to maintain a lamp in return for 2s p.a. for all suits. The tenements are now let for £4 13s 4d p.a. The church has a further 2 tenements of the yearly rent of £1 6s 8d, also given to the morrow mass priest. Of which, 2s quitrent to the king; 4s each to 9 poor people (total £1 16s); total deductions £1 18s p.a. Clear remainder £4 2s p.a.

Parish rooms: a room in the churchyard, built at the parishioners' expense, with under-rooms, let to the poor rent-free, 'where the parishioners do assemble'.

Memoranda: 1,400 communicants. Sir John Rixman, rector, receives £31 p.a. and 'serveth the cure with his curate only'.

1. E 101 names 2 priests here: Edward Thompson and William Underwood. BC has only Underwood, but with Richard Vyall, conduct.

153. [m.30] Hounslow
No lands are given for any 'priest, obit, lamp or any such like thing'.
Chapel: in the parish, adjoining the late friary, having no lands, maintained by the parishioners of Heston (Heyston) and Isleworth.
Almshouse: where poor and sick people are maintained by the inhabitants of the town who pay yearly 'to the lord thereof' 4d.[1]

> 1. No memoranda.

154. Kensington
Church house: now occupied by the poor 'of the sufferance of the parishioners'.
Memoranda: 100 communicants. The king is rector and patron. Sir John Pateson, vicar, receives £18 6s 8d p.a. and serves the cure himself.

155. St Mary Matfelon
Obit for the soul of John Ball and others: 10s p.a. rent from tenements in the parish bequeathed to the church, t. Martin Cowley and his wife.
Obit: 6s 8d p.a. is spent by Thomas Casse, 'but out of what lands it is not certified'.
Prayers: lands and tenements given by the abbot and convent of St Osyth's for a term of years still to run, 'to be prayed for by the curate or parson', £6 2s 8d p.a. Of which, 13s 4d rent to one [blank] Glasto 'for that he hath purchased the same lands as it is said'. Clear remainder £5 9s 4d p.a.
Memoranda: 670 communicants. Sir Edward Artwycke, rector, receives £31 17s 4d p.a. and serves the cure himself without finding any other.

156. Ealing (Yellinge)
Obit or anniversary: 4 acres of free land, t. John Pynner, bequeathed by William Turnor, sometime vicar, for his soul for ever, 6s p.a. Of which, 3s obit including 1s 3d to the poor; 5d quitrent to Mr Spilman; 6d quitrent to Mr Annsam; total deductions 3s 11d. Clear remainder 2s 1d p.a.
Obit: a customary cottage with a garden and 5½ acres, and an orchard called "Cockes Hawe", t. John Pynner, given by Sir Thomas Cowrtes for his and other souls, 17s 3d p.a. Of which, 2s obit; 4s to the bishop of London; 4d quitrent to the heirs of Clavell; total deductions 6s 4d. Clear remainder 10s 11d p.a.
Lamp: an acre of arable land in "Braynforde" field, t. Richard Edlyn, given by one Nedlar for ever, 1s 8d p.a. Of which, 1s quitrent to the bishop of London. Clear remainder 8d p.a.
Obit: 14s p.a. rent from a cottage, a curtilage and 5 acres of land in West Ealing, t. William Nelder who maintains the same 'according to the will and tenor of a copy to him made and granted by William Nedlar his father'. Of which, 6s 8d obit, including 5s to the poor; 1s 2d quitrent to the bishop of London; total deductions 7s 10d. Clear remainder 6s 2d p.a.
Memoranda: 360 communicants. Doctor Baughe, rector, receives £22 p.a. Sir William Haywarde, vicar, receives £13 6s 8d p.a. and serves the cure himself.
Church house: given by Master Frowycke 'to keep a drinking' for the relief of the poor.

Obit: kept by Richard Aylworthe, but for whom or from what lands is not certified.

Obit: William Ingram gave to Simon Coke certain cottages in order that Coke should maintain an obit for his soul spending 4s p.a. Coke has since sold the cottages to Richard Ingram, and for the past 2 years no obit has been kept.

157. [m.30d] FINCHLEY

Priest: £2 p.a. rent from a [tenement and two crofts][1] in the parish t. widow Lyster, with which Thomas Samy by his will enfeoffed various persons to find a priest for his soul for ever, 'if the king's Majesty's laws will suffer it',[2] or else his executors to sell it. Of which, 5½d quitrent to the bishop of London; 10d quitrent to "Billesworthe Place"; total deductions 1s 3½d. Clear remainder £1 18s 8½d p.a.

Repair of ornaments, mending of highways, and poor relief: £1 6s 8d p.a. rent from a croft in the parish with a house built on it, t. John Moncke senior, and a mease and garden, t. John Peter, with which Robert Warren enfeoffed various persons. Of which, Nil [sic] in quitrent to "Billesworthe Place"; 6s 8d to the poor; total deductions 6s 8d. Clear remainder £1 p.a.

Purpose unknown: 13s 4d p.a. rent from 4 crofts of land and meadow in the parish, called "Poyntelles", t. John Whitt, with which Thomas Samy enfeoffed various persons. Of which, 4s 4d quitrent to the bishop of London; 9s to the poor; total deductions 13s 4d. Clear remainder Nil.

Church house: built by the rector, churchwardens and parishioners at their own expense for their 'common assembly as well for matters of the king's as for the church and parish', let to John Slatter at will, 'permitting the said churchwardens notwithstanding to have their liberty of incoming into the same at all convenient times'.

Memoranda: 280 communicants. Sir John Spendlow, rector, receives £20 p.a. and serves the cure himself without help.

　　1. Illegible in the text, but confirmed in SC 6.
　　2. No priest is named here in E 101.

158. HANWELL

Purpose unspecified: a messuage and 'half a yardland customary', in the parish, and 8 acres of 'land of lords lands', t. John Wayland, given by one Hopkyns, £1 p.a. Of which, 7s 8d quitrent to the bishop of Westminster. Clear remainder 12s 4d p.a.

Memoranda: 53 communicants. Sir Thomas Cheney, rector, receives £20 p.a. and finds a priest to serve the cure.

159. ST MARY LE STRAND (Our Lady of Stronde)

Priest to sing for ever: a tenement or brewhouse called the "Flowre de Luyce", with 5 tenements belonging thereto, t. widow of John Henbury, bequeathed by James Atkinson who held a lease of the premises from the Duchy of Lancaster for a term of years not specified, £5 p.a. Of which, £2 quitrent to the king; £3 for part of the salary of Sir Anthony Torky singing for the said James; total deductions £5. Clear remainder Nil.

Memorandum: 'The parish church of Strand aforesaid before the dissolution of the same church[1] had belonging to it of houseling people 280, and that by the same dissolution there is neither vicar nor curate.'

1. It was demolished to make way for Somerset House in 1548: see R. Somerville, *The Savoy* (1960), 48–9.

160. St Marylebone
No lands etc.
Memoranda: 66 communicants. The king is rector and finds a priest to serve the cure.

161. Acton
No lands etc.
Memoranda: 158 communicants. Sir Hugh Twrnebull, rector, receives £14 p.a. and finds a priest to serve the cure.

162. [m.31] Harrow on the Hill
Lady mass priest: a messuage and 101½ acres of land, 5½ acres of meadow and 4s 4¼d rent given by William de Bosco, DD, to Thomas Akyng, chaplain of the said parish, and his successors as chaplains for his soul, £9 16s 5d p.a. Of which, 10s 5d quitrents to divers persons; £9 6s to Sir Thomas Parker 'now serving according to the foundation'; total deductions £9 16s 5d. Clear remainder Nil.
Augmenting and furniture of divine service: 10 acres of wheat, 2 oxen, 2 cows and a horse given by the same William de Bosco.
Lamp and poor relief: a close called "Danyelles", t. Robert Edlyn, given by Henry Parson, £1 2s 8d p.a. Of which, 2s 8d quitrent to Richard Redyng; £1 to the poor; total deductions £1 2s 8d. Clear remainder Nil.
Obit: a croft called "Hamoundes", given by the same Henry Parson for ever and now t. John Soles, 8s p.a. Of which, 4d quitrent to John Parson. Clear remainder 7s 8d p.a.
Obit: a piece of land, t. Thomas Bugbord, given by Agnes Agernehill, 8s p.a. Of which, 7d quitrent to Richard Redyng. Clear remainder 7s 5d p.a.
Memorandum: 'Within the said parish of Harrow is a free chapel called Tockington (Toddyngton) chapel, distant 2¼ miles from the said church, whereunto belongeth certain lands and tenements and the same chapel; by whom, how long time past, or to what use it was founded, the said parson and churchwardens know not, but time out of man's mind hath been belonging, and as a member taken, of the said parish church of Harrow until about 2 years past one John Fynche entered and ever since occupied the same by the grant of one William Leighton that affirmeth he hath purchased it[1] so that they meddle not with it, which chapel with the lands thereof is worth yearly £6.'
Memoranda: 1,000 communicants. Sir Edward North, kt., is rector. Arthur Leighton, vicar, receives £33 12s 8d p.a. and finds 2 priests to serve the cure.

1. Leighton, described as 'keeper or chaplain', had surrendered the chapel to Henry VIII and on 28 July 1546 was awarded an annuity of £4 13s 4d (*LP* xx (i) no. 748; xxi (ii), 435).

163. TOTTENHAM
Paschal light and poor relief: 2 tenements and 6 acres of ground, t. Thomas
Miles and John Hamond, bequeathed by William Cowrteman, £2 6s 8d p.a.
Of which, 3s 4d quitrent; the remainder to the poor, £2 3s 4d; total deduc-
tions £2 6s 8d. Clear remainder Nil.
Priest:[1] cows given by various people, now kept by the following: William
Cordall 1; Richard Tompson 4; William Morres 3; Peter Oldes 2; Master
Phesaunt 1; William Payle 1; Richard Clerke 1; John Petcher 1; John
Jones 1; Thomas Come 1; William Harberd 1; Thomas Miles 1; Robert
Bird 1; Richard Colfoxe 2; Robert Jeffreyson 1; John Cayser 2; William
Pakyngton 1; William Bone 2; Thomas Petcher 1; John Edrige 2; Richard
Dorman 1; John Oldes 1; Thomas Braknocke 1. Total 33 cows at 2s per
cow £3 6s p.a.
Memoranda: 356 communicants. The dean and chapter of St Paul's are
rectors 'and letten out by year for £19. Sir John Archer is vicar there whose
living yearly there is unknown.'

    1. No priest is recorded in E 101.

164. [STOKE] NEWINGTON
Purposes and donors not specified: 3 acres of land and an acre of wood.
Memoranda: 100 communicants. James Clyve, rector, receives £20 p.a.

165. HAYES
Maintenance of church: 2½ acres of land; unknown by whom given.
Lamp: ½ acre of land, t. John Nicholles, 8d p.a. Of which, 2½d quitrent to
Sir Edward Northe, kt. Clear remainder 5½d p.a.
*Lamp:** 2 acres of land in Hayes lately sold to ... , t. Nicholas ... , but
nothing paid for the past 3 years.
Memoranda: 260 communicants. The rectory is worth [blank] and the
vicarage £20 p.a.

166. [Number not used]

167. [m.31d] HANWORTH*
*Church house:** used for assembly.
Memoranda: [blank] communicants. Sir William Harbart, rector, receives
£10 p.a.

168. FULHAM
Church repairs: 2 acres of land, t. churchwardens, rented at 13s 4d p.a.
Memoranda: 444 communicants. Dr Haynes,[1] rector, receives £26 p.a.
Master Smyth, vicar, receives £10 p.a. and finds a priest to serve the cure.

    1. Simon Haynes STP and John Smyth STB (Hennessy, 160–1).

169. STEPNEY (Stebunheth)
Prayers: a tenement in Freby Street, Limehouse, in the parish, given by
Thomas Brett to be prayed for for ever, now t. John Phellipes, £1 13s 4d p.a.
Memoranda: 1,360 communicants. Sir Gabriel Donne, rector, receives
£50 p.a. Sir Henry More, vicar, receives £33 6s 8d p.a.

170. CHELSEA (Chelsey)
No lands etc. for these purposes.
Memoranda: 75 communicants. Sir Robert Richardson, vicar, receives
£13 6s 8d p.a.

171. EDGWARE
Lamp: a close containing 1 acre of ground and wood, 1s 8d p.a.
Memoranda: 120 communicants. Henry Page, rector, receives £9 p.a. and
finds a priest to 'keep the cure'.

172. GREAT STANMORE (Stanmer Magn')
Parish clerk: 8 acres of arable land, £1 p.a.
Memoranda: 130 communicants. Alfonsus Deselinus, rector, receives
£10 p.a. and finds a priest to serve the cure.

173. EDMONTON
Two chantry priests, light and obit: £13 6s 8d p.a. salary is paid to the 2
chantry priests[1] by the Chamber of the city of London which also pays
them 13s 4d 'to keep a light in a lamp', and 13s 4d to maintain an 'obit
which is dealt to the poor'. The vicar receives from the Chamber 6s 8d to
oversee the obit.
Property of the chantry: a chantry priests' house where they dwell, 13s 4d
p.a. A house with a back side, let to John Sadeler of London, 10s p.a.
A 4 acre field let to [blank] Ogle, widow, 10s p.a. A cottage with an orchard,
6 acres of ground and ½ acre of meadow in the common marsh of Edmonton (Edelmenton), let to Richard Askewe, merchant, £1 3s 4d p.a. An
orchard lying behind the barn of John Sadler, merchant, 3s 4d p.a. Of
which, 2s 8d is paid to the churchwardens for the repair of the church.
Clear remainder £2 17s 4d p.a.
Church repair: 2s 8d is paid by the chantry priests.[2] There are also 3 shops
built in the churchyard by the churchwardens with the help of the parishioners, and let for 6s p.a.; and a croft of 1 acre let for 6s p.a. Of which, 3s
'to the parson or his deputy'. Clear remainder Nil.
[m.32] *Memoranda:* 600 communicants. The dean and chapter of St Paul's
are rectors and receive £20 p.a. Sir Andrew Powes, vicar, receives £18 p.a.
and is resident.

1. John Pierson and John Naylet (BC).
2. As recorded above.

174. FELTHAM
No lands for these purposes.
Memoranda: 85 communicants. Sir Thomas Cotton, rector, receives £11
p.a. Sir Richard Penmentory, vicar, receives £8 p.a.

175. PADDINGTON
Purpose unspecified: lands and tenements, 8s p.a. Of which, 2s 4d to the
poor. Clear remainder 5s 8d p.a.
Memoranda: 74 communicants. The king is rector.

176. HARLINGTON
Church repair: 'the church half acre', value unknown.
Lamp: an acre called "Chylde lande", value unknown.
Purpose unknown: "St Nicholas half acre", value unknown.
Lamp: ½ acre called "Pluckyngtons landes", value unknown.
Light: a rood of land called "Taylors lande", value unknown.
Memoranda: 91 communicants. Sir Hugh Glasyer, rector, receives £24 p.a. and keeps a curate to serve the cure.

177. LALEHAM
No lands for these purposes.
Memoranda: 180 communicants. Sir John Myllest, vicar, receives £8 p.a.

178. KINGSBURY
Obit: church lands given by John Edward, £1 p.a., distributed yearly among the poor in meat, drink and money.
Obit: 8 cows given by Alice Cowper, 10s p.a. to be given to the poor.
Church house: a little close called "Hill Felde", given by John Edwardes 'to make a church house', 8s p.a.
Memoranda: 98 communicants. The dean of St Paul's is rector and receives £12 6s 8d p.a.

179. GREAT GREENFORD (Greneford the More)
Five lights before the image of the Trinity and Our Lady: 2 acres of arable land, t. John Lancton, given by Henry Collyn, 1s 4d;[1] and ½ acre of meadow, t. Robert Colley, 1s 8d;[2] total 3s p.a.
Quitrent: 1s 6d p.a. paid by John Milles.
Quitrent: 'Out of the lands of William Herne there ought to be paid the said parish church yearly' 6d.
Purpose and value unspecified: 'Sir Thomas Wedger, sometime parson there, gave unto the said church out of Thomas Hilles lands', now t. Simon Baranger, [blank].
Memoranda: 100 communicants. Sir Henry Thornton, rector, receives £20 p.a.

  1 and 2. The totals are entered as an afterthought above the line.

180. RUISLIP (Rueslyppe)
No lands for these purposes.
Memoranda: 480 communicants. The rectory is impropriate to the king's college of Windsor, £18 p.a. 'One Whithorne',[1] vicar, receives £8 p.a.

  1. George Whitehorne (Hennessy, 381).

181. WILLESDEN (Wyllesden)
Obit: a tenement called "Champnes", £1 10s p.a. Of which, 2s 6d quitrent to the lordship of "Bondes"; 3d quitrent to the lordship of "Brandes"; 6d obit; total deductions 3s 3d p.a. Clear remainder £1 6s 9d p.a.
[m.32d] *Masses and a light and lamp:* 5s 8d p.a. rent from a meadow called Long Mead and other ground. Of which, 4s 3d masses; 1s bread and ale

among the poor; 7d light 'or lamp'; 4d to the churchwardens; total deductions 6s 8d p.a. Clear remainder Nil.

A tenement in the churchyard: 16s 8d p.a. 'wherein Thomas Cockes dwelleth'.

Obit: a house with a garden plot given by Sir Thomas Pollett to John Pollett to keep the obit for his soul, 'and also for the maintenance of a sheep or wether and a calf and as much bread and drink as may be thought convenient to eat the same, and the same to be eaten and distributed to and among the poorest of the same parish only on the day of the obit to be kept', 6s 8d p.a.

Memoranda: 240 communicants. The dean and chapter of St Paul's are rectors and receive £14 p.a. Sir John Bushope, vicar, receives £14 p.a. and finds a priest to serve the cure.

182. [WEST] DRAYTON

No lands for these purposes.

Memoranda: 130 communicants. Sir John Hurst, rector, receives £8 13s 4d p.a. and serves the cure himself.

183. ICKENHAM (Ikenhame)

No lands for these purposes.

Memoranda: 80 communicants. Sir John Dyar, rector, receives £13 6s 8d p.a. and serves the cure himself.

184. LITTLETON

Chantry priest: £3 6s 8d p.a. from the court of Augmentations from the revenues of Chertsey abbey, to "Sir Phelipe Lymard,[1] a Frencheman", chantry priest.

Property of the chantry: a house, an orchard, a little croft or close containing a yardland, 7½ acres of arable land, 2 half acres of meadow and a yard, let by the chantry priest to John Taylor for £1 p.a.; 2s 2½d p.a. quitrents received by him: from Dame Blanche Wochan 9½d, from Richard Pennyson 1s and from John Sheperton 5d. Of which, 1s 4d quitrent to the manor of Laleham. Clear remainder £1 0s 10½d p.a. Also a tenement with a close containing an acre of ground, 14 acres of arable land and 3½ acres of meadow, which the chantry priest has for a term of years still to run, and lets at £1 18s 11d p.a. Of which, 12s 11d to Dame Blanche Vochan. Clear remainder £1 6s p.a.

Memoranda: 100 communicants. Sir Edmund Pyerson, rector, receives £14 p.a.

1. Leonard in E 101 and BC.

185. ENFIELD

Obit: a tenement, t. Robert Foster, bequeathed by Walter Forde, 13s 4d p.a. Of which, 2s 1d obit; 1s 8d quitrent to Robert Decro, grocer; total deductions 3s 9d. Clear remainder 9s 7d p.a.

Obit: a tenement, t. William Myller, given by one Rotheham, 10s p.a. Of which, 2s 1d obit; 2d quitrent to William Honnesdon; total deductions 2s 3d. Clear remainder 7s 9d p.a.

Obit: 2 acres of meadow, t. John Woodeham, given by Thomas Aylworthe, 6s 8d p.a. Of which, 2s 1d obit. Clear remainder 4s 7d p.a.

Obit: 2 crofts and an acre of land, t. William Wilson, given by Hugh Forde, 4s p.a. Of which, 2s 1d obit. Clear remainder 1s 11d p.a.

Brotherhood priest: a close and 3 acres of ground, t. Roger Gardener, given by John Forde, 11s p.a. Of which, 2s 6d quitrent to the king. Clear remainder 8s 6d p.a.

[m.33] *Maintenance of the same priest and obit:* a tenement, t. Johan Bennet, given by Maud Hamond, 7s p.a. Of which, 1s quitrent to Sir Thomas Wroith; 3s 4d obit; total deductions 4s 4d. Clear remainder 2s 8d p.a.

Light before the Lady altar: 3½ acres of meadow, t. Robert Stryngfelow, given by Walter Baldewyn, 5s p.a.

Brotherhood priest: 3 messuages, 200 acres of land, 100 acres of meadow, 200 acres of pasture, 50 acres of wood and 200 acres of marsh, in the towns of South Benfleet, Hadleigh and Thundersley, Essex, now t. one Jeffray, £10 p.a. Of which, £7 salary to Sir John Bridgeman.[1] Clear remainder £3 p.a.

Memoranda: 1,000 communicants. Sir Robert Stringfelowe, vicar, receives £26 p.a. and finds a curate to help serve the cure.

1. Edward Gooseman is also named here in E 101 and BC.

186. NORTHALL

Lamp before the high altar: 1½ acres of land in the common field, now t. William Sheppard and William Harte, 1s 4d p.a.

Memoranda: 100 communicants. Sir Ralph Standysche, rector, receives £26 p.a. and finds a curate.

187. HESTON

Obit: a messuage or tenement called North Hyde and 55½ acres of land, pasture and wood in Heston and Norwood, Middlesex, t. Walter Cole of Heston who holds them by indenture from Alice Danby of London, widow, on condition of maintaining the obit for her soul and others. Rent unknown.[1] Of which, 2s 4d 'in expenses at the obit, viz. amongst the parishioners there as much as may be made of 3 bushels of wheat and as much ale as can be made of 4 bushels of malt; in cheese 1s; to the choir according to the use and custom there; and to the 2 churchwardens 8d'.

Easter wafers: 14 acres of land 'given out of Groves Place' for the vicar to distribute to the parishioners as many wafers as can be made of 4 bushels of wheat, at Easter 'after they have taken their rights, and for default of so doing then the said land to remain to the said Grove Place', £1 p.a.

Rood light and church repair: one acre for a rood light: 1s 4d,[2] and 3 roods of land for repair: 11d,[3] 2s 3d p.a. Of which, 7d quitrent. Clear remainder 1s 11d p.a.

Purpose unspecified: an acre of land called Godfrey acre, t. Henry Cole, [value blank]. Of which, 2s to the poor on Good Friday, with 4d to the churchwardens. Clear remainder [blank].

Memoranda: 363 communicants. The king is rector and receives £24 p.a. [Blank]⁴ Whitt, vicar, receives £16 p.a.

1. £1 2s 3d (SC 6).
2 and 3. Totals entered as an afterthought above the line.
4. Thomas (Hennessy, 218).

188. TWICKENHAM

Obit: lands owned by the master and fellows of the college of St Giles, Norwich, £1 p.a. Of which, £1 is spent. Clear remainder Nil.
*Obit:** 6 acres of land, t. Robert Sandwell, held by Isabel Walker to keep the obit, 8s p.a. Of which, ... obit. Clear remainder ...
*Obit for the soul of George (?Hene):** kept by his executor, William Whitt, ...¹
Church lands: at a yearly rent of 7s 4d.
*Lady light:** an acre and 3 roods of land, held by Thomas Whitt, the acre at (?"Heygate") and the 3 roods at (?"Stakton"), 1s 9d p.a. Of which, 10d quitrent. Clear remainder 11d p.a.
Memoranda: 210 communicants. Sir Thomas² Stonard, rector, receives £11 p.a.

1. SC 6 has 6s 8d.
2. Thus Hennessy; the name is barely legible.

189. [m.33d] [ACTON: An exact duplicate of **161**. The remainder of this membrane blank.]

190. [m.34] THE LATE COLLEGE OF ST STEPHEN WESTMINSTER

[i]   SPIRITUALITIES

London and Middlesex: £5 p.a. pension from the court of Augmentations paid by Master Spylman¹ for an obit for king Henry VIII.
Huntingdonshire: the rectory of Fen Stanton and its tithes, given by Thomas, earl of Nottingham, £26 13s 4d p.a. Of which, 4d quitrent to the Lord Berkeley; £1 6s 8d to the poor; total deductions £1 7s. Clear remainder £25 6s 4d p.a.
Norfolk: the rectory of Gayton with its tithes, £13 6s 8d p.a. Of which, £3 6s 8d quitrent to the king; £1 6s 8d pension to the vicar; total deductions £4 13s 4d. Clear remainder £8 13s 4d p.a.
Buckinghamshire: the rectory of Bledlow with its tithes ("thenthes"), £20 5s 4d p.a. and "lands late Hitchecockes" belonging to the same, £1; total £21 5s 4d p.a. Of which, 7s quitrent to the provost of Eton; £2 pension to the bishop of Lincoln; 13s 4d to the archdeacon of Bucks; £5 pension to the vicar; 5s to the poor; total deductions £8 5s 4d. Clear remainder £13 p.a.
Yorkshire: the rents of 5 rectories,² including £4 10s for a mill, total £188 10s p.a. Of which, £3 to Sir John Constable, receiver; 6s 8d to the poor; total deductions £3 6s 8d. Clear remainder £185 3s 4d p.a.
Dorset: the rectory of Frampton, including £1 for the chapel of St Laurence, total £25 p.a. Of which, £3 9s 9d pension to the vicar. Clear remainder £21 10s 3d p.a.

[ii]   TEMPORALITIES
London and Middlesex: 3 farms, £220 17s 2d p.a. Of which, £3 6s 8d
pension to the dean and chapter; 1s 1d quitrent to the dean; £1 quitrent to
the Master of the Rolls; 6d quitrent to the warden of the Fleet; £16 16s 8d
fees, as follows: £8 10s to the auditor, £7 collector, 13s 4d bailiff of the
liberty, 13s 4d steward, £3 13s 4d fees of divers counsellors in the law
retained by the college; total deductions £24 19s 1d [sic]. Clear remainder
£195 18s 1d p.a.
Surrey: farms, assize rents and other rents, £9 4s 8d p.a. Of which, 6s 8d
quitrent to the archdeacon of Canterbury. Clear remainder £8 18s p.a.
Norfolk: rents, farms and profits of woods, £26 10s p.a. Of which, 6s 8d
bailiff's fee. Clear remainder £26 3s 4d p.a.
Hampshire: farm of the manor of Winchfield, £22 12s p.a. Of which,
13s 4d steward's fee. Clear remainder £21 18s 8d p.a.
Yorkshire: farm within the city of York, received from the sheriffs there,
£30 p.a.
Dorset: rents and farms of the manor of Frampton in divers towns, hamlets
and parishes, with the profits of courts, £92 13s 11d p.a. Of which, £2 head
steward's fee; 16s 8d understeward's fee; £1 bailiff's fee; 11s 6d stewards'
expenses; total deductions £4 8s 2d. Clear remainder £88 5s p.a.
Assize rents in Bincombe and profits of courts, £18 6s 1d p.a. Of which,
4s 3½d steward's fee. Clear remainder £18 1s 9½d p.a.
Assize rents in Winterborne,[3] £10 p.a.
Assize rents and farm of the manor of Burton with profits of courts,
£50 11s 11d p.a. Of which, 4s 3d steward's fee. Clear remainder £50 6s 8d
p.a.

[iii] [m.34d] *Kent, Sussex, Essex and Hertfordshire:* Assize rents of the
manor of [Elham][4] with farm of demesne lands, wood sales and profits of
courts, £87 13s 1d p.a. Of which, £5 bailiff's fee; 6s 10½d steward's expenses;
total deductions £5 6s 10½d. Clear remainder £82 6s 2½d p.a.
Rents and farms of Ashford (Esschetisforde) and divers towns, hamlets and
parishes, with wood sales and profits of courts, £96 16s 3d p.a. Of which,
1s 6¼d quitrent to the manor of Brabourne; £1 castle ward;[5] £1 to the earl
of Arundel for his manor of Postling; 14s 10d to the dean and chapter of
Canterbury; 4s 2¼d to the king for his manor of [blank];[6] £2 11s 2¼d to the
king for his manor of [blank];[7] total £5 11s 9½d; also £6 13s 4d bailiff's fee;
£2 head steward's fee; 3s 4d understeward's fee; 9s 4¾d understeward's
expenses at courts; total £9 6s 0¾d; grand total of deductions £14 17s 10¼d.
Clear remainder £81 18s 5¾d [sic] p.a.
Rents and farms of the manor of Queen Court and Painters, with demesne
lands, rent of a watermill, wood sales and profits of courts, £51 3s 1½d p.a.
Of which, 10s to Sir Roger Nicholas 'for a quiet of the manor' of Painters;
£3 6s 8d bailiff's fee; 4s 8d steward's expenses; total deductions £4 1s 4d.
Clear remainder £47 1s 9½d p.a.
Farm of the manor of North Court with demesne lands and wood sales,
£16 3s 4d p.a. Of which, £2 5s 8¼d castle ward. Clear remainder £13 17s 7¾d
p.a.
Assize rents of Meres Court in divers parishes and hamlets; farm of the

manor of Meres Court and Bredhurst with demesnes and wood sales, £24 11s 10d p.a. Of which, £2 to the bailiff and receiver. Clear remainder £21 11s 10d p.a.

Farm of lands and marshes in Iwade called Binwall Marsh, £8 p.a. Of which, 8s 3½d quitrent to John Norton; 1s 6d to Thomas Grovehurst; 1s to John Clerke; total deductions 10s 9½d. Clear remainder £7 9s 2½d p.a.

Farm of lands in Halstow 'late Stephen Bulles', £3 6s 8d p.a. Of which, 8s quitrent to John Norton; 2s 3¼d quitrent to the king; total deductions 10s 3¼d. Clear remainder £2 16s 4¾d p.a.

Assize rents of the manor of Witchling (Whitcheling), farm of demesne, wood sales, £12 2s 3½d p.a. Of which, 6d to the sheriff of Kent for blanch rent; £1 6s 1½d castle ward;[8] total deductions £1 6s 7½d. Clear remainder £10 15s 8d p.a.

[*Sussex*]: Farm of the manor of Cooden (Codyng)[9] and demesne, £19 p.a.

[*Essex and Hertfordshire*]: Fee farms in the counties of Essex and Hertford-shire received from the sheriffs, £2 10s p.a.

[iv] Total of all the possessions, 'the deductions not reprised', £1,080 19s 1¾d p.a. Of which, £105 16s 6d [sic] portion, or stipend, to Dr Chamber, dean, viz: £66 13s 4d for the deanery, £2 for his prebend, £4 18s 2d obits, £18 for his "resydeny", £14 for his dividend; £415 8s 8d to 11 canons[10] 'at £37 15s 4d the man by year in such profits as is aforesaid'; £125 16s 2¾d [sic] to 11 vicars[11] at £13 16s 0¼d each in all profits; £29 13s 4d to '4 chantry priests[12] chaplains' at £7 8s 4d each; £36 17s 1d to 4 lay clerks, viz: £11 2s 7¼d to Robert Lawney, £7 15s 11¼d to William Pampyon, £8 2s 7¼d to John Fuller, £9 15s 11¼d to Thomas Wallyes; £28 15s 9d to 7 choristers[13] according to the foundation at £4 2s 3d each; £13 3s 4d verger's fee[14] according to the foundation; £4 1s 6d sub-sexton's fee[15] by patent; £4 9s 8d wages and stipend of the clock-keeper,[16] including 9s 8d for obits; £13 10s spent as follows: £7 10s steward, £5 treasurer, £1 each to the dean and 2 canons auditors; £20 8s 2d tenths to the king. Total deductions £798 0s 2¾d. Clear remainder £282 18s 11d p.a.

[v] [m.35] Lands given by John Chamber, late dean of the college, for 8 poor people:

Middlesex: farm of rents in Staines, £16 p.a. Of which, £1 9s 6d quitrent to the king; 8d to Corpus Christi college, Oxford; total deductions £1 10s 2d. Clear remainder £14 9s 10d p.a.

Surrey: farm of the manor of Hall Place and High Graveney, £21 p.a.

Norfolk: farm of the manor of Setchey (Seche in Southe Lyn) £24, and of a tenement in Wiggenhall £3, total £27 p.a. Of which, 1s 6½d quitrent to the king; 10½d quitrent to the Lord of Oxford; 1s quitrent to the Lady Clifforde; total deductions 3s 5d. Clear remainder £26 16s 7d p.a.

Total lands, reprises not deducted: £64 p.a. Reprises £1 13s 7d. Clear remainder £62 6s 5d p.a.

Payments to 8 poor bedesmen, besides their house-room: £5 6s p.a. each to Robert Derker, Robert Wheler, Nicholas Nelson, John Massy, William Turkyngton, John Shawe, John Kithe, Margaret Charleton as follows: 1s 8d [each] per week (£3 18s p.a.); 3½ yards of cloth for livery at 4s per yard, 14s; 8 yards of cotton for lining, 5s 4d; and 'for the making thereof', 2s; wood and coal, 6s 8d; grand total £42 8s p.a.

Payments to officers: 6s 8d to Robert Derker for keeping the gate of the almshouses; £1 6s 8d to the treasurer for his pains; £7 to Master Reper for his annuity by patent; total £8 13s 4d p.a. Grand total for payments to bedesmen and officers £51 1s 4d. Clear remainder £8 5s 1d [sic] p.a.

SITE OF THE COLLEGE AND OTHER BUILDINGS
The church, cloister and other buildings and lodgings are valued at £25 p.a. as appears in a particular survey made by Philip Lentall. The lodgings in Cannon Row, including 13s 4d for a counting house, also valued by Lentall, £35 6s 8d p.a.

1. Thomas Spilman, receiver of Augmentations for London and Middlesex, see W. C. Richardson, *History of the Court of Augmentations* (Baton Rouge, 1961), 49.
2. Wakefield, Dewsbury, Sandal, Penniston and "Byrton", *Valor*, i, 428.
3. Winterborne Cane (idem).
4. Idem. Illegible here.
5. At Dover (*Valor*, 429).
6. Wye (idem).
7. "Say" in Wye (idem).
8. At Dover (idem).
9. *Valor* has "Codyngton".
10. Thomas Canner, Richard Cockes, William Ibrye, John Donne, John Harbart, Robert Brocke, Thomas Robertson, John Vaughan, Alan Cooke, Thomas Daie and John Rudde (BC).
11. John Virley, Robert Skelton, Richard Mathewe, William Crose, James Rabone, John Meere, John Markaunt, John Pulforde, William Langeborne, John Rogers and Alexander Peryn (BC).
12. John Fountayn, John Forster, Robert Skyres and Hugh Shepye (BC).
13. Thomas Clerke, Thomas Gilberte, William Clerke, John Lane, Nicholas Roddes, John Rudde and Richard Horpe (BC).
14. Nicholas Ludford (BC).
15. Christopher Barton (BC).
16. Bastian Lesney (BC).

190a. TOTAL VALUE OF LANDS IN MIDDLESEX: £1,414 9s 5½d.
TOTAL NUMBER OF COMMUNICANTS: 22,079.
[Signed] Roger Cholmeley; Nich Har; John Godsalve; Wymound Carew; Ric Goodrick; Richard Morysone; Hugh Losse.

[190b.] [m.35d] TOTALS FOR LONDON AND MIDDLESEX
Jewels, ornaments, vestments etc.
London: plate 1,675¾ oz.
    ornaments £252 10s 10d.
Middlesex (except St Stephen's college, whose inventory is with Sir John Godsalve): plate 251⅔ oz
    ornaments £26 11s 6d
Stocks of cattle
Hampton 1 cow; Harrow 1 cow, 1 horse;[1] Chiswick 1 cow; South Mimms 1 cow;[2] Cranford 4 sheep, 2 lambs; Hadley 4 cows; Friern Barnet 4 cows; Tottenham 33 cows: total[3] 69 cows, 1 horse, 4 sheep, 2 lambs.

Lead and bells
Nil, save what remains intact on the buildings of St Stephen's college, Mores chapel in Pardon churchyard and Haliwell chapel.
[Signed]: Roger Cholmeley; Nich Hare; John Godsalve; Wymounde Carew; Rico Goodrick; Richard Morysone; Hugh Losse.

1. But see **162**.
2. But see **117**.
3. See above, n. 1–2. The cattle at Kingsbury are omitted (see **178**), perhaps because they were given to the poor.

[m.36] CORPORATIONS AND COMPANIES OF THE CITY OF LONDON

191. SALTERS[1]
Priest in All Hallows Bread Street: lands given by Thomas Beamounde, £17 17s 4d p.a. Of which, £7 11s 8d to Sir John Cornysshe, priest;[2] 14s 8d quitrent to the king; £3 0s 9d obit; £1 lights; total deductions £12 7s 1d. Clear remainder £5 10s 3d p.a.
Priest in St Mary Magdalene and All Hallows Bread Street: lands given by the same Thomas for his soul for ever, £16 4s p.a. Of which, £6 13s 4d to Sir James Cade [priest]; 10s quitrent to the king; £4 9s 6½d obit; total deductions £11 12s 10½d. Clear remainder £4 11s 1½d p.a.
Priest in St Thomas the Apostle: lands given by Richard Chawrey for ever, £29 6s 8d p.a. Of which, £6 13s 4d to Sir Thomas Wawpole, priest; 10s obit; £1 to prisoners in Newgate; total deductions £8 3s 4d. Clear remainder £21 3s 4d p.a.
Priest and obit in St Matthew Friday Street: lands given by William Clerke, £32 6s 8d p.a. Of which, £7 6s 8d to Sir John Smythe, priest; £1 quitrent to the king; £1 13s 4d obit; total deductions £10. Clear remainder £22 6s 8d p.a.
Obit in the late house of the Friars Minor: lands given by Thomas Brown for ever, £8 p.a. Of which, £1 10s obit. Clear remainder £6 10s p.a.
Obit in St Stephen Walbrook for 20 years: lands given by Sir John Cotes, kt., £4 p.a. Of which, 13s 4d obit. Clear remainder £3 6s 8d p.a.

1. Cf. (for 1546) LR 2/241 fos 47–67, which includes a very full rental.
2. The original wording here, and in most similar entries below, is 'to X, priest, for his stipend'. It was to be an important consideration that these priests were stipendiaries and not endowed chantry priests.

192. SKINNERS[1]
Augmentation of the salary of a priest in St Anthony, and obit there: lands given by John Draper for his soul for ever, £7 10s 8d p.a. Of which, £2 13s 4d to the augmentation of "Gothams"[2] priest; £3 6s 8d to the rector of St Anthony's; £1 1s 8d obit; £1 8s 8d to the poor prisoners of Newgate; total deductions £8 10s 4d. Clear remainder Nil.
Priest and obit in St Mary Aldermary: lands and tenements given by John Uphavering for his soul for ever, £10 13s 4d p.a. Of which, £6 13s 4d to Sir Nicholas Dunston, priest; 6s 8d obit; £2 quitrent to the king; total deductions £9. Clear remainder £1 13s 4d p.a.

Priest in Guildhall chapel, and obit in the charnel house: lands given by Henry Burton for his soul for ever, £36 5s 4d p.a. Of which, £8 to Sir Robert Foxe, priest; £2 6s 8d obit; total deductions £10 6s 8d. Clear remainder £25 18s 8d p.a.

Priest and obit in St Mary Aldermary: lands given by John Clyff for his soul for ever, £17 6s 8d p.a. Of which, £6 13s 4d to Sir Thomas Garnet, priest; 5s quitrent to the king; 13s 4d obit; total deductions £7 11s 8d. Clear remainder £9 15s p.a.

Obits: in St Stephen Walbrook for John Foster; in St Mary Colechurch for William Wyken; in St Anthony for William Dalton; and in St Peter Cornhill for Thomas White: lands given by John Russell, £12 14s 4d p.a. Of which, £1 17s 5d for the 4 obits. Clear remainder £10 16s 11d p.a.

Torches and obits in the chapel of the charnel house: 200 marks were given by Thomas Mursen to buy lands for this purpose, and the master and wardens have entered into a deed of covenant with Mr Judge, late alderman of London,[3] to perform this, committing to this purpose lands worth £12 13s 4d p.a.

Obit in St Mary Aldermary: a tenement in the parish of St Martin Orgar, given by Thomas Welles for his soul for ever: 10s p.a. is spent at the obit.

Obit in St Anthony: lands given by William Gregorie, £2 13s 4d p.a. Of which, 13s 4d quitrent to the king; 5s obit; total deductions 18s 4d. Clear remainder £1 15s p.a.

Obit for John Russell in St Mary at Hill: a tenement, £1 16s 8d p.a. Of which, 17s 8d obit. Clear remainder 19s p.a.

[m.36d] *Two obits in St Botolph Billingsgate:* £2 p.a. spent.

Obit in All Hallows Barking: a tenement called the Ram's Head, given by Nicholas Jennens, £5 p.a. Of which, £1 10s 4d obit. Clear remainder £3 9s 4d p.a.

Priest in St John Walbrook, and obit at Greyfriars: lands and tenements given by John Barre, £12 4s 4d p.a. Of which, £6 13s 4d to Sir Ralph Shepard, priest;[4] 3s 4d obit; 1s 8d lights; total deductions £6 18s 4d. Clear remainder £5 6s p.a.

1. Cf. (for 1546) LR 2/242 fos 133–7, which gives detailed rentals but does not cover all the above endowments.
2. Perhaps *recte* Grauntham's priest, see **26**.
3. Andrew Judge.
4. BC has two priests from this endowment, the other being Richard Straunge.

193. VINTNERS

Chaplain in St Martin [in the Vintry]: lands given by Simon Adam, £7 6s 8d p.a. Of which, £8 to Sir Thomas More, priest. Clear remainder Nil.

Priest at Wilmslow (Wyndeslowe), Ches.: £3 6s 8d p.a. paid by the master and wardens in consideration of £100 given to them by Henry Trayforth.

Priest and obit at the late Friars Preachers: land given by Thomas Roger to yield 5 marks p.a. for a priest and to maintain an obit, £9 12s p.a. Of which, £3 6s 8d p.a. quitrent to the king; 6s 8d obit kept at St Martin's; total deductions £3 13s 4d. Clear remainder £5 18s 8d p.a.

Obit in St Martin in the Vintry: lands given by Thomas Bayne, £2 10s p.a. Of which, £1 obit. Clear remainder £1 10s p.a.

Obit in St James Garlickhithe: lands and tenements given by Nicholas Kent for his soul for ever, £6 p.a. Of which, 8s obit. Clear remainder £5 12s p.a.

Obit for the soul of John Nicholl in St Martin in the Vintry: lands given by Guy (Gwye) Shuldehame for ever, £7 p.a. Of which, 15s obit. Clear remainder £6 12s p.a.

Obit in St Botolph Billingsgate: lands and tenements given by Thomas Owston for his soul for ever, £12 p.a. Of which, 15s 6d obit. Clear remainder £11 4s 6d p.a.

Obit in St Martin in the Vintry: lands and tenements given by William Stafford for his soul for ever, £6 13s 4d p.a. Of which, £1 obit. Clear remainder £5 13s 4d p.a.

Obit in St Magnus: lands and tenements given by Thomas Lewes for his soul for ever, £2 10s p.a. Of which, 15s 5d obit. Clear remainder £1 14s 7d p.a.

194. MERCERS[1]
Obit for Sir William Estfelde in St Mary Aldermanbury; obit for Lymrelmershe in St Martin le Grand; priest in St Mary Aldermanbury: lands given by Sir William Estfelde, £18 4s p.a. Of which, £1 8s 4d for Estfelde's obit; 13s 4d for Lymrelmershe's obit; £6 13s 4d to Sir Edmund Giles, priest; total deductions £8 15s. Clear remainder £9 9s p.a.

Priest and 2 obits in Acon college: lands given by Richard Lakyn, £33 11s p.a. Of which, £1 4s 8d for Lakyn's obit; £1 8s 8d for William Marlere's obit; £6 13s 4d to the churchwardens of St Lawrence Old Jewry towards the Lady mass there; £8 to Sir William Digby, priest;[2] total deductions £17 6s 8d. Clear remainder £16 4s 4d p.a.

Priest and obits: lands and tenements given by William Brown for his soul for ever, £50 19s 4d p.a. Of which, £6 6s 8d quitrents to the king; £1 6s 8d for John Brown's obit in St Mary Magdalene [Milk Street]; £6 13s 4d to a priest singing there; 13s 4d for William Brown's obit in Acon college; £8 6s 8d to a priest singing there; total deductions £23 6s 8d. Clear remainder £27 12s 8d p.a.

Priest and free school at "Fingeringhoo",[3] Northants: lands given by John Abbott, £9 16s 8d p.a. Of which, £6 13s 4d to James Colles, priest. Clear remainder £3 3s 4d p.a.

Priest and obit in St Stephen Coleman Street: lands and tenements given by Dame Joan Bradbury for ever, £12 15s p.a. Of which, £1 13s 4d quitrent to the king; £7 13s 4d to Sir Robert Biging, priest; £3 6s 8d obit; total deductions £12 13s 4d. Clear remainder 1s 8d p.a.

Priest and obit for the soul of John Allen in Acon college: £7 16s 8d paid by the master and wardens under a deed of covenant with Allen who had given £300 for the building of their hall. Of which, £7 6s 8d to the priest; 10s obit.

Priest and obit in St Olave:[4] £200 cash and some lands of unknown value were given in 1516 by Sir Richard Haddon, kt., for his soul for ever. Of which, £7 to Sir Thomas Tickell, priest; £2 obit; total deductions £9. Clear remainder [blank].

[m.37] *Priest and obit in St Pancras:[5]* £233 6s 8d cash given by Margaret

Reynoldes for her soul for ever. Of which, £6 13s 4d to Sir William Stapleford, priest; £2 obit; total deductions £8 13s 4d. Clear remainder [blank].

1. Cf. (for 1546) LR 2/241 fos 27–45.
2. William Dingley in BC, which refers to the institution as the 'chapel of Acres in Cheap'. The Mercers had bought the chapel of the former hospital of St Thomas of Acon. Other priests named here in BC are Anthony Bradshawe, Humfrey Edwardes, Richard Baker and Thomas Harte.
3. *Recte* Farthingho (*Husting*, ii, 574).
4. Hart Street (BC).
5. See **28**.

195. WAXCHANDLERS
Obit in St Benet Grasschurch: lands and tenements given by Roger Brocket, £3 3s 4d p.a. Of which, 10s obit. Clear remainder £2 13s 4d p.a.
Obit in St Michael Queenhithe: lands and tenements given by John Thomson, £8 p.a. Of which, 14s quitrent to the king; £1 obit; 8s lights; £2 13s 3d to the poor; total deductions £4 15s 3d. Clear remainder £3 4s 9d p.a.

196. INNHOLDERS
Obit for 21 years at Hornchurch, Essex: £42 cash was given by John Gefford for his soul, £2 p.a.; 14 years are still to run, leaving £28. Of which, £2 obit. Clear remainder £26.

197. JOINERS
Obit in St James Garlickhithe: lands and tenements given by Agnes Sawmon, £2 p.a. Of which, 13s 4d quitrent to Whittington college; 6s 8d obit; total deductions £1. Clear remainder £1 p.a.

198. GREY TAWYERS
Lamp and obit in All Hallows London Wall: a tenement which is the common hall of the company, given by William Wilson, £4 p.a. Of which, 5s obit; 4s lamp; total deductions 9s. Clear remainder £3 1s p.a.

199. CURRIERS[1]
Obit in St Alphege: lands and tenements given by Thomas Stern, £7 0s 8d p.a. Of which, 16s 8d obit; £1 10s quitrent to the king; total deductions £2 6s 8d. Clear remainder £5 14s p.a.
Obit in St Stephen Coleman Street for Robert Alexaunder: the company are bound to keep this for a further 2 years, but 'how much they be bound thereat to spend for lack of evidence, unknown'.

1. Cf. (for 1546) a negative return in E 301/90.

200. COOPERS
Obit in St Michael Bassishaw: tenements given by John Bager for his soul for ever, £4 6s 8d p.a. Of which, 6s 8d quitrent to Eton college; £1 2s obit; £1 1s to the poor; total deductions £2 9s 8d. Clear remainder £1 17s p.a.

201. PEWTERERS[1]
Obit in St Mary Abchurch: lands and tenements given by Laurence Astelyn for his soul for ever, £5 10s p.a. Of which, 13s 4d quitrent to the king; 10s obit; total deductions £1 3s 4d. Clear remainder £4 6s 8d p.a.
Obit in "Chappesford",[2] Herts., for Robert Astelyn: 6s 8d p.a. quitrent paid to the petty canons of St Paul's who maintain the obit.
Obit for John Goteshame: £1 6s 8d p.a. quitrent paid to the petty canons of St Paul's.

   1. Cf. (for 1546) a negative return in PRO E 117/13/4.
   2. Sawbridgeworth, see *CPR 1549–51*, 400 and *CPR Index*.

202. CORDWAINERS
Obit in St Michael Queenhithe: £1 6s 8d p.a.
Obit in St Sepulchre for Peers Hill: 13s 4d p.a.
Obit in St Dunstan in the West: lands given by John Fyssher, £12 p.a. Of which, 13s 8d obit. Clear remainder £11 6s 4d p.a.

203. FOUNDERS
Contribution to Our Lady brotherhood in St Michael Queenhithe: £1 p.a.

204. CUTLERS
Obit in St Botolph Aldersgate: lands given by Simon Newington, £8 15s p.a. Of which, 9s 3d quitrent to the king; 13s 4d obit; total deductions £1 2s 7d. Clear remainder £7 12s 5d p.a.
Obit in Baldock for John Monke: £1 6s 8d p.a.

205. CARPENTERS
Obit in St Dionys Backchurch and St Andrew Undershaft: lands and tenements given by Thomas Markehame, £10 p.a. Of which, £1 obit. Clear remainder £9 p.a.

206. [m.37d] COOKS**
Obits: in St Dunstan in the West for ... Finche 12s 6d; in ... for John ... 10s 1d; in St Swithin for John S... . Total spent £1 12s 3d p.a.

207. BARBERS
Obit in St Dunstan in the East: lands given by John Johnson, £2 13s 4d p.a. Of which, 2s 8d obit. Clear remainder £2 10s 8d p.a.
Obit in All Hallows Lombard Street: certain plate, given by James Scot: 44 years are still to run at 4s p.a.
Obit in St Martin in the Vintry: a sum of money given by Robert Dalve: 14 years are still to run at 3s 4d p.a.
Obit in St Peter Cornhill: certain plate given by Thomas Grove for his soul for ever [sic]; 7 years are still to run [sic] at 10s p.a.

208. FLETCHERS
Obit: 4s p.a.

209. FISHMONGERS

Obits in St Botolph Aldgate and St Nicholas Cole Abbey: lands given by Henry Jurden, £40 10s 6d p.a. Of which, £7 to Sir John William, priest; £1 14s 8d obit; 6s 8d quitrent to the fraternity of St Giles; £1 15s quitrent to Bow church; 13s 4d quitrent to the king; total deductions £11 9s 8d. Clear remainder £29 0s 10d p.a.

Two priests in St Mary Mounthaw and obit in St Nicholas Cole Abbey: lands and tenements given by John Gloucestor, £14 2s p.a. Of which, £10 to Robert Knight and Wyberd Gilby, priests (£5 each); 3s 4d quitrent to St Mildred's; 13s 4d obit; total deductions £10 16s 8d. Clear remainder £3 5s 4d p.a.

Priest at St Austin Hackney; contribution of £3 6s 8d to the rector of Ilford, Essex, and obits in St Margaret Moses and St Margaret Bridge Street: lands and tenements given by John Heron, £22 6s 8d p.a. Of which, £6 13s 4d to a priest in Hackney; £3 6s 8d to the rector of Ilford; 13s 4d obits; total deductions £10 13s 4d. Clear remainder £11 13s 4d p.a.

Obit in St Peter West Cheap:[1] lands and tenements given by Agnes (Annes) Palmer, £15 13s 4d p.a. Of which, £6 13s 4d to Sir Christopher Reynoldes, priest; £1 6s 8d obit; £1 14s to St Leonard's church; total deductions £9 14s. Clear remainder £5 19s 4d p.a.

Two obits in Guildhall chapel: lands given by Thomas Knesworthe, £98 7s p.a. Of which, £4 5s 4d obit. Clear remainder £94 1s 8d p.a.

Obit in St Margaret Bridge Street: lands given by Richard Knight, £7 8s p.a. Of which, 13s 4d obit. Clear remainder £6 14s 8d p.a.

Obit in St Mary at Hill: lands given by John Mougeshame, £4 p.a. Of which, 10s obit. Clear remainder £3 10s p.a.

Obit in St Botolph Billingsgate: lands given by Lettice Smyth, £4 p.a. Of which, 10s obit. Clear remainder £3 10s p.a.

Obit in St Michael Crooked Lane: lands given by John Awood, £7 6s 8d p.a. Of which, £1 1s 2d obit. Clear remainder £6 5s 6d p.a.

Obit in St Mildred: lands given by William Copinger, £4 16s 8d p.a. Of which, 6s 2d quitrent to the king; 4s obit; total deductions 10s 2d. Clear remainder £4 6s 6d p.a.

Obit in St Sepulchre: lands and tenements given by John Aston, £12 1s 8d p.a. Of which, 6s quitrent to the king; 1s 1d quitrent to St Sepulchre's; 13s 4d obit; total deductions £1 0s 5d. Clear remainder £11 1s 3d p.a.

Obit in St Mary Somerset: lands given by Elizabeth Wilford, £4 2s 4d p.a. Of which, £1 obit. Clear remainder £3 2s 4d p.a.

Obit in St Mary at Hill: lands given by William Remington, £2 16s p.a. Of which, 15s obit. Clear remainder £2 1s p.a.

Obit in St Mary at Hill for Henry Gyfford: 6s 8d p.a. is spent.

Obits in St Magnus and in St Michael Crooked Lane: £1 13s 4d p.a. is spent.

Two torches in St Paul's cathedral: £1 4s p.a.

Lamp in St Mary Somerset: 4s p.a.

1. Originally a chantry and obit. See the original return for St Peter's in 1546 (E301/120). Cf. **99**.

210. IRONMONGERS

Obit in St Nicholas Olave:[1] £140 cash, and lands and tenements amounting to £11 6s 8d p.a., given by Thomas Michell. Of which, 2s 6d quitrent to the king; £6 13s 4d to Sir William Bucknell, priest; £1 6s 6d obit; total deductions £8 2s 4d. Clear remainder £3 4s 4d p.a.

[m.38] *Obits in St Mary at Hill and St Leonard East Cheap:*[2] lands and tenements given by Humphrey Barnes, £11 p.a. Of which, £2 3s 4d obits. Clear remainder £8 16s 8d p.a.

Obit in St Leonard East Cheap for 80 years to come: lands and tenements given by Elizabeth Gyva, £6 13s 4d p.a. Of which, £1 6s 8d obits. Clear remainder £5 6s 8d p.a.

Obit: £40 cash given by Thomas Dorchester for his soul for ever, 8s p.a.

Priest in St Mary Colechurch for seven years to come: £7 p.a. paid Sir Robert Sandewiche.

Obit in St Benet Grasschurch for Robert Smyth: £2 16s p.a. is spent.

1. BC has this in St Olave Jewry.
2. '. . . the one within the church of St Mary at Hill and the other within the church of St Mary at Hill Leonards East Cheap'.

211. MERCHANT TAYLORS[1]

Priest at the North side of St Paul's and obit: lands and tenements given by Thomas Carleton for ever, £9 8s p.a. Of which, £6 13s 4d to Sir John Turnor, priest; 10s obit; total deductions £7 3s 4d. Clear remainder £3 4s 8d p.a.

Priest and lamp in St Martin Outwich: lands and tenements given by John Churcheman, £30 6s 8d p.a. Of which, £6 13s 4d to Sir John Wilkenson, priest; £3 6s 8d augmentation of a priest's living; 17s quitrent to the king; 6s obit; 16s lamp; total deductions £11 19s. Clear remainder £18 7s 8d p.a.

Obit in St Mary Abchurch: lands and tenements given by William Turnell, £2 p.a. Of which, 15s 1d obit. Clear remainder £1 4s 11d p.a.

Obit in St Mary Aldermary: lands and tenements given by Ralph Hollande, £6 16s 8d p.a. Of which, 13s 4d obit. Clear remainder £6 3s 4d p.a.

Obit in St Martin Outwich: lands given by Edith Hilliat, £4 16s 4d p.a. Of which, 6s 8d obit. Clear remainder £4 9s 8d p.a.

Obit in St Mary Abchurch: lands given by Ellen Langewiche, £12 6s 8d p.a. Of which, £2 6s 2d quitrent to the king; 16s 8d obit; total deductions £3 2s 10d. Clear remainder £9 3s 10d p.a.

Obit in St Martin Outwich: lands given by Hugh Candysshe, £20 13s 4d p.a. Of which, 16s 8d obit. Clear remainder £19 16s 8d p.a.

Priest and obit for the soul of Thomas Hoddam for ever in St Mary Abchurch: £333 6s 8d cash and some plate was bequeathed by Hoddam. Of which, £7 3s 4d to the priest;[2] £1 7s obit, including 12s 9d to the poor; total deductions £8 10s 4d p.a.

Two priests and obit in St Mary Woolnoth: lands and tenements given by John Percevall, £43 p.a. Of which, £6 13s 4d to Sir John Palmer, priest; £6 13s 4d to Sir Thomas Somerton, priest; £2 10s obit; total deductions £15 16s 8d. Clear remainder £27 3s 4d p.a.

Augmentation of the same priests' livings: lands given by Dame Thomasine (Thamesyn) Percevall, £18 13s 4d p.a. Of which, £2 13s 4d augmentation; £2 6s 8d for an anthem and beam light; £2 1s 10d for an obit; total deductions £7 1s 10d. Clear remainder £11 11s 6d p.a.

Priest and obit in All Hallows Bread Street for 2 years to come: £7 p.a. paid to Sir Harry [blank], incumbent; 13s 4d spent at obit including 1s 9d to the poor. Total spent £7 13s 4d p.a.

Priest and obit in St Mary Woolnoth for 72 years to come: in return for £200 given by Joan Hilton. The present priest, John Fyssher, receives £7 p.a. and the obit costs 13s 4d including 1s 11d to the poor. Total spent £7 13s 4d p.a.

Priest in St Martin Outwich: lands bought from ready cash given by Matthew Pemerton, £24 14s 8d p.a. Of which, £8 to Sir George Sharpe, priest; 12s quitrent to the king; total deductions £8 12s Clear remainder £16 2s 8d p.a.

Obit in St Martin Outwich for the soul of Gerard Braysebroke: £2 p.a. spent.

Obit in St Mary Colechurch for ever: in return for £100 given by John Kirkebie £1 p.a. is spent.

Obit in St Pancras for John Hadley: £1 p.a. is spent.

Priest in St Peter Cornhill: £7 p.a. given to Sir Robert Stockes.

Beam light in St Peter Cornhill: 13s 4d p.a. is spent.

*Obit in St Michael Cornhill:** lands given by Robert Shether, £4 1s p.a. Of which [16s 5d][3] obit. Clear remainder [£3 4s 7d p.a.][4]

[m.38d] *Obit:** ... £1 6s 8d p.a. spent.

*Obit in St Mary Abchurch:** lands given by Richard S... , £6 ... p.a. Of which, £1 0s 6d obit. Clear remainder £5... p.a.

Obit in St Anthony for Thomas Speight for 26 years to come, with 4s 6d to the poor, £1 p.a.

Obit in St Leonard East Cheap for John Palmer with one year to come: £1 6s 8d p.a. including 12s 9d to the poor.

Obit in St Mary Aldermary for John Britton with 15 years to come: 15s p.a. spent including 3s 4d to the poor.

Obit in St Martin Outwich for Hugh Talbot: 4s 11d spent including 1s 2d to the poor; unknown how long it is to run.

1. Cf. (for 1546) LR 2/241 fos 7–19.
2. Robert Waterhouse (E 101); Robert Waterall (BC).
3. Supplied from Guildhall Microfilm 298.
4. Calculated from the preceding figures.

212. GROCERS[1]

Obit in St Anthony:[2] lands given by Simon Streat, £2 6s 8d p.a. Of which, £1 obit including 4s to the poor. Clear remainder £1 6s 8d p.a.

Obit in St Dunstan in the East: lands given by John Maldon, £5 6s 8d p.a. Of which, 9s quitrent to the king; £1 obit; total deductions £1 9s. Clear remainder £3 17s 8d p.a.

Priest and obit in St Stephen Walbrook: lands and tenements given by Elizabeth Burell, £16 6s 8d p.a. Of which, £8 to [Sir][3] Henry Cockes, priest; £1 10s to a chantry priest in St Paul's cathedral; 6s quitrent to the king; £2 obit; total deductions £11 16s. Clear remainder £4 10s 8d p.a.

Priest and obit in St Mary Aldermary: lands and tenements given by Henry Kebell for ever, £28 p.a. Of which, £3 8s obit; £7 3s 8d to Sir Thomas Artes, priest; total deductions £10 11s 8d. Clear remainder £17 8s 4d p.a.

Priest and obit in Biddenham, Beds. and obit 'in London':[4] lands and tenements given by Sir William Buttler, kt., £25 7s 8d p.a. Of which, 6s quitrent to the king; £6 to Sir Henry Atkinson, priest; £4 18s 4d obit; £1 to the poor sisters of Elsing Spittal; total deductions £12 4s 4d. Clear remainder £13 3s 4d p.a.

Obit for John Pechye in "Bullington",[5] *Kent:* £3 p.a. spent including £1 6s 8d to the poor.

Priest and obit in St Peter Cornhill: lands and tenements given by Henry Ade, £28 15s 4d p.a. Of which, £7 10s to Sir Nicholas Jackeson; £6 16s 8d obit; total deductions £14 6s 8d. Clear remainder £14 8s 8d p.a.

Two priests and obit in the chapel of Hallywell, Midd.: lands given by John Billesdon for his soul for ever, £33 16s 8d p.a. Of which, £10 to a priest[6] at Thorpe Salvin, Yorks; £8 to Sir James Hurst, priest; £8 to Sir Richard Maryf; £1 18s 4d obit; total deductions £27 18s 4d p.a. Clear remainder £5 18s 4d p.a.

Obit:[7] in return for £100 given by Sir Nicholas Lamberd, £2 p.a. is spent, including 14s to the poor.

Obit in St Botolph Billingsgate: lands and tenements given by Nicholas West, £4 p.a. Of which, £1 10s obit. Clear remainder £2 10s p.a.

Obit in St Mary Woolchurch for the soul of John Trystram: £1 7s 4d p.a. spent, 'but for how long it is not known'.

Priest in Glynde, Suss.: lands given by Thomas Crull for ever, £7 13s 4d p.a. Of which, 13s 4d quitrent to the king; £6 13s 4d to Sir Brian Newton, priest; total deductions £7 6s 8d. Clear remainder 6s 8d p.a.

Priest and obit in St Mary Magdalene Milk Street: in return for £180 given by Sir Thomas Exmewe, kt., £7 6s 8d p.a. is spent.

1. Cf. (for 1546) LR 2/243 fos 93–102, which includes an inventory. This entry has also been compared with the company accounts in Guildhall MS. 11571/5.
2. For Sir Stephen Brown (MS. 11571/5).
3. Ibid.
4. At St Stephen Walbrook (idem).
5. Sic. MS. 11571/5 and *Husting*, ii, 255 have Lullingstone.
6. Sir George Oxley (MS. 11571/5). The other two priests were at Haliwell (BC).
7. In St Stephen Walbrook (MS. 11571/5).

213. SADDLERS[1]

Two priests in the Long chapel at St Paul's cathedral: £21 1s 8d p.a. given to the dean and chapter of St Paul's.

Two chaplains for the soul of Walter Waldesheff in Boylstone, Derb.: £9 p.a. is spent.

Obit in St Vedast: lands and tenements given by William Caldewell, £10 16s 8d p.a. Of which, £1 6s 8d obit including 6s 8d to the poor. Clear remainder £9 10s p.a.

Obit in St Vedast: lands given by John Aston, £6 2s 4d p.a. Of which, 18s 2d obit including 4d to the poor. Clear remainder £5 4s 2d p.a.

1. Cf. (for 1546) LR 2/243 fos 109–11.

214. TALLOW CHANDLERS

Priest and obit in St Botolph Bishopsgate: lands given by Edward Steward, £19 18s 8d p.a. Of which, 18s quitrent to the king; £6 13s 4d to Sir Richard

Nelson, priest; £1 12s 6d obit; total deductions £9 3s 10d. Clear remainder £10 14s 10d p.a.
Obit in St Margaret: lands given by Stephen Lyttlebaker, £5 p.a. Of which, £1 5s 4d obit including 12s to the poor. Clear remainder £3 14s 8d p.a.

215. [m.39] ARMOURERS[1]
Priest and obit in St Peter the Poor[2] and augmentation of Barnard's chaplain: lands and tenements given by William at Stocke for ever, £24 10s p.a. Of which, £6 13s 4d to Sir James Payn, priest; £2 6s 8d to augment Barnard's chaplain;[3] £1 obit; total deductions £10. Clear remainder £14 10s p.a.
Obit in St Sepulchre: lands given by John Buttler, £9 p.a. Of which, 11s obit; 5s quitrent to St Sepulchre; total deductions 16s. Clear remainder £8 4s p.a.

1. Cf. Guildhall MS. 12140/2 for greater detail, and for 1546, MS. 12140/1.
2. *Recte* St Peter the Less (Paul's Wharf).
3. Cf. **60**.

216. CLOTHWORKERS[1]
Priest at Chilham, Kent: lands and tenements given by Robert Pele, £19 6s 8d p.a. Of which, 1s obit; £9 6s 8d to the priest; total deductions £9 7s 8d. Clear remainder £9 19s p.a.
Obit in Whittington college and divine lecture[2] thrice every week: lands given by James Finche, £30 0s 4d p.a. Of which, £10 to the reader of the lecture; £2 obit; £3 6s 8d quitrent to the church of All Hallows the Great; total deductions £15 6s 8d. Clear remainder £14 13s 4d p.a.
Obit in All Hallows the Great, Thames Street: lands and tenements given by William Gardener, £14 7s p.a. Of which, £4 quitrent to the king; 10s 6d obit; total deductions £4 10s 6d. Clear remainder £9 16s 6d p.a.
Obit in St Bartholomew the Less: lands given by John Felde, £11 10s p.a. Of which, 6d quitrent to the king; 10s obit; total deductions 10s 6d. Clear remainder £10 9s 6d p.a.
Obit in St Martin Outwich: lands given by Richard Gardener, £5 4s p.a. Of which, £1 3s 4d obit with 4s 4d to the poor. Clear remainder £4 0s 8d p.a.
Obit in Whittington college: lands and tenements given by Margaret, countess of Kent, £11 16s 8d p.a. Of which, £3 11s 8d obit. Clear remainder £7 5s [sic] p.a.
Obits in St Anthony for Dr Taylor and in St Mary Aldermary for John Shepard: maintained by the company but not endowed with land: respectively 7s 2d and 10s, total 17s 2d p.a.

1. Cf. (for 1546) LR 2/242 fos 127–30.
2. Lectures of divinity (ibid. fo. 129).

217. ALE BREWERS[1]
Priest and obit in St James Garlickhithe: lands and tenements given by Isabel Harte, £30 p.a. Of which, £8 to Sir Henry George, priest; £3 6s obit; total deductions £11 6s. Clear remainder £18 14s p.a.
Priest in St Dunstan in the West: lands and tenements given by John Knapp, £20 5s 4d p.a. Of which, £7 to Sir Edmund Elye, priest; 19s quitrent to the king; total deductions £7 19s. Clear remainder £12 6s 4d p.a.

Obit in St Mary Matfelon: lands given by John Leving, £3 p.a. Of which, 10s obit including 3s 4d to the poor. Clear remainder £2 10s p.a.

Obit in All Hallows Barking, for Edward Jones for 14 years to come: 10s p.a. is spent.

Priest in St Mary Aldermary: £6 13s 4d p.a. stipend.

    1. Cf. (for 1546) LR 2/243 fos 103–8.

218. CLERKS[1]

Four obits in Guildhall chapel: lands given by William Dwight for ever, £5 8s 5d p.a. Of which, 8d quitrent to the king; 8s obit; total deductions 8s 8d. Clear remainder £5 p.a.

Obits: in St Giles Cripplegate for Alexander Walshe and in the hospital of St Katharine by the Tower for Hugh Grey: lands given by Richard Wright, £3 p.a. Of which, 6s 7d for Walshe's obit including 6d to the poor; 13s 8d for Grey's obit including 3s 7d to the poor; total deductions £1 0s 3d. Clear remainder £1 19s 9d p.a.

    1. The Parish Clerks' Company was judged by the court of Augmentations not to be a craft or mystery, and was ordered to surrender all its assets shortly afterwards, see PRO E 315/105 fo. 212. For the subsequent history of the company, see R. H. Adams, *The Parish Clerks of London* (1971).

219. LEATHERSELLERS

Priest and obit in St Mary Magdalene, Southwark, Surrey: John Scrages gave lands for these purposes, which the company have long since sold, but they keep up the payments, viz.: £7 1s 8d to the priest; £2 4s 4d obit; £1 6s 8d to the poor; 6s 8d to the prisoners in Newgate; total deductions £10 19s 4d. Clear remainder [blank].

220. [m.39d] HABERDASHERS

Two priests and obit for the soul of Dr Dowman at the altar of St Martha in St Paul's cathedral: £22 p.a. rent given to the dean and chapter who pay £8 p.a. each to the priests and spend £6 on the obit.

Priest to sing for Thomas Justice at Reading, Berks: £7 p.a. rent given to the mayor and burgesses of Reading who pay £6 to the priest and retain £1 for their pains. In consideration of 400 marks given to the company by Justice.

Obit in St Michael Hogen Lane: lands and tenements given by Thomas Exmeux for ever, £3 6s 8d p.a. Of which, £1 13s 4d obit including 16s 2d to the poor. Clear remainder £1 13s 4d p.a.

Obit in St Katherine Cree: lands and tenements given by Stephen Smyth, £3 6s 8d p.a. Of which, £1 10s obit. Clear remainder £1 16s 8d p.a.

Obit in St George Botolph Lane for the soul of Thomas Gale: £1 6s 8d p.a. is spent, including 4s to the poor.

Obit in St Mary Staining for the soul of Henry Somner: £1 10s p.a. including 12s for the poor.

Obit in St Martin for the soul of Stephen Pecocke: £6 2s 8d p.a. is spent, including £1 5s 4d to the poor.

Obit in St Paul's cathedral for the soul of John Gothame: £1 1s 8d p.a. is paid to the petty canons.

Obit in St Andrew Undershaft for the soul of John Godyne: 10s p.a. is spent.

221. DYERS

Priest and obit in St Peter the Poor for the soul of Robert Lunde: £5 6s 8d p.a. is spent. Of which, £1 obit including 16s 3d to the poor; £4 6s 8d to the priest.

Stipendiary priest in St Michael, Coventry for the soul of John Tate: £5 6s 8d p.a. is paid.

222. GOLDSMITHS

Two priests and obits in All Hallows Bread Street and St Peter West Cheap: lands and tenements given by John Walpole, £31 10s p.a. Of which, £13 6s 8d to the priests; £1 6s 8d quitrent to St Paul's cathedral; 13s 4d quitrent to the king; total deductions £15 6s 8d. Clear remainder £16 3s 4d p.a.

Priest and obit in St John Zachary: lands and tenements given by Hugh Wetherby, £14 8s 2d p.a. Of which, £6 13s 4d to the priest; £1 11s 2d obit; total deductions £8 4s 6d. Clear remainder £6 3s 8d p.a.

Two priests in St Michael Crooked Lane: lands and tenements given by John Patesley, £49 p.a. Of which, 12s quitrent to the king; £2 6s 8d to a chantry priest in St Paul's cathedral; £14 13s 4d to the two priests; 13s 4d obit; total deductions £18 5s 4d. Clear remainder £30 14s 8d p.a.

Priest and obit in Cromer, Norfolk: lands and tenements given by Bartholomew Rede for his soul for ever, £50 10s 8d p.a. Of which, £12 3s 4d to a priest; £2 6s 8d obit; total deductions £14 10s. Clear remainder £36 0s 8d p.a.

Priest and obit in St Matthew Friday Street: lands and tenements given by Thomas Polle, £15 13s 4d p.a. Of which, £6 to the priest; 13s 4d obit; total deductions £6 13s 4d. Clear remainder £9 p.a.

Priest and obit: 400 marks formerly given to this use by Thomas Exmeux for his soul for ever was surrendered to the crown while Wolsey was Chancellor, as witnessed by a tripartite indenture.

Priest in St Foster: 500 marks formerly given by John Thurston for his soul for ever was surrendered as above.

Priest in St Vedast: lands and tenements given by William Stamelden for ever, £7 6s 8d p.a. Of which, £6 13s 4d to the priest; 13s 4d obit; total deductions £7 6s 8d. Clear remainder Nil.

Priest and obit in St Foster: lands and tenements given by John Carbonell for ever, £14 16s 8d p.a. Of which, 15s quitrent to the king; £6 13s 4d to Sir James Serle, priest; 13s 4d obit; total deductions £8 1s 8d. Clear remainder £6 15s p.a.

Chaplain at Longdendale, Ches., and grammar school master and obit at Stockport (Topford), Ches.: lands given by Thomas Fereby, £51 2s 8d p.a. Of which, 13s 4d quitrent to the king; £10 to the school master, who is to be well learned; £4 6s 8d to the chaplain, 'for the ease of the people being far distant from the parish church'; £2 1s 4d obit; 12s to the poor; total deductions £17 13s 4d. Clear remainder £33 9s 4d p.a.

[m.40] *Chantry lands:* £14 8s 8d p.a. Of which, 9s 1d quitrent to the king; £6 13s 4d to the chantry priest; total deductions £7 2s 5d. Clear remainder £7 6s 3d p.a.

Relief of the company's blind, lame and weak, and obit in St John Zachary:

lands given by John Frauncis, £18 17s 8d p.a. Of which, £2 quitrent to the king; 14s obit; total deductions £2 14s. Clear remainder £16 3s 8d p.a.

Lamp and obit: lands given to the rector of St Foster and to the company by John Standolf for his soul for ever, £8 18s 4d p.a. Of which, £1 0s 4d obit; £1 1s 8d to 13 poor goldsmiths; 8s lamp; total deductions £2 10s. Clear remainder £6 8s 4d p.a.

Gowns to 13 poor goldsmiths every third year, and obit of Hugh Barrentine: lands given by John Hilles, £18 17s 8d p.a. Of which, 16s to the keeper of Our Lady's light at St Paul's cathedral; £2 12s to the poor in coal; £4 17s 6d black gowns given to 13 poor men every third year; total deductions £8 5s 6d. Clear remainder £2 12s 6d p.a.

Relief of the blind, sick and lame of the company and obit in St Peter Cheap: lands given by John Carler, £7 3s 4d p.a. Of which, 1s quitrent to St Bride's; £1 3s 4d obit; 6s 6d to 13 poor almsmen; 6d to the beadle, a poor man; total deductions £1 11s 4d. Clear remainder £5 12s p.a.

Obit in St Vedast: lands given by John Edmundes for his soul for ever, £4 9s 4d p.a. Of which, £1 5s 10d obit; 6s 8d to the poor; total deductions £1 12s 6d. Clear remainder £2 16s 10d p.a.

Obit in St Peter West Cheap, and relief of the poor: lands and tenements given by William Walton, £22 6s 8d p.a. Of which, £13 14s 8d to 4 almsmen; £1 13s 4d obit; 3s 4d to the poor; total deductions £15 11s 4d. Clear remainder £5 15s 4d p.a.

Obit in St John Zachary: lands given by Robert Fenrother, £2 p.a. Of which, £1 18s 8d obit. Clear remainder 1s 4d p.a.

Obit in St Martin[1] Friday Street and 1s 4d a week to two poor widows: lands given by Agas Harding, £9 13s 4d p.a. Of which, £3 9s 4d to 2 almswomen; £1 4s obit; 2s 8d to the poor; total deductions £4 16s. Clear remainder £4 17s 4d p.a.

Obit in St Alphege and £5 4s to the poor: lands given by Alice (Ales) Lupsett for ever, £6 p.a. Of which, 7s 8d obit; 8d to the poor 'resorting thither'; £5 4s to 12 almsmen; total deductions £5 12s 4d. Clear remainder 7s 8d p.a.

Obit in St Foster: lands given by William Button for ever, £11 13s 4d p.a. Of which, 8s 4d quitrent; £6 13s 4d to a priest there; £1 obit; total deductions £8 1s 8d. Clear remainder £3 11s 8d p.a.

Obit in St Leonard, and relief of 2 poor men: lands and tenements given by Oliver Davy for ever, £20 16s 8d p.a. Of which, 15s quitrent to the king; £1 2s 10d obit; 3s 10d to the poor; £6 1s 4d to two almsmen; total deductions £8 3s. Clear remainder £12 13s 8d p.a.

Obit in St Foster, and poor relief: lands given by Richard Bradocke, £1 17s p.a. Of which, 6s quitrent to the king; 17s 8d obit; 13s 4d to the poor; total deductions £1 17s. Clear remainder Nil.

Four other obits: £3 0s 4d p.a. spent: no lands.

Quitrent to St Martin Ludgate: £3 6s 8d p.a.

Lamp in St Edmund Lombard Street: £1 p.a.

Obit in St Foster: lands given by John Alen for ever, £32 13s 4d p.a. Of which, £3 2s quitrent to the king; £1 3s 2d obit; total deductions £4 5s 2d. Clear remainder £28 8s 2d p.a.

1. *Recte* St Matthew.

223. WHITE BAKERS

Augmentation of a priest in St Martin Pomery: lands given by Robert Brocket for his soul and others, £11 10s p.a. Brocket provided in his will that if no priest was found 'for lack of honest behaving himself' or any other reason the money, limited to £2 16s 8d p.a., should be given to provide bread for prisoners in the 4 prisons of London, and for an obit in St Martin, and other charges. Now spent as follows: 13s 4d obit; 10s to the poor; £1 to Alice Brocked [sic] for life; £2 16s 8d to prisoners in the 4 prisons; total deductions £5. Clear remainder £6 10s p.a.

224. DRAPERS*1

Two chantry priests, and relief of the poor brethren and sisters of the company: lands and tenements given by Maud at Vine and Robert Clopton for ever, £33 11s 4d p.a. Of which, £6 13s 4d to a chantry priest in St Edmund Lombard Street; £6 13s 4d to the rector of Clopton, Cambs; total deductions £13 6s 8d. Clear remainder £20 4s 8d p.a.

Priest and obit: lands given by William Cawley for his soul for ever, £21 6s 8d p.a. Of which, £5 quitrent to the king; £6 13s 4d stipend of a priest;2 16s 8d obit; 4s 8d to the poor; total deductions £12 14s [8d].3 Clear remainder £8 12s p.a.

[m.40d] *Priest and obit [in St Christopher]:* lands and tenements given by Alice [Harlewyn], £31 1s 4d p.a. Of which, £6 13s 4d to Sir William [Widensor]; 13s 8d obit; 13s 4d lamp; 16s 8d …;4 total deductions £8… Clear remainder £22 2s 8d [sic] p.a.

Lady priest and obit in St Mary Abchurch for the soul of Henry Eburton for a further 20 years: £1 p.a. is spent, including 4s 4d to the poor.

Priest and obit: lands given by William Brothers for ever, £19 14s p.a. Of which, £9 6s 8d to Sir William Baylie, priest; £1 11s obit; 9s to the poor; total deductions £11 6s 8d [sic]. Clear remainder £8 7s 4d p.a.

Obit: lands and tenements given by Sir John Ruddeston, kt., for his soul for ever, £3 10s p.a. Of which, £1 13s 4d obit; 6s 8d to the poor; total deductions £2. Clear remainder £1 10s p.a.

Obit: lands and tenements given by Thomas Cartar for his soul for ever, £5 p.a. Of which, £1 3s 6d obit; 3s 2d to the poor; total deductions £1 6s 8d. Clear remainder £3 13s 4d p.a.

Obit: lands given by William Brothers as above, for his soul for ever, £6 1s 8d p.a. Of which, £1 10s obit; 16s 8d to the poor; total deductions £2 6s 8d. Clear remainder £3 15s p.a.

Obit: lands and tenements given by John Norman, £13 p.a. Of which, 13s 4d quitrent to All Hallows;5 10s quitrent to Sir Thomas [Hawes]; 15s obit; 5s to the poor; total deductions £2 13s 4d. Clear remainder £10 16s 8d p.a.

Obit: lands and tenements given by Maud Wylde for her soul for ever, £6 3s 4d p.a. Of which, 5s quitrent to the king; 13s 4d obit; 3s 4d to the poor; total deductions £1 1s 8d. Clear remainder £5 1s 8d p.a.

Obit: lands and tenements given by Alice Hungerford for her soul for ever, £4 p.a. Of which, 19s 8d obit; 7s 6d to the poor; total deductions £1 7s 2d. Clear remainder £2 12s 10d p.a.

Obit: lands and tenements given by William Whyte for his soul for ever,

£5 16s p.a. Of which, 16s 8d obit; 9s 4d to the poor; total deductions £1 6s. Clear remainder £4 10s p.a.

Obit for Richard Norman: formerly kept in the church of the Austin Friars, £2 13s 4d p.a. Now paid to Hugh Losse Esq. for the king.

Obit: a further £1 p.a. is spent 'of their own devotion'.

Obit: lands and tenements given by Thomas Carter for ever, £1 9s 4d p.a. Of which, £1 6s 10d obit; 2s 6d to the poor; total deductions £1 9s 4d. Clear remainder Nil.

Obit: lands and tenements given by William Prowde for ever, £9 p.a. Of which, £1 3s 4d obit; £4 10s to the poor; total deductions £5 13s 4d. Clear remainder £3 6s 8d p.a.

Obit: lands given by William Cawley, £4[6] p.a. Of which, 18s 4d obit; 2s 8d to the poor; total deductions £1 1s. Clear remainder £3 19s p.a.

Obit in St Michael Cornhill for John Tole, draper, with 20 years still to run: £2 3s p.a. including 16s 6d to the poor.

Obits in the Austin Friars (£1 6s 8d) and at Winchester college (£1 6s 8d): lands given by William Cawley, £17 8s p.a. Of which, 10s blankets and sheets to the poor of Winchester; 3s 4d to the mayor and bailiffs there; 3s 4d to the wardens and others there; 3s 4d to the poor; £1 10s to the poor for '3,000 of tallwood'; 13s 4d to the provider of the same; total deductions £2 13s 4d. Clear remainder £14 14s 8d p.a.

1. Parts of this entry are badly faded owing to its being on the final membrane, used effectively as the wrapper in the past. Names supplied in square brackets without comment are taken from a later copy of the original certificate, in the possession of the Drapers' Company (A III. 129) and printed in A. H. Johnson, *History of the Worshipful Company of the Drapers*, ii (Oxford, 1915), 343–79. This contains much additional detail on the properties, the names of churches where the obits were celebrated, and extensive notes.
2. Sir Thomas Welles (A III. 129).
3. Margin damaged.
4. These deductions are almost illegible. In A III. 129 they are in any case quite different: £1 9s obit; 1s to a poor clerk; 3s to other poor; 13s 4d in coals to the poor; total deductions £2 6s 4d.
5. Honey Lane.
6. There is a blot over this figure, which should read £5 if the sums are to balance.

224a. TOTALS FOR THE COMPANIES

Lands etc. £1,050 4s 8d p.a.

Deductions £960 5s 0½d.

Clear remainder £89 19s 7[½]d[1] p.a.

[Signed] Richard Chulmely; Nich. Hare; John Car[rell];[2] Wymounde Carew; Rico Goodrick; Richard Moryson; Hugh Losse.

1–2. Margin torn.

INDEX OF PERSONS AND PLACES

References in Roman numerals are to pages in the Introduction; those in Arabic numerals are to serial. numbers in the calendar. Names of tenements appear under 'tenements, named' in the Subject Index.

Henry IV, xvi, 102
Henry VI, 152
Henry VII, 112
Henry VIII, obit for, 190(i)
Herford, *see* Harford
Herne, William, 179
Heron, John, 209
Hertfordshire, rents etc. in, 190(iii)
Herwode, *see* Harwood
Heston (Midd.), 187; parishioners of, 153;
    "Godfrey Acre", "Grove Place", and
    "North Hyde", 187
Hewlet, Philip, 132
Hey-, *see* Hay-
Hickley, John, priest, 139
Hickmans, Thurstan, priest, 109
Hilday (Hylday), John, poulter, 100
Hill
    John, 107
    John, priest, 108
    Peers, 202
    Thomas, 179
Hillard, Helen, 133
Hilliat, Edith, 211
Hillingdon (Midd.), xxxi *bis*, 128
Hills, John, 222
Hiltoft, John, 108
Hilton, Joan, 211
Hinde, *see* Hynde
Hoddam, Thomas, 211
Hodson, Thomas, 114; *cf.* Hudson
Hogget, William, priest, 32
Holland (Hollonde)
    Edward, priest, 23b
    Henry, 21
    John, priest, 60
    Ralph, 88, 211
Holleghe, John de, 77
Holmes, Mother, 20
Holmes college, *see* St Paul's
Holy Trinity Aldgate, priory ('college'
    of Christchurch), 19
Holy Trinity the Less, xxvi, 85
Home, Roger, chancellor of St Paul's, 108
Honnesdon, William, 185
Honylande, William, priest, 53
Hope
    John, priest, 15n
    Robert, 2
    William, 63
Hopkins, — , 158
Hopper, Alice, 20
Hopton, John, priest, 51
Horde, Thomas, priest, 32n
Horlyn, Roger, 75
Hornchurch (Essex), 196
Horner, Thomas, conduct, 31a
Hornsey (Midd.), xxxi, 129; manor, 129
Horpe, Richard, chorister, 190n
Horsey, John, 119

Horsham, Thomas, 20
Hough, William, priest, 109
Hounslow (Midd.), xxxii *bis*, 145, 153
Hubthorne, Henry, kt., 90
Hude, Joan, 151
Hudson
    John, 114
    John, priest, 41
    Richard, priest, 41
    cf. Hodson
Hungerford, Alice, 224
Hunt
    Andrew, 24, 25
    Richard, 117
Huntley, Thomas and Katherine his wife,
    32
Hurar, Isabel, 46
Hurst
    James, priest, 212
    John, priest, 182
Husband, Nicholas, 112
Hyat, Alice, 146
Hynde (Hinde)
    Austin, 77, 105
    George, 12

Ibrye, William, priest, 190n
Ickenham (Midd.), 183
Idesworth, Henry, archdeacon, 111
Iford, John, 42
Ilford (Essex), 209
Illingworth, Richard, kt., xix, 57
Inglesby, Richard, priest, 116
Ingram
    Richard, 156
    William, 156
Innholders' Company, 196
Ipport, John, 37
Ireland, Thomas, 11
Ironmonger (Iremonger) Lane, 56
Ironmongers' Company, 210
Isleworth (Midd.), 145; parishioners, 153
Islington (Midd.), 121
Ivorne, William, 97
Ivory, William, 31b
Iwade (Kent), Binwall Marsh in, 190(iii)

Jackelyng (Jacklyn, Jackeson), Robert,
    priest, 57 and n
Jackson (Jackeson, Jackesonn)
    Nicholas, priest, 33n, 212
    Peter, priest, xxvii, 10
    William, priest, 89
Jakes, Margaret, 107
James, Bartholomew, kt., 151
Jay
    Bartholomew, kt., 21
    Richard, 23a
Je-, *see also* Ge-
Jecket, Bartholomew, 17

INDEX OF SUBJECTS

This is a select index of subjects mentioned in the calendar.

animals, 190b; cattle, 117, 118, 123, 131, 135, 137, 143, 162, 163, 178, 181; horse, 162; oxen, 162; sheep, 149

Augmentations, court, 30, 32, 37, 50, 64, 82, 85, 91, 101, 104, 139, 184, 190(i), 218n; treasurer, 16; pensions paid by, 3, 10, 11, 21n, 30, 50, 53

brotherhoods and fraternities, 23a, 125, 185 *bis*; Corpus Christi, 18n, 100; Holy Rood, 43; Holy Trinity, 48; Holy Trinity and Our Lady, 151; Jesus, 106, 121; Our Lady, 22, 96, 107, 119, 139, 203; Our Lady and St Dunstan, 20; Our Lady and St Giles, 18, 95; Our Lady and St John Baptist, 7; Our Lady and St Stephen, 14; Papey, 67, 105; St Anne and Our Lady, 12; St George, 64n; St Giles, 33, 209; St Katherine, 93; St Mary Rouncival, 139; St Michael, 12; St Nicholas, 95; St Sythe, 75; *Salve Regina*, 25; Sixty Priests, 62, 72

buildings
  brewhouses, 37, 74, 159
  chapels, 133, 153; built by parishioners, 119; of ease, 56; free, 162; Corpus Christi, 100
  church houses, 127, 154, 156, 167, 178; built by parish, 151, 157; parish rooms, 152
  lazar house, 151
  privies (Fleet jakes), 107
  see also clergy: houses

castle ward, 190 *passim*

church fabric, works, 46, 75; repair and maintenance, 20, 21, 22, 24, 36, 37, 43, 44, 53, 54, 107, 129, 131, 138, 141, 144, 149, 151, 165, 168, 173 *bis*, 176

church furniture
  altars (dedications specified): Jesus, 21; Lady, 6, 21, 24, 43 *bis*, 185; St Anne, 20; St Martha, 220; St Peter, 38
  bell, 77
  organs, 9; *see also* officials: organist
  rood loft, 126; *see also* lights

church goods, 14, 21, 23a, 48, 190b; goods and plate, 31a; plate, 1n, 12, 14, 23a, 207 *bis*; chalice, 9; jewels, 1n, 20; linen, washing of, 66; vestments (ornaments), 1n, 12, 13, 14, 20, 41, 63, 66, 108n, 111, 151, 157; inventories (mentioned), 2, 7, 12, 20n, 23n, 31a, 47, 48, 66, 67, 72, 93n, 100, 105n, 107 and n, 115, 125, 139; image of Our Lady, 1, 4, 9, 102, 179

church income, candle silver on Easter day, 65; housling dues, 126; offerings, 126; tithes, 190

clergy, breakfast for, 97; houses etc., 27, 85, 108, 109, 113n, 125, 126, 173; additional clergy at Easter, 3; preachers, 18, 23a, 51, 66, 96; shortage of clergy, 36n

copyhold land, 131, 146, 151 *bis*, 156, 158

education, schools and teaching, 9 and n, 10, 40n, 55, 194, 222; student exhibitions, 108, 109; lecture, 216

festivals, Corpus Christi, 57; Easter, 126; sepulchre, 65; wafers, 187

highways, repair of, 129, 157

Husting court, 95

licences in mortmain, 1, 21, 66, 100, 102 *bis*, 115

lights, lamps and torches, *passim*; specific locations and dedications: beam light, 33, 39, 43, 74, 77, 211; rood light, 2, 43, 57, 91; high cross, 78; high altar, 16, 186; Lady light (before Lady altar, before Lady image), 1, 4, 185, 188, 222; paschal, 1, 11, 23a, 33, 34, 42, 65, 126, 163; before the Sacrament, 2, 17, 19, 20, 27, 30 *bis*, 75, 77, 107; St Anne's light, 43; St Michael's light, 91

liturgy, anthems, 24, 57, 74, 211; antiphons, 24n; *diriges*, 43; Five Wounds devotion, 152; masses (specific dedications): Jesus, 5; Lady, 5, 24n, 34, 47n, 162, 194, 224; morrow mass, 16, 30, 35, 39, 43, 55n, 71, 74n, 77, 97, 126, 134, 152; books for, 41; cost of masses, 98; obit by note, 95; prayers from pulpit, 37; *Salve Regina*, 4, 5, 23a, 24, 98

officials
  auditors, bailiffs and collectors, 51, 84, 108 *bis*, 109, 119, 190(ii), 190(iii)
  choir, 145, 187; choristers (singing children), 21n, 40n, 96, 108, 109, 190(iv); singing men, 16

LONDON RECORD SOCIETY

The London Record Society was founded in December 1964 to publish transcripts, abstracts and lists of the primary sources for the history of London, and generally to stimulate interest in archives relating to London. Membership is open to any individual or institution; the annual subscription is £5 ($12) for individuals and £8 ($20) for institutions, which entitles a member to receive one copy of each volume published during the year and to attend and vote at meetings of the Society. Prospective members should apply to the Hon. Secretary, Miss Heather Creaton, c/o Institute of Historical Research, Senate House, London, WC1E 7HU.

The following volumes have already been published:
1. *London Possessory Assizes: a calendar*, edited by Helena M. Chew (1965)
2. *London Inhabitants within the Walls, 1695*, with an introduction by D. V. Glass (1966)
3. *London Consistory Court Wills, 1492–1547*, edited by Ida Darlington (1967)
4. *Scriveners' Company Common Paper, 1357–1628, with a continuation to 1678*, edited by Francis W. Steer (1968)
5. *London Radicalism, 1830–1843: a selection from the papers of Francis Place*, edited by D. J. Rowe (1970)
6. *The London Eyre of 1244*, edited by Helena M. Chew and Martin Weinbaum (1970)
7. *The Cartulary of Holy Trinity Aldgate*, edited by Gerald A. J. Hodgett (1971)
8. *The Port and Trade of Early Elizabethan London: documents*, edited by Brian Dietz (1972)
9. *The Spanish Company*, by Pauline Croft (1973)
10. *London Assize of Nuisance, 1301–1431: a calendar*, edited by Helena M. Chew and William Kellaway (1973)
11. *Two Calvinistic Methodist Chapels, 1743–1811: the London Tabernacle and Spa Fields Chapel*, edited by Edwin Welch (1975)
12. *The London Eyre of 1276*, edited by Martin Weinbaum (1976)
13. *The Church in London, 1375–1392*, edited by A. K. McHardy (1977)
14. *Committees for Repeal of the Test and Corporation Acts: Minutes, 1786–90 and 1827–8*, edited by Thomas W. Davis (1978)
15. *Joshua Johnson's Letterbook, 1771–4: letters from a merchant in London to his partners in Maryland*, edited by Jacob M. Price (1979)
16. *London and Middlesex Chantry Certificate, 1548*, edited by C. J. Kitching (1980)

All volumes are still in print; apply to Hon. Secretary. Price to individual members £5 ($12) each; to institutional members £8 ($20) each; and to non-members £10 ($25) each.

The following Occasional Publication is also available:
London and Middlesex Published Records, compiled by J. M. Sims (1970)